AGAINST
— *the* —
WAVES

JON HARRIS

AGAINST
— *the* —
WAVES

Christian Order in
a Liberal Age

truthscript | press

www.worldviewconversation.com

Produced by TruthScript Press

ISBN 978-1-967020-00-3 (Paperback)
ISBN 978-1-967020-01-0 (E-book)
ISBN 978-1-967020-02-7 (Audiobook)

Cover Design and Interior Layout: AuthorSupport.com
Cover Image: *View Across Frenchman's Bay from Mount Desert Island, After a Squall,* Thomas Cole, 1845 (Public Domain)

FIRST EDITION

*To my mother, whose example
and guidance prepared me to live a disciplined
and fulfilling life in God's incredible world.*

CONTENTS

APPENDICES

INTRODUCTION

I wrote this book to encourage those skeptical of modern life to embrace the ordered liberty that flows from God's creation. While my previous two books focused on critically examining social justice theory, this work aims to craft a positive social vision of divine order, natural relationships, and localized community. The need for these things is great, as we currently live in a disoriented age—an era defined by unorthodox ideas and novelty. Our communities, adjusting to the requirements of an open liberal society, are not yet prepared for the cruelty that this society will inevitably bring. Barriers once taken for granted, such as the gender binary and national distinctions, are already being questioned.

The compromises of 2020 regarding totalitarian control and DEI ideology served as a wake-up call for many. Some have struggled to make sense of the brave new world they find themselves in, searching for where society went astray in the hope of rediscovering the path to truth. I believe the way back can always be found because God is present. His general purposes are evident in the world He created. Though sinful people may suppress the truth about God, His witness remains ever-present in both creation and His Word.

I believe we are living in a unique window of opportunity. People who recognize that they have been lied to—on everything from history to nutrition—are more open to Christianity than they have been in decades. It was Christianity that made the West truly great by affirming human worth, inspiring virtue, and channeling passion into selfless service to God and others. This vision was upheld by institutions that were accountable to God, fostering leaders who recognized their obligations to those under their authority, thus minimizing corruption and promoting justice.

It is my prayer this book inspires these conditions once again for a new era, in our homes, churches, and society. May we rediscover the timeless traditions, heroes, and wisdom of the past, passing them down to our children. May we also find the humility to recognize when some of our modern assumptions—such as the idea of a proposition nation or a religiously neutral society—are not only misguided but also dangerous. These dangers are becoming more evident than ever before. May we have the courage to embrace the truth and humbly submit ourselves to the merciful God of Scripture and Creation, who sent Christ to redeem humanity from the stain of sin and promises eternal life to those who believe in Him.

"The conclusion, when all has been heard, is: fear God and keep His commandments, because this applies to every person."

Ecclesiastes 12:13

1

REGAINING REALITY

Whatever of order, truth, equity and good government is to be found among the sons of men, they are solely indebted for to this everlasting Counsellor, this Prince of Peace.

Rev. Jacob Duché–Colonial Preacher

There is no malady afflicting the modern world disconnected from the rejection of divine order. It is evident in every facet of life, including issues relating to sexuality, nationality, and the role of the state. Even political efforts to defend traditional morality as manifested in the Republican Party and various conservative organizations eventually adopt positions they once opposed. Unfortunately, the institutional church, which previous generations trusted would anchor society against loosening standards, also follows current trends, even if from a respectable distance.

It is popular for political conservatives to attribute their losses to secondary causes. Dark money, the deep state, and famous celebrities influence society in negative ways, but their influence cannot sufficiently explain our current condition. Some Christian

interpretations are equally inadequate. Debates concerning eschatology, baptism, and many other theological issues are important
but do not hold the key to understanding our present demise. Our
problems are more fundamental.

Humanist ideologies like nominalism, Darwinism, and Marxism
have eroded divine boundaries in the minds of Western man for centuries. By disregarding revelation we threw away our blueprint. By
disregarding the past we cannot remember where we left it. We are
now forced to live with the results: A world where chaotic forces
endlessly assault basic definitions while the modern state increases
its stranglehold over every facet of life. Drag queen story hours
(DQSH) in local libraries are perhaps the most recent egregious and
recognizable symptom of this decay.

A WORLD WITHOUT ANCHORS

Previous generations could not conceive of accepting such confusion. In the name of sexual liberation, political leaders erode the
barriers between education and titillation, innocence and carnality,
male and female, and child and adult. Unfortunately, most conservative opponents offer inadequate critiques by basing their complaint
on personal intuition or majority opinion. Appeals to the fact that
it is "inappropriate" for children, or the pressure to be on the "right
side of history" when such displays are hypothetically shut down,
may have merit but they are not principled positions.[1] Today's political conservatives simply repeat failed tactics used against same-sex
marriage ceremonies two decades ago.

Ironically, influential self-described evangelicals are not united
on the issue. Some are vocal in their opposition, most are silent,
and many attempt to neutralize concern. The neutralizers tend to
incorporate DQSH under the umbrella of protected assembly or

---

[1] Tomi Lahren, *Tomi Lahren: Drag queen story hours are inappropriate*, interview by Jason Chaffetz,
December 11, 2022, https://www.youtube.com/watch?v=JarIrd6dlUs; Sara Gonzolas, *What does an all-
ages drag brunch look like?*, interview by Tucker Carlson, October 19, 2022, https://www.youtube.com/
watch?v=JGrdJ3_4VUY.

downplay it in the face of issues of more seeming importance.[2] The effect is that some professing Christians suspect bad motives on the part of those who vigorously oppose DQSH. This lackluster response to what would be considered egregious even a few years ago illustrates modern man's gradual rejection of transcendent standards. It was not always this way.

Pre-modern people believed they were responsible to conform the particulars of their temporal existence to an eternal order. Christians saw divine revelation as guiding them to fulfill this calling. This is why many of America's Founders commonly refer to Providence. They saw God directing existence toward higher ends that people were to submit themselves to. Submission complemented rather than conflicted with people's special interests. Even those who filled subordinate social stations played meaningful parts in a divine drama. This providential outlook provided structure for society and promoted personal contentment.

George Washington articulated the general understanding of his day when he wrote in 1789 that "human happiness and moral duty are inseparably connected."[3] Now people disassociate these conditions to the point that it is standard to reject moral duties in the pursuit of happiness. It seems the only obligations people have are to fulfill their own temporal desires and to ensure that social institutions, notably the state, function to assist others in doing the same. Hardly anyone asks what their ultimate desires should be. The results of this thinking are negative.

Despite surrounding ourselves with convenience, entertainment, instant communication, and unlimited access to neurological drugs, we are a society increasingly marked by depression. With no purpose beyond the immediate, people fail to find an ultimate reason for

2 Benjamin Wallace-Wells, "David French, Sohrab Ahmari, and the Battle for the Future of Conservatism," *The New Yorker*, September 12, 2019, https://www.newyorker.com/news/the-political-scene/david-french-sohrab-ahmari-and-the-battle-for-the-future-of-conservatism; Phil Vischer [@philvischer], "@William_E_Wolfe You Never Mentioned Gun Control. 4500 Kids Died Last Year from Bullet Wounds. Drag Queen Story Time Didn't Kill Nearly That Many.," Tweet, *Twitter*, January 26, 2023, https://twitter.com/philvischer/status/1618457804511252481.
3 George Washington to the Protestant Episcopal Church, August 19, 1789, *The Papers of George Washington Digital Edition*, https://rotunda.upress.virginia.edu/founders/default.xqy?keys=GEWN-print-05-03-02-0289&mode=deref.

existence. This is especially true for young people. A report "on data from counseling centers at 180 colleges and universities" showed a gradual increase in students' anxiety and depression during the past decade.[4] Governments made the situation worse when they prioritized immediate safety over deeper human needs during the reaction to Covid-19. One study claimed an over twenty-five percent worldwide increase in anxiety and depressive disorders during this time.[5] Interestingly, this is all happening when there are "more [professional] support services, mental health facilities, and other interventions available than ever before."[6] Perhaps the professionals concerned with these matters have no real answer on the question of purpose.

For example, leading experts featured at the World Economic Forum suggest things like installing electronic brain implants or "getting involved in the fight against climate change" as ways to fight depression.[7] The now dominant political left has a long history of channeling the natural desire for meaning into activism. Yet they ignore the major reason for the rising tide of social angst. Modern man's attempt to find ultimate significance within self, society, or other aspects of creation leaves him fragmented and without a transcendent reference point. The Apostle Paul argues that the confusion normalized all around us is fundamentally an issue of worship.

People descend into lower forms of depravity and its chaotic results when they treat something created as if it were the Creator.[8] After rejecting the Architect, they discard His blueprint and are left without absolute authority or design. This leaves them open to things like DQSH. It is not because they reject all moral limitations. Rather, they endorse standards that reflect and support

---

4   "Trauma and Social Anxiety Are Growing Mental-Health Concerns for College Students," *The Chronicle of Higher Education*, January 25, 2023, https://www.chronicle.com/article/trauma-and-social-anxiety-are-growing-mental-health-concerns-for-college-students.

5   Lantie Jorandby, "Depression and Anxiety Are on the Rise Globally," *Psychology Today*, November 1, 2021, https://www.psychologytoday.com/us/blog/use-your-brain/202111/depression-and-anxiety-are-the-rise-globally.

6   Jorandby.

7   Sean Fleming, "Could This 'Pacemaker for the Brain' Be the Solution to Severe Depression?," *World Economic Forum*, October 8, 2021, https://www.weforum.org/agenda/2021/10/brain-implant-could-cure-depression/; Katherine Grill, "Eco-Anxiety Is a Growing Mental Health Crisis," *World Economic Forum*, November 1, 2022, https://www.weforum.org/agenda/2022/11/children-mental-health-eco-anxiety/.

8   Rom 1:25.

their twisted desires, although they cannot justify these standards in any meaningful way. The problem lies in their attempt to extract ultimate meaning from transient or contingent things like pleasurable experience or principles of equality. No particular thing in creation is capable of correctly ordering human life. This is where both Christians and political conservatives—who owe much of their foundation to the Bible—need to focus their attention.

The world of tomorrow is here and it is no utopia. It is filled with horrors unimaginable to previous generations, from the sexual anarchy one click away, to regular mass shootings and surveillance states increasingly bent on controlling all human activity. John Lennon's *Imagine* predicted that a world without religion, national allegiance, and private property would lead to a global brotherhood filled with peace and contentment. It was all an allusion. The fact is, the closer society gets to approaching this world, the less it enjoys peace and contentment.

A *Wall Street Journal* poll found that Americans are shedding their dedication to religion and patriotism at unprecedented levels.[9] At the same time issues like family breakdown, domestic violence, and suicide are climbing. Devout Christians are much less inclined to participate in these trends.[10] They are living reminders of what used to be and if society is to return to a sense of virtue it will once again need to pass through the gate of historic Christianity.

The great debt Western Civilization owes to Christianity starts with its notion that mankind's purpose is found in the eternal, absolute, and unchanging Creator. In his classic work *The City of God*, Augustine wrote: "For, though Himself eternal, and without beginning, yet [God] caused time to have a beginning; and man, whom He had not previously made, He made in time, not from a

---

9 Aaron Zitner, "America Pulls Back From Values That Once Defined It, WSJ-NORC Poll Finds," *Wall Street Journal*, March 27, 2023, sec. US, https://www.wsj.com/articles/americans-pull-back-from-values-that-once-defined-u-s-wsj-norc-poll-finds-df8534cd.
10 Brian Hollar, "Regular Church Attenders Marry More and Divorce Less Than Their Less Devout Peers," *Institute for Family Studies*, March 4, 2020, https://ifstudies.org/blog/regular-church-attenders-marry-more-and-divorce-less-than-their-less-devout-peers; Christopher G. Ellison et al., "Race/Ethnicity, Religious Involvement, and Domestic Violence," *Violence Against Women* 13, no. 11 (November 1, 2007), 1105; Norko, Michael, et al. "Can Religion Protect Against Suicide?". *The Journal of Nervous and Mental Disease*, vol. 205, no. 1, January 2017, pp. 9-14. doi: 10.1097/NMD.0000000000000615.

new and sudden resolution, but by His unchangeable and eternal design." This universal design determines mankind's roles, responsibilities, and rights. For example, Augustine states: "It is quite clear that [people] were created male and female, with bodies of different sexes, for the very purpose of begetting offspring, and so increasing, multiplying, and replenishing the earth." He adds, "It is great folly to oppose so plain a fact."[11] It was this basic framework that kept the state in check and led to many of the freedoms we still enjoy. This is easily seen in most of Anglo-America's significant legal documents.

The 9th century Legal Code of Alfred the Great instructed "God's servants" to "hold their proper rule according to [a] law" primarily based upon the Ten Commandments.[12] This understanding of limited government was vital in the development of English common law. Four centuries later the Magna Carta restrained the king's authority by allowing the church and barons to enjoy certain liberties. The document states the crown "granted all these things for God."[13] The famous English jurist William Blackstone wrote in his *Commentaries on the Laws of England*, "It is necessary that [mankind] should in all points conform to his maker's will."[14] This meant in part that "no human legislature has the power to abridge or destroy" God-ordained "natural rights, such as are life and liberty." Blackstone's doctrine is evident in famous American documents like The Virginia Declaration of Rights and the Declaration of Independence. Without this basis in divine order there is nothing to prevent societal disintegration and the emergence of a dystopian state.

A COMPASS FOR THE RIGHT

In order to safeguard order and repel the surveillance state, American believers must recover the legacy of their forefathers who developed

---

[11] Augustine, *The City of God*, Volumes I & II, ed. Anthony Uyl and Marcus Dods (Ontario, CA: Devoted Publishing, 2017), 213, 252.

[12] Stefan Jurasinski and Lisi Oliver, *The Laws of Alfred: The Domboc and the Making of Anglo-Saxon Law*, Studies in Legal History (Cambridge: Cambridge University Press, 2021), 371.

[13] "English Translation of Magna Carta" (British Library, July 28, 2014), https://www.bl.uk/magna-carta/articles/magna-carta-english-translation.

[14] William Blackstone, *Commentaries on the Laws of England* (Oxford: 1768), 39.

the conservative tradition. Likewise, modern political conservatives must remember their indebtedness to Christianity. The current social controversies are not over facts or practical concerns. They are over definitions and principles. It is not enough to advocate for majority opinion, what stimulates business, or what promises safety. Christians must base their arguments on what is objectively good, true, and beautiful. They must forge their political vision by appealing to noble ends.

Political philosopher Richard Weaver, in commenting on the demise of the Whig Party in Great Britain, observed, "A party must have its own principle of movement and must not be content to serve as a brake on the movements of others." When politically opposing a stronger force he argued the need for a "group sufficiently indifferent to success to oppose the ruling group on principle rather than according to opportunity for success."[15] This posture is clearly lacking in modern political conservatism.

As a whole, the political Left is more willing than the Right to make sacrifices, such as accepting lower paying jobs or donating time and resources to achieve their utopian ideals. They tend to reward radical activists, excuse corrupt leaders, and ignore charges of hypocrisy. They aggressively focus their energy on concrete goals regardless of how unattainable these initially appear. In contrast, the political Right strives to avoid the discomfort of being labeled things like "racist," "misogynist," or "transphobic." They allow the Left to gate-keep their ranks by setting the bar of acceptable behavior. They abandon previously-held positions when it becomes expedient. In short, the Right is reactionary while the Left is revolutionary.

Contrary to the course some new members of the Right want to take, mimicking the Left will not defeat them. Appealing to their standards of behavior by calling them "racists," for example, fails to be taken seriously and instead persuades conservatives to adopt the Left's framework. Likewise, disregarding personal morality contradicts efforts to reinforce social morality. Also, seeing

---

15 Richard Weaver, *The Ethics of Rhetoric* (Echo Point Books & Media, 2015), 73, 78.

previous progressive movements such as first-wave feminism, the move to nationalize education, or homosexual normalization as being somehow "conservative" or "American" undercuts efforts to oppose causes downstream from them. We need a better approach.

Recognizing divine purpose once again must be a Christian's uncompromising political objective. It will first need to be recovered in the ranks of conservatism and then applied more broadly. When this happens, major social issues will start rectifying themselves. People will again have a basis for embracing the gender binary, the necessity of family, and the reality of nations. They will reject gender fluidity, unconventional families, and the proposition nation. Pioneering this shift does include risk. The Left currently enjoys unlimited capacity to publicly smear those who represent what they wish to deconstruct. This should be expected.

Most successful social movements, including the Marxist revolutions, initially require great sacrifices for an even greater cause. A movement to reassert reality is no exception. Those who sacrifice for the cause should be recognized, yet there can be no room for personal ambition. The movement must have reachable objectives but there can be no fundamental compromise with evil to achieve them. Gaining political power is necessary but it cannot replace confidence in God. It must remain pure, principled, and patient, or it will revert to the current "shadow that follows Radicalism as it moves forward towards perdition."[16]

The starting point of any movement is believing that success is possible. This is difficult for those who wish to reestablish earlier understandings in a world that prizes innovation and progress. Yet, the Reformation and Renaissance are both successful examples of movements that sought to restore previous convictions. Though these dark times make any return to virtuous standards seem unreachable, we should remember that not long ago social institutions assumed and reinforced a divine order. Public leaders upheld rather than suppressed what God made clearly evident in creation.[17] They did so

---

[16] Robert Dabney, *The Southern Magazine*, vol. 8 (Baltimore: Murdoch, Browne & Hill, 1871), 327.
[17] Rom 1:19

imperfectly, as has every civilization, but even unregenerate people understood the importance of *telos*.[18]

Christians should lead the move to recover divine order, but this does not mean others cannot participate. Christians believe that in addition to God's atoning work for sinners He also providentially works through civil authorities for the "public good" and "disposeth all things to the good [of His church]." Only the redeemed are capable of "that which is spiritually good." But, "works done by unregenerate men . . . may be things which God commands, and of good use both to themselves and others."[19] Augustine observed this when he wrote about the "earthly city," that although "in bondage to vice," nonetheless it desires "human good" such as "earthly peace," "enjoying earthly goods," and a just victory. These he describes as "good things, and without doubt the gifts of God."[20]

The direction formerly Christianized societies will go remains to be seen, although one thing is clear: In a short period of time the contest will not be between Christianity and some version of a religiously-neutral liberal order. It will be between Christianity and a return to paganism. By some accounts it already is. While hope remains to rouse the minds of even unbelievers toward action in defending the natural order, Christians must remember the spiritual war behind the culture war. The spiritual goal is not ultimately found in a return to cultural Christianity, but in transferring the redeemed to the heavenly city. The Christian hope is that along with Augustine other sinners would say: "And thy purposes were profoundly impressed upon me; and rejoicing in faith, I praised thy name."[21]

---

18 *Telos* is a Greek term referring to ultimate end or final purpose.
19 "The Westminster Confession of Faith," Ligonier Ministries, 21.1, 5.7, 9.4, 16.7, https://www.ligonier.org/learn/articles/westminster-confession-faith/.
20 Augustine, *City of God*, 260.
21 Augustine, *The Works of Aurelius Augustine: A New Translation*, ed. Marcus Dods, vol. XIV. (Edinburgh: T. & T. Clark, 1886), 217.

2

APPRECIATING
NATURE

*We see, indeed, the world with our eyes, we tread the earth with
our feet, we touch innumerable kinds of God's works with our
hands, we inhale a sweet and pleasant fragrance from herbs and
flowers, we enjoy boundless benefits; but in those very things of
which we attain some knowledge, there dwells such an immensity
of divine power, goodness, and wisdom, as absorbs all our senses.*

John Calvin

I f we are to recover an understanding and appreciation for
God's natural order, we should spend more time in it. Most of
our ancestors who lived in agrarian societies spent far more of
their lives outdoors than we do. For the current generation of digital
natives, going outside is optional. A 2017 study showed that most
American adults were satisfied "spending five hours or less in nature
each week."[1] In contrast, the average American spends one third of
their waking hours on a mobile device and almost seven hours of

---

1 "U.S. Study Shows Widening Disconnect with Nature, and Potential Solutions," Yale University, April 27, 2017, https://e360.yale.edu/digest/u-s-study-shows-widening-disconnect-with-nature-and-potential-solutions.

their day online.[2] This new sedentary lifestyle negatively impacts more than just physical health.

Digital tycoons promise to give people the limitless ability to control their lives. Instead, they deliver them into what for many is a meaningless world of addiction and exploitation. Global advertisers now spend almost three quarters of their advertising budgets on digital platforms.[3] The number of pornography, video game, and binge-watching addicts is increasing. Online users exasperate cyberbullying and cancel culture by putting more stock in digital footprint than intimate experience. As technology advances, virtue retreats. Unfortunately conservatives and Christians commonly misunderstand the level at which these issues operate.

VIRTUAL LIVES AND PLASTIC WORLDS

Believers often conceive of digital-age problems strictly in terms of vice and choice. People use digital devices to fulfill sinful desires. Spiritual advisers rightly encourage Christians engaged in such activities to repent, seek accountability, and overcome temptation. Expanding spiritual disciplines like Scripture memorization and prayer are likewise important responses. However, there is an often neglected metaphysical dimension in addition to an ethical one.

Minds that stay indoors and online are capable of immersing themselves into a kind of artificial reality. It is easy for them to believe they can create a better world than the one that actually exists. This is not achieved by overcoming real challenges through work and discipline. Rather, it entails drawing a new blueprint for reality itself. Technology makes this dream seem possible. People have pleasurable experiences without the obligations that naturally accompany them, including sex without intimacy, friendship without obligation, and

---

2   Robert Hart, "Record 3.8 Trillion Hours Spent On Mobile Apps During 2021 In Another Blockbuster Year For Digital Economy," *Forbes*, January 13, 2022, https://www.forbes.com/sites/roberthart/2022/01/12/record-38-trillion-hours-spent-on-mobile-apps-during-2021-in-another-blockbuster-year-for-digital-economy/; Simon Kemp, "Digital 2023: Global Overview Report," *DataReportal*, January 26, 2023, https://datareportal.com/reports/digital-2023-global-overview-report.
3   Kemp.

adventure without risk. Internet natives tend to impose this manu-factured ideal onto reality itself.

Debates surrounding public accommodations for people who think of themselves as transgender are suddenly commonplace. One school in Jefferson County, Colorado, even experienced a controversy over accommodating students who thought of them-selves as anthropomorphic.[4] Members of a generation who grew up immersed in a world of online avatars, virtual reality, and social media are blurring the lines between the limitless experience facili-tated through technology and experience in the real world. The sub-sequent demand that actual communities recognize these artificial identities is related to this metaphysical outlook.

In the minds of many, reality is not fixed. People can edit existence with the swipe of a finger, choosing what pictures of themselves to show, erasing previous partners after break-ups, and curating a com-munity that reinforces their interests and decisions. Things as basic as identity in this fluid existence are socially generated and legiti-mized within a matrix of other public experiences. This outlook is an amplified version of the way urban dwellers started to think during the industrial revolution as people moved to cities that promised prosperity and equality.

Southern agrarian thinkers from the New Deal and World War II eras were foremost in critiquing this way of living. Many of their concerns about urbanization are prescient. Richard Weaver observed that "in Megalopolis the sentiment of friendship wastes away" in favor of new arrangements based on work, pleasure, or personality.[5] Lyle Lanier warned that urban populations contributed to internal dissension because they lacked the social anchors of land and reli-gion. Herman Clarence Nixon likewise connected the decline of the Roman Empire to "neglect of agriculture and the growth of an idle urban proletariat of unwieldy proportions."[6] This is related to

---

4   Shaun Boyd, "Emails Show JeffCo School Administrators Knew 'Furries' Were an Issue but Publicly Denied It," October 31, 2022, https://www.cbsnews.com/colorado/news/emails-show-jeffco-school-administrators-knew-furries-were-issue-publicly-denied/.
5   Richard Weaver, *Ideas Have Consequences* (University of Chicago Press, 2013), 29-31.
6   John Crowe Ransom et al., *I'll Take My Stand: The South and the Agrarian Tradition* (LSU Press, 2006),

Donald Davidson's concern that an urban mindset socialized medicine, education, and more.[7] In each case, these authors from almost a century ago tried to prevent the world most of us now live in. What was once unique to cities is now common in every region. Shallow friendships, deep social divides, and a welfare state are simply features of modern living.

Richard Weaver summarized the agrarian's concerns as a "conspiracy" against civilization to substitute "sensation for reflection." He argued that technology made urban living and mass communication possible on a scale previously unrealized. Cities existed since the time of Cain, but not the metropolises of the industrial age. For example, in 1800 the population of New York City was sixty thousand compared to over ten million in 1930.[8] This new arrangement fostered a "spoiled-child" mentality that detached people from lasting connections to land and relationships.

Weaver observed that city-dwellers lived with immediate access to "man-made comforts" and limitless information. Media outlets gained success by infusing people's dull mechanical lives with sensational or obscene content, constituting an attack on privacy. Politicians consolidated power by appeasing immediate desires. This short-circuited the "relationship between effort and reward." Urbanites began to believe there was "nothing [they could not] know . . . and nothing [they could not] have." This continual state of stimulation in the present erased reminders of human frailty and obligation to the past or future. The world was simply a machine existing for the purpose of supplying people with comfort.

As people depended more on this "complicated system of human exchange," they became "forgetful of the overriding mystery of creation." Weaver wrote that "an artificial environment causes [people] to lose sight of the great system not subject to man's control." Religion, which helped man "realize the presence of something

---

150, 195-196.

[7] Donald Davidson, *The Southern Agrarians and the New Deal: Essays After I'll Take My Stand*, ed. Emily Bingham and Thomas A. Underwood (University of Virginia Press, 2001), 113.

[8] "New York Urbanized Area: Population & Density from 1800 (Provisional)," accessed May 26, 2023, http://demographia.com/db-nyuza1800.htm.

greater than self," was the only hope urban-dwellers had of conserv-ing something of lasting value.[9] Weaver's reflections are more potent now than they were in 1948 when he originally made them.

Today, people carry the megalopolis in their pocket and bring it with them wherever they go, ready at any moment to interrupt reflection with sensation. For previous generations it was necessary to consider and contend with creation for survival. Today, it appears to be optional. Rejecting constant stimulation and the rewards asso-ciated with it like dopamine hits, entertainment, and distraction from the problems of life is difficult. It is especially hard if it is all someone knows. Nevertheless, contact with nature is necessary for healthy, productive, and honest living—and it is also possible. If we are to return to a sense of divine purpose, we will need to step into creation. It is here where we most naturally conform our will to our Creator's. It is here where unnatural notions are most easily extin-guished in light of the sublime and the beautiful.

BEAUTY, SUBLIMITY, AND LUST

Edmund Burke, the 18th century Irish statesman and pioneer of modern conservative thought, emphasized the importance of expe-riencing the sublime and the beautiful in his famous pre-Romantic work on aesthetics. He believed the sublime dwelled on great and terrible objects while beauty dwelled on small and pleasing ones. Later critics thought Burke's contrast paralleled gender differences.[10] Sublimity included qualities like ruggedness, vastness, magnificence, and power, whereas beauty carried with it qualities of smoothness, gradualness, delicacy, and grace. Consider Solomon's description of the shepherd bride in chapter four of Song of Songs.

Her eyes are like doves, her hair a flock of goats, her neck an ornate tower, and her breasts fawns among lilies. He also describes more than what is seen by praising the smell of her fragrance and taste of

---

9 Weaver, *Ideas*, 30, 61, 113-115.
10 Thomas De Quincey, *The Uncollected Writings of Thomas De Quincey* (S. Sonnenschein & Company, 1890), 38.

her lips. Such flowing, soft, elegant, tender, and sweet descriptions inspire the young suitor's heart to beat faster. This is a good illustration of Burke's conception of beauty. Another example is found in David's surroundings in the twenty-third Psalm. David states, "He makes me lie down in green pastures; He leads me beside quiet waters." The result comes in the next verse: "He restores my soul." For centuries people cherished these beautiful verses as reminders that life was worthwhile, even in the midst of suffering. The degraded art and literature of today does little to produce these effects. In short, there is little of beauty in it.

The problem is that modern media, instead of lifting people to a higher order, seeks to emancipate them from it. In the words of Sir Roger Scruton, they "attempt to recreate the world as though love were not part of it."[11] Burke believed beauty inspired love, which then compelled people to give themselves to something they found to be precious. This is quite the opposite of lust, which takes and uses and consumes. In modern art things are often reduced to animalistic function. People focus entirely on themselves and miss the world beyond them. The world is no longer their home but an absurd and dangerous place they must survive while extracting any pleasure they can. A good example of this is pornography.

Pornography assumes a freedom to cross natural boundaries that when attempted in reality leads to pain and chaos. Pleasure comes purely from mechanical actions detached from obligation and security. The world is a machine with no higher purpose than the present. One of Burke's contemporaries, the French revolutionary Marquis de Sade, from whom we get the term "sadism," pioneered this philosophy.

He encouraged young people to abandon religion, embrace atheism, and sacrifice everything to their own pleasure. This was the only way for the "poor creature who goes under the name of Man . . . to sow a smattering of roses atop the thorny path of life."[12] One easily

---

[11] "Why Beauty Matters" (BBC, 2009), http://archive.org/details/whybeautymatters.
[12] Marquis de Sade, *Justine, Philosophy in the Bedroom, and Other Writings*, trans. Richard Seaver and Austryn Wainhouse (New York: Grove Press, 1965), 185-188.

sees his resentment toward God and anyone who might represent Him in his writings. Instead of God, Marquis de Sade assumed he was obeying the voice of nature by fulfilling his perverted tastes. In reality he was trampling on nature by gratifying his own lusts. De Sade spent thirty-two years of his life in prison for crimes related to kidnaping, rape, and violence.

Contrary to de Sade, things are not beautiful just because they are useful to us. Beauty expresses design and purpose. It is not found in function but in form. The pleasure derived from beauty does not terminate in physical objects; rather, it infuses our experience with ultimate value. When we view a breathtaking scene, we forget ourselves and focus on what surrounds us. We put our interests on hold and take in the moment. Our enjoyment comes from being part of something bigger than us. Our appreciation is not arbitrary, but it is connected to something objective—something that can be appreciated by others in similar ways. Beauty shares some of its qualities with sublimity, but there are distinctions as well.

In both experiences we begin to cooperate with something outside ourselves. Yet while beauty charms us, sublimity commands us. For example, people respond to flowers differently than to volcanos. Beauty inspires love and sublimity evokes admiration. Burke thought of the sublime as great commanding conceptions beyond our comprehension. Standing in the presence of an important king, or experiencing an irresistible force such as a dark storm or a rugged mountain, evokes a sense of awe or even dread. People feel small when their minds are filled with thoughts of eternity, grandeur, and mystery. Burke observed "we submit to what we admire."[13] Two good examples of this are found at the end of Job and in Psalm 139.

The central question of the book of Job concerns why God allows the righteous to suffer. Instead of answering this question directly, God reminds man of his own limitations. Speaking to Job from a whirlwind, God challenges him. "Have you entered into the springs of the sea or walked in the recesses of the deep?" Burke particularly

13 Edmund Burke, *A Philosophical Enquiry into the Origin of Our Ideas of the Sublime and Beautiful: And Other Pre-Revolutionary Writings*, ed. David Womersley, Penguin Classics (London: Penguin Books, 1998), 311.

highlighted God's description of certain animals whose strength allowed them to defy domestication. Concerning Leviathan God asked Job: "Can you draw out Leviathan with a fishhook? Or press down his tongue with a cord? Can you put a rope in his nose or pierce his jaw with a hook? Will he make many supplications to you, or will he speak to you soft words? Will he make a covenant with you? Will you take him for a servant forever?"[14] These overwhelming descriptions reminded Job of his own insignificance. Consequently, he abandoned attempts to understand and instead surrendered to God's mysterious plan. Similarly, Burke wrote of King David that when he "contemplated the wonders of wisdom and power which are displayed in the economy of man, he seems to be struck with a sort of divine horror, and cries out, fearfully and wonderfully am I made!"[15] The feeling of smallness Job and David experienced was once encouraged every Sunday.

When Christians gained the ability to finance places of worship they built breathtaking cathedrals and magnificent churches. Features like large domes, ornate arches, and tall steeples reminded them of God's greatness. Many walked past the graves of their ancestors into sanctuaries where a symphony of heavenly music greeted them. Together they then listened to God's voice from Scripture and pledged themselves to follow it. Burke noticed that while all religions incorporated a sense of dread, power, and fear, Christianity also emphasized love. Unfortunately, this is now the only quality, in a somewhat shriveled form, that many Christians are encouraged toward.

FINDING MOUNTAINTOP MOMENTS

Modern churches often succumb to modernity by purposely ignoring the sublime in the pursuit of love, specifically love of self. Theologian David Wells believes churches in the 20th century shifted focus toward activities intended to meet felt needs. Smiling people, happy music, and professional speakers produced sentimentality,

---

[14] Job 38:16; 41:1-4.
[15] Burke, 168.

but so did organizations that were not religious at all. Without theology at the center, Christianity lost its distinctiveness. Many churches intentionally did this by giving the impression they were not churches at all. They used corporate sounding names, replaced crosses with logos, and designed buildings to look like businesses. Steeples, graveyards, and hymns became things of the past. Gradually Christian outlets that once contained theological content now published self-help and pop-culture material.[16] Christianity became less sublime and as a result less religious.

Some movements, like the Emergent Church, tried to reinstate a sense of transcendence by replacing traditional belief with things like social activism and practices associated with the New Age movement. This did nothing to increase sublimity because it reduced God to the level of His creation. People confused connection to the world with connection to the divine. As a result, man's power increased and God's decreased. There was no longer a reason to fear God or to conform one's life to His will.

People can lose themselves in all kinds of activities, from drug trips to contemplative prayer, but if they are not encouraged to think of themselves as distinct and fragile creatures in the face of overwhelming majesty or power, they will not gain a sense of the sublime. Today it is clear that these necessary reminders are not automatic. We must choose to deliberately integrate sublimity into our lives. Nature is and has always been the place where people go to experience this most directly. Burke described the "passion caused by the great and sublime in nature" in vivid terms:

> Astonishment is that state of the soul, in which all its motions are suspended, with some degree of horror. In this case the mind is so entirely filled with its object, that it cannot entertain any other, nor by consequence reason on that object which employs it. Hence arises the great power of the sublime, that far from being produced by them, it anticipates our reasonings,

---

16 David Wells, *No Place for Truth: Or Whatever Happened to Evangelical Theology?* (Wm. B. Eerdmans Publishing, 1994), 207-210.

and hurries us on by an irresistible force. Astonishment, as I have said, is the effect of the sublime in its highest degree; the inferior effects are admiration, reverence and respect.[17]

There are numerous examples throughout the Psalms where people respond to God's creative works in nature with this attitude. In Psalm 33 David recounted how God made the heavens and ocean, commanding the response: "Let all the earth fear the Lord; let all the inhabitants of the world stand in awe of Him." In Psalm 36 he said, "Your righteousness is like the mountains of God; Your judgements are like a great deep." The wicked ignored what should be obvious because "there is no fear of God before [their] eyes." David asked God to keep him from this pride and the consequences of it. In Psalm 97 he referred to the way lightning made the people of earth tremble. Truly "the heavens are telling of the glory of God, And their expanse is declaring the work of His hands."[18]

It is obvious that this admiration, reverence, and respect are significantly diminished in our world, as is the fear of God that produces such qualities. If this sense cannot be found in most churches, we surely cannot expect it to show up in places of education, enterprise, or entertainment. This is why we must go outside. From God instructing Moses in the wilderness to remove his sandals because he stood on holy ground, to Jesus crying out in a garden, "Not My will, but Yours be done," there is a long tradition of what are sometimes called "mountaintop experiences."[19] Natural settings are not required to communicate with God, but often it is in these settings, frequently on mountains, that God reveals Himself in profound ways.

God wrestled with Jacob in a secluded place. He revealed His law to Moses on Mount Sinai. He first appeared to David on Mount Moriah, and later He communed there with His people who gathered at Solomon's temple. He miraculously answered Elijah's prayer on Mount Carmel by sending fire from heaven. He

---

[17] Burke, 156-157.
[18] Psalm 33:8; 36:1,6,11-12; 97:4; 19:1.
[19] Ex 3:5, Luke 22:42.

transfigured Himself before Peter, James, and John on the Mount of Transfiguration. Jesus set the ultimate example for Christians by frequently slipping away to pray in the wilderness during His earthly ministry.[20] If Jesus needed time alone with God in nature in an agrarian context, how much more so do Christians who are surrounded by modern technology?

While preachers often use our Lord's actions to demonstrate the importance of prayer, they sometimes neglect calling attention to where He chose to pray, often hiking up mountains to enjoy the solitude of nature. When all other voices are eliminated, the voice of God is more discernable. Theodore Cuyler, a Presbyterian pastor in Brooklyn during the Industrial Revolution, expressed the need for Christians to plan these kind of mountaintop experiences for themselves in light of city life.

Cuyler asked, "Can Christian dwellers in the cities and the towns discover no time or places for meditation, for prayer, for spiritual reading, for their Bibles, or for heart-converse with their Saviour?" He concluded, "Yes, they may if they will resolutely determine so." He then gave examples of businessmen who managed to incorporate contemplation into the rhythm of their busy lives. This is the challenge Christians today must continue to engage as technology changes and distractions increase.

The 19th century American painter Thomas Cole spent much time contemplating the American landscape from his home in New York between the Hudson River and Catskill Mountains. Progress made its mark during his life. Lumberjacks, tanners, and railroad workers penetrated the Hudson Valley, motivating him to preserve nature's sublimity in its pure form through art. Cole's Christianity appears in many of his writings and paintings. In a famous lecture on American scenery, Cole stated:

> It has not been in vain—the good, the enlightened of all ages
> and nations, have found pleasure and consolation in the beauty
> of the rural earth. Prophets of old retired into the solitudes of

---

20 Gen 32:24-32, Ex 31:18, 2 Chronicles 3:1, 1 Kings 18:36-38, Matt 17:1-9, Luke 5:16

nature to wait the inspiration of heaven. It was on Mount Horeb that Elijah witnessed the mighty wind, the earthquake, and the fire; and heard the "still small voice"—that voice is YET heard among the mountains! St. John preached in the desert;— the wilderness is YET a fitting place to speak of God.[21]

Cole sensed a connection to God in nature and it frustrated him when others devalued this experience. To pursue trivial entertainment in a scenic area was to Cole "a desecration of the place where nature offered a feast of higher holier enjoyment."[22] To appreciate a painting is to appreciate the painter who made it.

Cole is considered one of the first American conservationists. He knew human progress was necessary but did not want to see it destroy "the sublimity of the wilderness." Behind this were not the musings of Transcendentalists like Henry David Thoreau, to whom nature was an abstract utopia capable of emancipating man from oppressive social attachment. Cole believed people, including himself, were sinners in need of grace, and he took his responsibilities to family, friends, and society seriously. Nature did not free man from obligation; rather it helped him honor his obligations more freely. The lessons of nature said something about God, not man. Nature pointed to a higher eternal existence beyond the temporal world of suffering and pain.

Cole wrote in his journal that "every great artist works to God, forgetful of the whims, caprices, prejudices, and even the desires of men. He labours to gratify his soul's devotion to the beautiful and true which are centered in God." Experiencing the sublime and beautiful in nature was in a certain way experiencing the hand of a good and powerful God. Cole testified that "those scenes of solitude from which the hand of nature has never been lifted, affect the mind with a more deep toned emotion than aught which the hand of man has touched. Amid them the consequent associations are of God the

---

[21] Thomas Cole, "Essay on American Scenery," *American Monthly Magazine*, January 1836, 2.

[22] Thomas Cole, *Thoughts & Occurrences: Journal of Thomas Cole* (Thomas Cole National Historic Site, 2022), 17.

creator—they are his undefiled works, and the mind is cast into the contemplation of eternal things."[23]

However, immersing ourselves in nature will not solve all our problems. One only needs to consider primitive pagan societies. According to Scripture, they suppress what they know about God and worship His creation instead. Environmentalism commits the same kind of error. They fail to approach creation with what John Calvin called a "sober, docile, mild, and humble spirit."[24] Yet, if the testimony of Scripture is correct that creation says to us something about our Creator, then we would do well to put ourselves in places where we can listen to its voice.

When we walk into nature with eyes to see and ears to hear, our hearts are filled with the presence of something beyond us, something that reminds us of how small we are but which comforts us at the same time. We realize the artificial world mediated through flat screens and earphones is nothing like the real world before us, and we are relieved. We startle at the terror of thunder and sigh at the refreshment of a gentle breeze. Whether the sublime or the beautiful surrounds us, both assure us we are not alone. There is a plan for nature and there is a plan for us. Finally, our minds are set on the things above. It is then we can sing in agreement with the lyrics of an old Swedish hymn.

> When through the woods and forest glades I wander,
> And hear the birds sing sweetly in the trees,
> When I look down from lofty mountain grandeur
> And see the brook and feel the gentle breeze.
>
> Then sings my soul, my Saviour God, to Thee,
> How great Thou art, how great Thou art!
> Then sings my soul, my Saviour God to Thee,
> How great Thou art, how great Thou art!

---

[23] Ibid., 123, 84-85.
[24] John Calvin, *Commentary on Genesis*, vol. 1 (Christian Classics Ethereal Library), accessed May 31, 2023, https://ccel.org/ccel/calvin/calcom01/calcom01.vi.html.

3

FRIENDSHIP AND COMMUNITY

Dear George, remember no man is a failure who has friends.

Clarence—It's a Wonderful Life

etachment from others is a feature built into the normal course of life now more than ever. According to the U.S. Bureau of Labor, employees stay in the same job for less time than they did a decade ago.[1] The average American now moves almost twelve times during the course of their life.[2] Voluntary and civic organizations have decreased dramatically.[3] In short, people are not around each other or working in close proximity for as long as they used to. Add to this trend growing family dysfunction, political

---

1 "The median number of years that wage and salary workers had been with their current employer was 4.1years in January 2022." It was 4.6 years in 2012. See: "News Release: Employee Tenure in 2022," *Bureau of Labor Statistics*, September 22, 2022.

2 "Calculating Migration Expectancy Using ACS Data," *Census Bureau*, December 3, 2021, https://www.census.gov/topics/population/migration/guidance/calculating-migration-expectancy.html.

3 Putnam, "The Strange Death of Civic America," *The Independent*, March 11, 1996, sec. Voices, https://www.independent.co.uk/voices/the-strange-death-of-civic-america-1341522.html; Linda Poon, "Why Americans Stopped Volunteering," Bloomberg.Com, September 12, 2019, https://www.bloomberg.com/news/articles/2019-09-12/america-has-a-post-9-11-volunteerism-slump.

polarization, and increased time spent connected to media sources, and it should come as no surprise that people today feel isolated.

Though these trends started before 2020, the Covid-19 lockdowns certainly did not help. A 2021 American Perspectives Survey found "that Americans report having fewer close friendships than they once did, talking to their friends less often, and relying less on their friends for personal support."[4] This revelation sparked concerns in major media outlets like *The New York Times,* which tallied up the implications of this increase from "serious loneliness" to "heart disease and stroke[s]."[5] *Fortune Magazine* called it a "friendship epidemic."[6]

Some Christians see a chance to attract new members by offering community in response to the "friendship epidemic," but churches face these isolation issues too.[7] Organizations like *The Gospel Coalition*, *9 Marks*, and *G3 Ministries* offer solutions to the crisis in things like being more intentionally social at church, participating in Bible studies, and treating church membership as a command despite feeling disconnected.[8] Most of these approaches are nothing new, but some try to package them in innovative ways. For example, the magazine *Christianity Today* ran a piece suggesting forming what the author called a "Q place" to deal with disconnected young people. This entailed a few Christians creating a group to "explore spiritual truths" by asking questions and reading Scripture without the constraints imposed by authority figures. People used to call that

---

4   Daniel Cox, "The State of American Friendship: Change, Challenges, and Loss," *The Survey Center on American Life,* June 8, 2021, https://www.americansurveycenter.org/research/the-state-of-american-friendship-change-challenges-and-loss/.

5   Catherine Pearson, "How Many Friends Do You Really Need?," *The New York Times,* May 7, 2022, sec. Well, https://www.nytimes.com/2022/05/07/well/live/adult-friendships-number.html.

6   Trey Williams, "It's Not Just You. Our Friendships Really Are Worse Now—and It's Getting Harder to Make New Ones," *Fortune,* February 5, 2023, https://fortune.com/2023/02/05/why-friendships-are-worse-now/.

7   In 2010, Southern Baptist leading thinkers published a blueprint for maintaining and expanding their denomination. It focused in part on the need to "model community in ways our increasingly urbanized and technologically isolated population craves." See: Adam Greenway and Chuck Lawless, *The Great Commission Resurgence: Fulfilling God's Mandate in Our Time* (B&H Publishing Group, 2010), 228.

8   Erik Raymond, "Help for Those Who Feel 'Disconnected' at Church," *The Gospel Coalition,* September 8, 2014, https://www.thegospelcoalition.org/blogs/erik-raymond/help-for-those-who-feel-disconnected-at-church/; Carrie Russell, "Open Your Bible, Bless Your Church," *9Marks,* October 4, 2019, https://www.9marks.org/article/open-your-bible-bless-your-church/; *Josh Buice,* "The Necessity to Prioritize the Local Church," G3 Ministries, November 22, 2022, https://g3min.org/the-necessity-to-prioritize-the-local-church/.

having friends over. Now it is a new strategy to prevent young people from leaving. All of these things can be helpful, but they are rather formulaic and fail to address the root issues.[9]

CLOSE PROXIMITY AND SHARED EXPERIENCE

Until recently, people did not choose friends based on superficial factors like hobbies or entertainment preferences. They simply lived, worked, and married near their neighbors, forming bonds as life unfolded. People were less distracted, more reliant on each other, and understood their responsibilities within family, community, and church. In some ways, our grandparents' lives resembled the world of Christ's time more than our own.

Jesus ministered in an area smaller than Rhode Island, among a close-knit, culturally homogeneous people who shared the same worship practices and relied on each other for survival. He worked closely with the same twelve disciples daily. Hospitality was common, and people often invited Jesus into their homes, leaving doors open for others to join.[10] With no private barriers like earphones or tinted windows, people lived openly, singing and traveling together. While this may seem overwhelming to introverts, it fostered strong friendships and a sense of belonging—key elements in the growth of the early church.

Christ's close connection with His disciples came in the context of physically living together for three years. It is what made Judas's betrayal an actual betrayal. It explains why Jesus was disappointed when James, John, and Peter fell asleep in the Garden of Gethsemane. It is also why unbelievers who did not know the Lord persecuted Christians who did.[11] Luke recorded that anti-Christian Jewish opponents recognized Peter and John "as having been with Jesus."[12] This shared intimacy is also why sorrow filled the disciples'

---

9 Emily Capo Sauerman, "How Can We Reach the Younger Generation?," *Christianity Today*, September 11, 2012, https://www.christianitytoday.com/biblestudies/bible-answers/spirituallife/younger-generation.html.
10 Luke 7:37 records how a woman came into Simon's house to wash Jesus' feet. This kind of openness was common.
11 John 15:21, 16:3
12 Acts 4:13

hearts at the prospect of Jesus leaving.[13] Christ's instruction to His disciples to "abide" in Him reinforces this call for proximity.[14] The word translated "abide" (μένω) means to "remain in a place." It is the opposite of "to go away."[15] Believers, loyal to their Savior, are meant to stay close to Him, just as He remains with them.[16] This connection is maintained by obeying His command to love one another.

Love should be the goal in all our relationships, but within the community of faith it bears a special significance. Christ portrayed His command to "love one another" as a "new commandment."[17] It could not have been "new" in the sense that God did not previously command it. Indeed, in Leviticus 19:18 God commanded the people of Israel to "love [their] neighbor as [themselves]." Yet the text indicates this command applied to "the sons of your people," meaning those with whom they shared ethnic ties. Thus, Jesus gave a "new commandment" by creating a community of love grounded not in the earthly realm, but in an eternal bond through the Holy Spirit. John Calvin said of this, "Because the image of God shines more brightly in those who have been regenerated, it is proper that the bond of love, among the disciples of Christ, should be far more close."[18] The outgrowth of this deep abiding love for each other is naturally what we know as friendship.

After commanding them to love each other, Jesus told His disciples, "No longer do I call you slaves, for the slave does not know what his master is doing; but I have called you friends, for all things that I have heard from My Father I have made known to you." In other words, Jesus had every divine right to maintain a strictly hierarchal relationship with His followers where they would keep His commandments simply on the basis of His authority. Yet Jesus condescended further by befriending sinful humans and treating them

---

[13] John 16:16

[14] John 15:4, 15:10, 15:25, 14:17.

[15] Geoffrey William Bromiley, *Theological Dictionary of the New Testament*, vol. 4 (Wm. B. Eerdmans Publishing, 1964), 574.

[16] Hebrews 13:5, Matt 10:33.

[17] John 13:34.

[18] John Calvin, John 13, *Calvin's Commentaries* (Christian Classics Ethereal Library), accessed August 12, 2023, https://biblehub.com/commentaries/calvin/john/13.htm.

with the familiarity shared between friends who enjoy disclosing important matters to each other. Jesus did this in person with the original disciples and does so now through the Holy Spirit.[19] This bond is only made possible through the gospel wherein God reconciled Himself to repentant sinners through the application of the merits of Christ's life, death, and resurrection. This is the "greater love" that compelled Jesus to "lay down his life for his friends."[20]

Thus, in Christ's example is a solution to the "friendship epidemic." Jesus' friendship with His disciples sprang from a mutual love built on shared experience. He walked with them through joy, sorrow, service, and sacrifice. Scripture says, "He loved them to the end."[21] In one sense, the church is a new spiritual fellowship, but in another, it mirrors natural relationships that form organically. This is why Peter describes the church using familiar terms like "a chosen race, a royal priesthood, a holy nation, [and] a people for God's own possession."[22] The secret to Christ's friendship with His disciples is really no secret at all. But it did require time, effort, and something in common.

ESTABLISHING CONNECTION

Christians share the love of Christ, families share ancestry, workers share goals, neighbors share interactions, and citizens share culture— all of which create opportunities for love and friendship to grow. Unfortunately, many people are now reluctant to make the effort to connect. In the past, life's demands required forming friendships, but today, technology allows us to avoid even basic interactions like checking our groceries out with an actual person. Because of this, social skills have atrophied and people have forgotten how to be a friend. Some fear rejection, while others are distracted by addictions. Whatever the reason, without the social trust that comes from mutual affection, our institutions will eventually deteriorate and nothing but brute force will hold them together. If we exclude

---

19 John 15:15, John 16:15.
20 John 16:13.
21 John 13:1.
22 1 Peter 2:9.

brothers and sisters from our Christian lives, we will likewise face spiritual ruin. We need each other.

Throughout Scripture God commends sharing fellowship with others. Psalm 133 states: "Behold, how good and how pleasant it is for brothers to dwell together in unity! It is like the precious oil upon the head, coming down upon the beard, even Aaron's beard, coming down upon the edge of his robes. It is like the dew of Hermon coming down upon the mountains of Zion; for there the Lord commanded the blessing—life forever."

In this short Psalm, King David celebrated worshipers journeying to Jerusalem for an annual feast. Throughout history, people applied the first sentence to everything from university mottos to Masonic lodges to rich estates, but in context it refers to the fellowship national citizens enjoyed in corporate worship. The Psalmist compares this unity to two symbols: costly oil, representing God's blessing for spiritual service, and dew on Israel's highest peak, which nourishes the land. Both images point to a rich and valuable social harmony.

God also commends the bonds people form in marriage, family, and friendship. Consider Solomon's words from Proverbs: "A friend loves at all times, and a brother is born for adversity."[23] "Faithful are the wounds of a friend, but deceitful are the kisses of an enemy."[24] "Oil and perfume make the heart glad, so a man's counsel is sweet to his friend."[25] He also talked about "a friend who sticks closer than a brother."[26] He may have been thinking about his father's friendship with Jonathan, which Scripture describes as "more wonderful than the love of women" because "the soul of Jonathan was knit to the soul of David, and Jonathan loved him as himself."[27] The picture is clear. True friendship involves support, honesty, and understanding.

Without close friendships it is unlikely Daniel, Hananiah, Mishael, and Azariah would be as strong as they were to challenge

---

[23] Prov 17:17.
[24] Prov 27:6.
[25] Prov 27:9.
[26] Prov 18:24.
[27] 2 Sam 1:26, 1 Sam 18:1

the Babylonian Empire. Moses needed Aaron, Elisha needed Elijah, Ruth needed Naomi, and Timothy needed Paul. Solomon observed:

> Two are better than one because they have a good return for their labor. For if either of them falls, the one will lift up his companion. But woe to the one who falls when there is not another to lift him up. Furthermore, if two lie down together they keep warm, but how can one be warm alone? And if one can overpower him who is alone, two can resist him. A cord of three strands is not quickly torn apart.

If our homes, churches, and country are weakening, perhaps it is related to a lack of human connection.

This is not a call to bury strained lives in more activities or to force unsuitable friendships.[28] Instead, it is a warning to not avoid friendships because of the risks involved. When Martha hosted Jesus, He pointed out that she was "worried and distracted by many things," causing her to miss the fellowship Mary had with Him.[29] Friendship may take time away from other tasks, but those tasks are often not as important. It takes work to be part of someone's life, but the rewards are worth it.

Three things seem to drive the current "friendship epidemic" more than anything else. First, people are afraid of rejection. Younger generations, who were often shielded by overprotective parenting and given trophies by sports teams regardless of performance, have not fully developed the emotional resilience needed to handle rejection. When it inevitably comes, some of them question their very existence. Rejection is an inevitable part of life, as Jesus' example demonstrates. It is hard to get to know someone until time is spent with them, and in that process, bonds often form—sometimes before the character of a person is fully understood.

---

28 Solomon warned about people who did not make suitable friends. He noted that "A perverse man spreads strife, and a slanderer separates intimate friends." (Prov 16:28). He also warned "not [to] associate with a man given to anger or go with a hot-tempered man." (Prov 22:24) Some relationships are detrimental because they set people up for betrayal, influence us in negative ways, or take away from relationships that are more important.

29 Luke 10:41.

Second, modern people have a tendency toward passivity. Political philosopher Robert Putnam examined the question of why civic organizations were declining as far back as 1996. He concluded "the culprit is television." This was at a time when Americans looked at screens for only "roughly four hours a day." Technology, including entertainment media, can be beneficial when it directs our attention to meaningful or uplifting pursuits. However, excessive use can dull the mind and place it in a consumptive, instead of productive, mode.

Third, some people do not know what being a friend is because they have never observed it in practice. Family dysfunction and social breakdown placed them in positions where they had no examples to follow. They may not know how to invite someone over for a meal or let someone know they care through a sympathy card or birthday present. Fortunately, ignorance is easily cured. The Bible is filled with examples of friendship.

In his letter to the Colossians, Paul outlines how Christians should live together, highlighting four key principles that can be grouped into two categories. First, he calls on Christians to actively cultivate kindness and love. Second, he encourages them to passively allow the peace of Christ and the word of Christ to shape their lives. He says:

> So, as those who have been chosen of God, holy and beloved, put on a heart of compassion, kindness, humility, gentleness and patience; bearing with one another, and forgiving each other, whoever has a complaint against anyone; just as the Lord forgave you, so also should you. Beyond all these things put on love, which is the perfect bond of unity. Let the peace of Christ rule in your hearts, to which indeed you were called in one body; and be thankful. Let the word of Christ richly dwell within you, with all wisdom teaching and admonishing one another with psalms and hymns and spiritual songs, singing with thankfulness in your hearts to God.[30]

---

[30] Col 3:12-16

The crown jewel of the passage is verse fourteen, where Paul says "Beyond all these things put on love." This inevitably takes work. It may mean helping someone instead of doom scrolling. This however is "the perfect bond of unity." There is no true unity without it. Love is the glue that binds people to each other and to Christ.

The good news is that God provides the patience and love people need through His peace and His Word. His peace dispels the fear of rejection, as Christians know they are always welcomed into His presence. Nothing done for others is wasted when it is done for God first. His Word offers examples of true friendship, curbs the desires for distractions that hinder relationships, and provides the strength and wisdom needed to nurture them.

4

A Rightly Ordered Love

Love is not love
Which alters when it alteration finds,
Or bends with the remover to remove:
O, no! it is an ever-fixed mark,
That looks on tempests and is never shaken.

William Shakespeare

I n our day it is common to think of love in terms of subjective personal preferences. Love can be found in both the devoted elderly couple and the casual sexual rendezvous. It can be displayed at a Veterans Day parade or a Pride month celebration. It can refer just as much to a stranger on social media as it can to a family member. Love does not need the boundaries set by mutual obligation, proximity, or trust. In fact, rejecting these boundaries is the only absolute condition that defines it. The slogan "love is love" captures this. It communicates the idea that various experiences producing different kinds of love are all equally legitimate.

Under this thinking, to place a limitation on what qualifies as love is to be unloving. We must accept people for who they are, which means affirming their professed identities and the choices that allegedly flow from those identities. Relegating the "love" label to certain displays and failing to extend it to others is condemned as hate and reserved for ignorant bigots who cling to prejudices that favor themselves, their people, and their God. This means natural affections and religious sentiments that discriminate against vice are now at odds with the modern definition of love. Even though this paradigm is self-refuting, since it also discriminates against competing definitions, many professing Christians seem to accept it.

In mainline churches it is common to assume that uncritical acceptance and the Bible's conception of love are the same thing. In light of this, they dismiss passages that limit worship to God and sexuality to marriage. Evangelical leaders often take a more complicated approach. They seek to uphold biblical teachings while also engaging with modern values to some degree. By publicly condemning those with more controversial reputations, they aim to present themselves as loving and thereby win approval from secular elites with social influence. However, it is becoming clear that while this strategy may create a temporary distinction between them and fringe "hate groups," the effects are short-lived. Increasingly, government officials and corporate leaders are pressuring Christians and traditional conservatives to embrace pluralism and sexual freedom. In this context, how should we respond when our core virtue—love—is used against us?

Jesus set an example during His battles with the Pharisees, who often subverted God's intended meaning. They justified fleshly desires by prioritizing perverted interpretations of certain passages, while ignoring other more relevant teachings. For example, Mark 7:9-13 recounts the way they justified failing to provide for their own parents by placing their funds in a ministry-directed safe harbor where it would inevitably benefit themselves. Likewise, Mark 10:2-12 describes the way they used Mosaic law to vindicate freely divorcing their own wives. In both cases, Jesus confronts them for disobeying God's clear design concerning honoring parents and marital fidelity. Ultimately, they distorted the definition of love by undermining the natural obligations that guide it, all in the pursuit of sin.

Today, we face a similar, yet more revolutionary, threat. Its goal is to subvert the created order and reshape us into "lovers of pleasure rather than lovers of God."[1] Just as Jesus challenged the Pharisees, we must challenge the present world system and embrace God's ordering.[2] This begins with recognizing how we are manipulated into accepting a false hollowed-out definition of love.

LOVE CORRUPTED

The term "love" has earned its positive reputation through generations of heartfelt expressions and acts: families were nurtured, soldiers sacrificed, and Jesus gave His life. At its core, love has always involved willingly embracing actions and fulfilling duties for the benefit of those with whom one shares a bond. This broad concept of love was recognized by secular and Christian thinkers alike. The Roman historian Livy (59 BC – AD 17) wrote that "true patriotism. . . [was] founded upon respect for family and love of the soil." The fictional Mentoria, who in colonial times instructed soon-to-be women to love their parents, said: "With love and duty both this I indite, and these lines dear parent I impart, the tender feelings of a grateful heart."[3]

Premodern people generally understood that for most human relationships, a natural design guided love and love motivated duty. Even if someone did not feel like fulfilling their duty, they should still fulfill it on the basis of a higher love for God and others. Eventually, affection for the object of their duty would follow. For example, a book on courtship from the 17th century told young women in the case of royal arranged marriages to "sacrifice [their] love where duty

---

1 2 Tim 3:4
2 Rom 12:2
3 Livy, *History of Rome* (Penguin Books, 1971), 105; Joanne Bailey, *Parenting in England 1760-1830: Emotion, Identity, and Generation* (OUP Oxford, 2012), 189.

ordains it."[4] In this case, benefitting one's family initially became the basis for selecting a spouse, while mutual love for that spouse came later through time and experience. This formulation offends modern sensibilities.

This is because in addition to the traditional view, we also inherit a Pre-Romantic outlook that sees love and duty as almost in opposition. Philosopher Immanuel Kant (1724-1804) said "inclinations . . . are always burdensome to a rational being," meaning that feelings conflicted with actions based in reason. This devalued passions as if they were not important.[5] Romantic-era philosophers tried to recover the importance of passion by grounding it in "a cosmic spirituality that underlay the apparent materialism of nature."[6] Unfortunately, they instead introduced a rationale that justified love on emotional grounds separate from any guiding principle. What came next effectively synthesized rational and emotional approaches to love.

In *The Origin of Species*, Darwin claimed "maternal love or maternal hatred . . . is all the same to the inexorable principle of natural selection."[7] This evolutionary teaching reduced people to animals. Love was simply an instinct derived from blind amoral biology. This did more than explain why people loved—it also destroyed the ability to set limits on legitimate instincts. Over time hormonal impulses became associated with love, and duties that conflicted with them were delegitimized as relics from the Dark Ages. For the next century, philosophers and psychologists wrestled with questions of love and duty, but they never returned to the transcendent view that placed them in their proper places. It is easy to see how we arrived at the current situation where divine explanations for love are non-binding and we are daily deceived to think of it more in selfish than sacrificial ways.

A constant drumbeat in our ears encourages us not only to reject duty and let our passions run wild, but also to think of this as love.

---

4   *The Art of Making Love: Or Rules for the Conduct of Ladies and Gallants in Their Amours* (J. Cotterel, 1676), 139.
5   Immanuel Kant, *The Critique of Practical Reason*, trans. Thomas Kingsmill Abbott (Project Gutenberg, 1778), https://www.gutenberg.org/files/5683/5683-h/5683-h.htm.
6   Irving Singer, *The Nature of Love, Volume 3: The Modern World* (MIT Press, 2009), 383.
7   Charles Darwin, *The Origin of Species* (P. F. Collier, 1909), 215.

Enlightened activists, supposedly free from bias and welcoming to all, simply want love—even if it means burning down a building. Spouses are motivated by self-love to end marriages they feel do not reflect their authentic selves. Friends destroy relationships when they cut someone out of their lives for failing to affirm a lifestyle choice. In each case, what was once considered unloving is now accomplished in the name of love. This approach to love ironically seeks to limit those who believe in limits. It "call[s] evil good, and good evil" and accomplishes the mission of Satan to "steal and kill and destroy."[8] This means the term is now dead, and if it is to mean anything again, we must recover its good name and adorn it with truth.

LOVE RESTORED

The greatest commandment in the Bible is to love God "with all [our] heart, and with all [our] soul, and with all [our] mind, and with all [our] strength."[9] From this flows our love for those made in His image. This means the entirety of the Christian life is characterized by love. It should motivate spiritual service and natural obligation. Jesus instructed His followers to love even their enemies.[10]

The word *agape* was rarely used in pagan literature, but it is the term most often translated as love in the New Testament, appearing 116 times. It is popular for preachers to describe it is as a love that acts rather than feels. But it is more than an action that must be chosen. The Pharisees preoccupied themselves with keeping the technical details of Mosaic law. They were known, according to Josephus, to be "accurate expositors" in this.[11] Yet in Luke 11:42, Jesus indicts them for paying "tithes of mint, rue, and every kind of garden herb" while ignoring "justice and the love of God." None of their religious actions produced legitimate *agape*. This is because *agape* also "carries the sense of affectionate regard or benevolence toward someone."[12]

---

8 Is 5:20, John 10:10
9 Mark 12:30
10 1 Cor 13:13, Eph 5:25, Matt 5:44.
11 Flavius Josephus, *The Jewish War*, ed. Robert Traill, vol. I (London: Houlston and Stoneman, 1851), 205.
12 Douglas Mangum, ed., *Lexham Theological Wordbook* (Bellingham, WA: Lexham Press, 2014).

We find in Luke 16 that the Pharisees "were lovers of money" and scoffed at Jesus' teaching that one "cannot serve God and wealth." They also liked "the chief seats in the synagogues and the respectful greetings in the market places."[13] Their willful attempts to follow God's law proceeded from a desire for success and comfort rather than a love for God. Their motives, rooted in what Jesus identified as evil hearts, ultimately became their ruin.[14]

In contrast, Jesus' actions came from a love for God and others. He set the law in its proper place where it honored God's intentions and served man. When the Pharisees confronted Him because His disciples picked grain on the Sabbath, He declared: "The Sabbath was made for man, and not man for the Sabbath."[15] His love did not terminate with the letter of the law. He could see beyond it to the people it governed. When James and John asked to sit on His right and left in glory, Jesus did not say "follow rules." He said they should be "slave[s] of all."[16] He exemplified this before His death in the upper room where He dressed as a slave and "wash[ed] the disciples' feet."[17]

No better tribute to Christ's love may be found than in the ancient *Carmen Christi* hymn from Philippians 2. Paul precedes the hymn with instructions to the church at Philippi to "not merely look out for [their] own personal interests, but also for the interests of others." This preference for other church members is part of what Paul called "maintaining the same love." He then promoted Christ's attitude as the example they should follow: "Who, although He existed in the form of God, did not regard equality with God a thing to be grasped, but emptied Himself, taking the form of a bond-servant, and being made in the likeness of men. Being found in appearance as a man, He humbled Himself by becoming obedient to the point of death, even death on a cross."[18] In this supreme act of love, the God of creation

---

[13] Luke 16:13-14, Luke 11:43
[14] Matt 15:18
[15] Mark 2:27
[16] Matt 10:43
[17] John 13:5
[18] Phil 2:4, 2:2, 2:6-8

willingly suffered slander, betrayal, rejection, humiliation, pain, and death for His people.

This is how "God demonstrate[d] His own love toward" believers, according to Romans 5:8. Yet this demonstration simply displayed what was already present. In Romans 8:28-30, what theologians call the Golden Chain of Redemption, teaches that God "foreknew," "predestined," "called," "justified," and "glorified" His people. This means before their birth, God already loved them. On this basis, Paul claimed that no "created thing will be able to separate us from the love of God, which is in Christ Jesus our Lord."[19] Christ's *agape* preceded His sacrifice.

Some incorrectly teach the reason God loves believers is because they first choose Him. This conflicts with numerous passages that show a Christian's love for God is actually preceded by God's love for them: "the kindness of God leads you to repentance."[20] Salvation is not based on human "deeds . . . done in righteousness," but on the mercy of God "according to the kind intention of His will."[21] This desire to show mercy and kindness to someone else is central to *agape*. Not only does it provide the basis for salvation and spiritual service, but it is necessary for the formation and maintenance of any healthy society. In a certain sense love does make the world go 'round.

THE BOUNDS OF LOVE

God's covenantal love for both Israel and the church is unconditional, everlasting, and exclusive. He does not love other nations or institutions like He does Israel and the church. For the church He gave special favor based upon what Christ accomplished in redemption. Christians in turn reflect this love of God to each other. The "new commandment" Jesus gave to His disciples "to love one another" inaugurated a new spiritual community composed of people from different tribes, tongues, and nations all adopted into God's family.

---

[19] Rom 8:39
[20] Rom 2:4
[21] Titus 3:5, Eph 1:5

Christ did not say others would know them by miracles, customs, or community involvement, but by their "love [for] one another."[22] This was the "the perfect bond of unity" coloring their interactions with each other.[23] It meant that while God commanded them to "do good to all people," their first priority was to care for members "of the household of the faith."[24]

One important difference between the church and Israel is that the universal church exists on a spiritual level. It does not provide a substitution for the temporal associations people belong to related to gender, family, nation, community, citizenship, labor, or voluntary association. Galatians 3:28 says: "There is neither Jew nor Greek, there is neither slave nor free man, there is neither male nor female; for you are all one in Christ Jesus." Nevertheless, Augustine explained: "Difference of race or condition or sex is indeed taken away by the unity of faith, but it remains imbedded in our mortal interactions, and in the journey of this life."[25] For example, a woman does not cease to be a married female of Italian heritage when she converts to Christianity. This is important, because it orchestrates the way God beautifully arranges how love is channeled in natural ways rooted in creation and not just in spiritual ways rooted in redemption. In Israel we see this more clearly.

There, God established a spiritual community within the boundaries of natural relationships. Although everything in their religious system—from animal sacrifices to religious celebrations pointed national members toward spiritual redemption—they nevertheless remained members of ethnic Israel. One only needed to be born a Jew to receive the temporal covenant blessings that came through things like law and land. Paul said that to Israel belonged "the adoption as sons, and the glory and the covenants and the giving of the Law and the temple service and the promises."[26]

Just as God commanded the church as a spiritual community to

---

22 John 13:35
23 Col 3:14, 1 Cor 16:14
24 Gal 6:10
25 Mark Edwards and Thomas Oden, *Galatians, Ephesians, Philippians* (InterVarsity Press, 2014), 49.
26 Rom 9:4b-5

prioritize fellow Christians, He also commanded Israel to prioritize their fellow countryman. For example, Christians and Israelites were both to provide for destitute members of their groups.[27] They were both to seek spiritual mediation instead of court adjudication concerning challenging personal disagreements.[28] They were both to "give preference to one another" in tangible ways. For Israel, this included laws concerning slavery, worship, and land rights that favored their countryman over others.[29]

It is common for modern people to get uncomfortable at this point and start asking whether such laws reflect bigotries and hatred for outsiders. Should Americans or any other country or region set up laws that protect or benefit themselves and not others? Today these questions surround things like border security and voting rights. The important thing to remember is that God's law, when implemented from a pure heart, is the definition of love. Jesus said that the entire law rested on the commands to love God and neighbor.[30]

When Israel walked with God, they took their responsibility to be "a light of the nations so that [His] salvation may reach to the end of the earth" seriously.[31] God told them to treat strangers with the love they had for themselves by doing them no wrong.[32] Yet this equality before the law did not erase the special love they had for each other. This is apparent in the New Testament when Jesus wept over Jerusalem or when Paul wished he "were accursed . . . for the sake of . . . [his] kinsmen according to the flesh."[33]

The natural feelings we share for familiar places like home, the comradery of old friends, and the love of country inspire us to sacrifice for those with whom we share fellowship. We love the things we are connected to through mutual obligation, proximity, and trust. This is the essence of loving our neighbors as ourselves. The

---

[27] Is 58:7, James 2:15
[28] Deut 17:8, 1 Cor 6:4
[29] Ex 21:2-6, Lev 25:44-46, Ezekiel 44:9, Deut 23:3-7, Lev 25:10, Rom 12:10
[30] Matt 22:40
[31] Is 49:6
[32] Lev 19:33-34
[33] Luke 19:41, Rom 9:3

English term neighbor comes from two words meaning "near" and "dweller."[34] A neighbor is "any person who is near us."[35]

Under the influence of the modern concept of love, real people are often sacrificed to abstract notions of equity, diversity, inclusion, and freedom. People dehumanize others who do not fit into their utopian political vision. Everyone loves humanity in the abstract, but not always the individuals they live with, especially when those people disrupt their plans. However, loving neighbors is not a love for propositions, principles, or ideas. It is a love for the tangible people we encounter in our everyday lives.

The other Greek terms translated "love" channel *agape* toward different relationships. *Phileo* refers to affection developed through experience, like friendships. *Storge* refers to intimate connections such as kinship. *Eros* refers to romantic or sexual love. Each of these relationships, when properly exercised, represent the connection humans share as part of God's good design. They even serve to illustrate heavenly realities such as the brotherly affection and deep devotion Christians have for one another as well as the mysterious love Christ has for His church. We learn to love our brothers and sisters in Christ by first understanding what it is to love our actual brothers and sisters.[36]

Paul instructs Christians engaged in different earthly relationships to "walk in love" in specific ways. This includes wives respecting husbands, husbands loving wives, children honoring parents, fathers not provoking children, slaves obeying masters, and masters caring for slaves.[37] Jesus Himself cared for His mother, submitted to His Father, preached to and healed the "lost sheep of the house of Israel," and laid down His life for His sheep.[38] John recounts that "Jesus, knowing that His hour had come that He would depart out

---

[34] "Neighbor" (Online Etymology Dictionary), accessed July 2, 2023, https://www.etymonline.com/word/neighbor.

[35] Charles Spurgeon, "Love Thy Neighbour," https://www.spurgeon.org/resource-library/sermons/love-thy-neighbour/.

[36] Heb 13:1, Rom 12:10

[37] Eph 5:1, 5:22-6:9

[38] John 19:25-27, John 6:38, Matt 15:24, John 10:15

of this world to the Father, having loved His own who were in the world, He loved them to the end."[39]

The answer to the question, "Who is my neighbor?" is actually fairly straightforward. Duty and proximity are linked. Extending out from the center of our most intimate relationships are people we share life with. Our obligation to them diminishes as our proximity decreases, but it still remains. Charles Spurgeon said of the Good Samaritan that "when he saw the wounded man on the road to Jericho, [he] felt that he was in his neighbourhood, and that therefore he was his neighbour, and he was bound to love him."[40] In the same way we are to love even our personal enemies whom we cross paths with, which means doing what is best for them even at our own expense.

---

[39] John 13:1
[40] Spurgeon.

5

THE RELIGION OF
LIBERALISM

*The great line of division in modern politics . . . is not between
totalitarians on the one hand and liberals (or libertarians) on
the other; rather, it lies between all those who believe in some sort
of transcendent moral order, on one side, and on the other side
all those who take this ephemeral existence of ours for the be-all
and end-all to be devoted chiefly to producing and consuming.*

Russell Kirk

For conservative Christians, the past few years have been particularly tumultuous. After weathering a social justice storm
and the Covid-19 hysteria, many believed they were no longer
wanted in the medical, military, and educational establishments. To
make matters worse, rank and file evangelicals felt betrayed by their
own trusted institutions, including churches. As a result, embattled
believers put faith in the few institutions remaining they thought
resisted the impulses of 2020. Ministries like The Gospel Coalition,
Together for the Gospel, and 9Marks became synonymous with

compromise, subversion, and weakness, while G3, Founders, and Canon Press gained from their demise.

At the time, only a handful of people could see what is now unfolding—that despite battle fatigue, evangelicals would continue to fracture over ideology. Whether people are aware or not, the main disagreement this time seems to involve a clash of conservative instincts with liberalism. Unlike the conflict over social justice, which Americans who remembered the Cold War era better understood, this division is more difficult to navigate, because it requires people to examine their ingrained assumptions.

SOCIAL JUSTICE AND LIBERALISM

Christians on the Right reject things like Black Lives Matter in part because it reminds them of previous enemies such as the Bolsheviks, Nazis, and various socialist movements. Yet, liberalism and the post-WWII consensus which reinforced it are largely taken for granted.[1] It is easier for the religious Right to spot the issues with foreign-born socialism that it is to recognize similar features embedded in their own country's liberal order. Unlike Westerners who are generally unaware of the gradual changes transforming their societies from Christian to totalitarian, immigrants from communist countries tend to see the shift more clearly.

In Ryszard Legutko's book *The Demon in Democracy*, a man who lived under Soviet control in Poland describes his dismay upon discovering that Western liberal democracy was similar to the communism he thought he left. Both were all-encompassing ideologies that sought to change reality into a utopian ideal. The world was "like a machine to be ... perfected by new inventions" that could free people

---

[1] It is typical in modern treatments of liberalism, usually from Classical Liberals who wish to distinguish themselves from progressives, to make sharp distinctions between different forms of liberalism. I do not go into great detail about these differences and developments since my focus is on commonly shared traits. "We continue to define ourselves culturally, even spiritually, as anti-totalitarian, anti-fascist, anti-racist, and anti-nationalist. I call the atmosphere of opinion that sustains these anti imperatives the 'postwar consensus.'" See: R. R. Reno, *Return of the Strong Gods: Nationalism, Populism, and the Future of the West* (Simon and Schuster, 2019), X.

from an oppressive past.[2] People were required to replace their older obligations with allegiance to a certain political system. In Eastern-Bloc countries, every institution was politicized and expected to prove their commitment to the party. In Western democracies, similar requirements emerged to defend liberalism and its features such as the democratic process, venerating minorities, and free sexual expression. The architects of these abstract systems, whether high-ranking communist party members or liberal Ivy League professors, thought they would inevitably succeed since history was on their side. This is one reason Legutko believes former communist elites succeeded better in Western liberal democracies than they did against their more religious anti-communist opponents in former Soviet states.

It is important to understand that modernity gave birth to both liberalism and Marxist-influenced social justice as tools to undermine previous traditional civilizations.[3] In the name of democracy, freedom, and progress both contribute to social pluralism, cultural decay, and increased state control. Some might think the two are not easily distinguished, but there are differences. The main one is that liberals see the individual as the basic social unit, and thus they advocate for the expansion of a neutral society which guarantees people's sacred autonomy. Social justice proponents, on the other hand, argue that certain identity groups are more fundamental, and thus they advocate for the expansion of a society that guarantees the prosperity of underperforming identities. These shades of difference produce heated political debate today, but in the end, both sides force traditional societies to conform to rigid innovative ideologies. Liberals are fond of saying they are the alternative to communism and fascism, but in reality they join the ranks of both against sacredness, social bonds, and custom.

---

2 Ryszard Legutko, *The Demon in Democracy: Totalitarian Temptations in Free Societies* (Encounter Books, 2018), 6.
3 By modernity I refer to secularizing forces that reduce man to a scientific or economic unit.

THE LIBERAL RIGHT

Generally speaking, most modern Right-wing media figures reject overt social justice, but often embrace a form of classical liberalism on issues like religious pluralism, multiculturalism, and marital recognition. For example, then candidate Mitt Romney's 2007 *Faith in America* speech was almost universally praised by political conservatives.[4] Rush Limbaugh called it "uplifting," "optimistic," and "inspiring."[5] Sean Hannity thought it was unfortunate Romney had to defend himself against people who were "attacking religion" by harboring reservations about the possibility of a Mormon president.[6] Yet, the driving point of Romney's speech was that America possessed a "political religion" transcending all faiths, thus making religion a personal necessity that did not reflect a binding reality. The assumption that Americans should take seriously a religiously neutral "common creed" in public while privatizing their religious beliefs is now the standard assumption in politically conservative circles.[7] Most influencers on the Right treat culture the way they treat religion—as operating alongside other cultures in a neutral society that does not favor one culture over others.

The United States started shifting away from its dominant Anglo-Protestant culture most significantly after the 1965 Immigration Act, which allegedly "infuse[d] justice into our immigration policy" by overturning restrictions that favored certain nationalities.[8] While modern conservatives oppose illegal immigration, few are willing to entertain the idea that this continuing development presents a challenge for social stability. Instead, they tend to attribute racial and religious tensions to different disembodied "ideas" that could be rectified if all residents simply held universal American beliefs.

4　Modern political conservatives tend toward classical liberalism. Traditional or paleoconservatives reject liberalism.
5　"Romney Speech Freaks Out Libs," *The Rush Limbaugh Show*, December 7, 2007, https://www.rushlimbaugh.com/daily/2007/12/07/romney_speech_freaks_out_libs/.
6　"Evangelical Leaders On Romney's Speech," *Hannity and Colmes* (Fox News, December 6, 2007), https://www.realclearpolitics.com/articles/2007/12/evangelical_leaders_on_romneys.html.
7　Mitt Romney, "Transcript: Mitt Romney's Faith Speech," https://www.npr.org/templates/story/story.php?storyId=16969460.
8　"First Session on H.R. 2580 to Amend the Immigration and Nationality Act, and for Other Purposes" (U.S. Government Printing Office, 1965).

Republican politicians like Paul Ryan and Ted Cruz repeat slogans used by the Left, such as "we are a nation of immigrants," to promote the idea that immigrants are "critical for our economic well-being" or that they share our belief in "freedom."[9] Whether these conservatives realize it or not, this culture-blind approach undermines longstanding ways of life in communities across Europe and the United States.

The institution of marriage has not been threatened by foreign cultures as much as it has been by domestic liberalism. Commentators like Ben Shapiro and Charlie Kirk defended religious liberty, yet they have also voiced support for the right to marry someone of the same sex. Shapiro reasoned that consensual sexual activity carried no social "externalities," while Kirk argued that Republicans were "the party of freedom" and that same-sex marriages "should have all the same tax benefits."[10] Although this notion was a relatively new one for popular conservative thinkers, it became almost universal overnight. When media personality Dave Rubin announced that he and his alleged husband were having children via surrogacy, they were congratulated by popular conservative media personalities like Christopher Rufo, Matt Whitlock, and Megyn Kelly, in addition to social media platforms such as The Blaze and Prager U.[11]

Of course, none of these positions are actually conservative in the traditional sense and have only been adopted over time as more liberalism gained inroads on the Right. During the 2015 Republican presidential primaries, popular commentator Glenn Beck told his radio audience: "I really think we have to start calling ourselves Classic Liberals." For him this meant appealing to people on the Left who rejected the conservative label but wanted to stop the

9 Paul Ryan, "10 Questions With Paul Ryan," interview by Belinda Luscombe, *Time*, August 21, 2014, https://time.com/3153350/10-questions-with-paul-ryan/.; Ted Cruz [@tedcruz], "We Are a Nation of Immigrants. The Right Way to Come Is Legally by Following the Rule of Law. The Wrong Way to Come Is by Putting Children in the Custody of Human Traffickers and Crossing Illegally. Https://T.Co/zLDKkzhtaa," *Twitter*, March 27, 2021, https://twitter.com/tedcruz/status/1375613541269467138;

10 Ben Shapiro, *Joe Rogan Experience #1276*, interview by Joe Rogan, April 3, 2019, https://www.youtube.com/watch?v=sCD9zjf_YRU; Charlie Kirk, *Millennial Conservative on Trump, Social Issues, & Religion | Charlie Kirk | POLITICS | Rubin Report*, interview by Dave Rubin, January 19, 2018, https://www.youtube.com/watch?v=dZ8Cy4wULxg.

11 Dave Rubin [@RubinReport], "It's True. All of It. Https://T.Co/IV4rUIn13j," *Twitter*, March 16, 2022, https://twitter.com/RubinReport/status/1504128589201039360.

government from violating their freedom.[12] Evangelical elites have largely gone along with this sea change by defending a more neutral society in the public realm, while simultaneously holding on to their unique religious beliefs within the confines of church and home.

Much of the debate over so-called "Christian Nationalism" displays this mindset. Scott Aniol, the Executive Vice President of G3 Ministries, believes Christians should pursue public office "not so they can enforce Christian law" but instead to "prevent pagans from enforcing pagan law."[13] Though Aniol believes Christians still have a duty to "uphold the Constitution" and "be active in the political process," they should reject "the establishment of 'cultural Christianity'" with its customs and laws.[14] He called the Pilgrims' motivation in founding the Plymouth Colony "for the Glory of God, and Advancement of the Christian Faith," "unbiblical."[15] Under this thinking, Christians should work toward a "universal common kingdom of God" in which no religion is favored more than any other.[16]

Interestingly, modern evangelical thinkers have also started to help Christians suppress whatever urge they may have to conserve their more homogeneous cultures against the forces of globalism. It goes without saying that evangelical elites habitually misinterpret Revelation 7:9 as a mandate for Western Christians to diversify their churches and countries. It is also standard for the most conservative voices at Christian conferences to promote the teaching from Critical Race Theory that race is simply a "social construct."[17] While

---

12 Wilson, "Glenn: I'm a Liberal...," January 30, 2015, https://www.glennbeck.com/2015/01/30/glenn-im-a-liberal/.

13 Scott Aniol [@ScottAniol], "@MarcusGustavus Yes You Are, and God Has given You Very Limited Enumerated Powers to Preserve Peace and Order in This Present Evil Age. Faithfulness to Your Calling Means Staying in Your God Ordained Lane. And, by the Way, I Want as Many Christians as Possibly in Public Office, Not so They Can...," *Twitter*, April 22, 2023, https://twitter.com/ScottAniol/status/1649763477576204289.

14 Scott Aniol, "Christian Faithfulness: The Biblical Alternative to Christian Nationalism," *G3 Ministries* (blog), May 3, 2023, https://g3min.org/christian-faithfulness-the-biblical-alternative-to-christian-nationalism/; Scott Aniol, "The Mixed Blessings of a Christian Nation," *G3 Ministries* (blog), April 26, 2023, https://g3min.org/the-mixed-blessings-of-a-christian-nation/.

15 Scott Aniol [@ScottAniol], "@MarcusGustavus Unbiblical.," Twitter, April 17, 2023, https://twitter.com/ScottAniol/status/1648001840628260868.

16 Aniol, "The Mixed Blessings of a Christian Nation."

17 The Dallas Statement on Social Justice states: "'Race' is not a biblical category, but rather a social construct that often has been used to classify groups of people in terms of inferiority and superiority." Some of the more prominent signers have also individually expressed their agreement. See: Craig Mitchell, "Race / Ethnicity," March 13, 2019, https://statementonsocialjustice.com/author_speaker/craig-mitchell.

these teachings seem to conflict, they both easily contribute to a reductionistic approach to man that downplays his national identity, either confining its importance to a spiritual dimension, or questioning its reality, while placing ultimate importance on the ideas that exist in his mind. The only social requirement to be part of a liberal democracy involves a profession of faith in liberal democracy. Things like heritage, lineage, and language are ultimately irrelevant.

Even some postmillennialists, who would likely disagree with religious pluralism, find multiculturalism acceptable. For example, Peter Leithart believes that when it comes to public policy, affinity for the universal church should outweigh cultural affinities. In his mind, Western Christians have nothing to fear from members of other nationalities immigrating in large numbers, since they allegedly boost the economy and reinvigorate Christian institutions.[18] Leithart essentially justifies his belief in a proposition nation based on universal principles by appealing to Christianity. He says "it's not hard" to turn "people from every corner of the globe into devoted Americans," and that doing so will help us "resemble that final kingdom assembled from all tribes, tongues, nations, and peoples."[19] An approach to public policy that promotes the interests of a particular nation instead of the universal church conflicts with "the universal political vision of Christianity."[20] Instead, Christians should "rigorously attempt to make the Church, rather than the nation-state, the heart of our geopolitics."[21] This same penchant to devalue the importance of religion or culture in a body politic is also starting to apply to marriage and gender.

Adopting beliefs that blatantly justify same-sex marriage ceremonies or transgenderism are still causes for expulsion from conservative evangelicalism. Yet two developments undermine Christians' ability

---

[18] Peter Leithart, "Stay in the Story: A Response to Alastair Roberts," *Theopolis Institute* (blog), June 13, 2019, https://theopolisinstitute.com/conversations/stay-in-the-story-a-response-to-alastair-roberts/.

[19] Peter Leithart, "The Nation, the Church, and the Immigrants," *First Things* (blog), July 31, 2015, https://www.firstthings.com/web-exclusives/2015/07/the-nation-the-church-and-the-immigrants.

[20] Peter Leithart, "Against National Conservatism," *First Things* (blog), August 19, 2022, https://www.firstthings.com/web-exclusives/2022/08/against-national-conservatism.

[21] Peter Leithart, "Conservatism's Putin Problem, Revisited," *Patheos* (blog), July 25, 2017, https://www.patheos.com/blogs/leithart/2017/07/conservatisms-putin-problem-revisited/.

to apply biblical morality to these matters in the public square. The first is a commitment to a neutrality where Christians and LGBTQ+ activists can both operate publicly on an equal footing. Even if their ideas are sinful and damaging, that in itself is not seen as a reason to prohibit their public advocacy.

The second is the gradual adoption of a non-sinful homosexual orientation which can easily justify public acceptance of accompanying behavior.[22] Organizations designed to appeal to evangelicals, like Revoice and The Center for Faith, Sexuality & Gender, support the idea that same sex attraction is permissible. Yet if only homosexual actions are sinful, but not the temptations, inclinations, or desires that lead to them, there is little reason to prohibit the advancement of homosexual ideology in public unless it blatantly includes stimulating sexual activity. This is where Moms for Liberty and other parental rights groups craft arguments to prohibit blatantly pro-LGBTQ+ books in schools only on the basis that they are graphic, while ignoring their homosexual component. At the very least, evangelicals who adopt this belief do still try to advocate for Christian morality, but they do so while operating with a self-inflicted disadvantage. While the soft-peddling orientation approach harms orthodoxy, the neutral public square approach is more directly serious.

George Marsden called this neutral commitment "principled pluralism" and describes it as an "attempt to take the differences among varieties of both religious and nonreligious perspectives seriously."[23] When prominent pastors like J.D. Greear call homosexuality a sin, yet instruct Christians to be "the fiercest advocates for dignity and rights to be extended to . . . gay and lesbian people," they are applying this rationale.[24] Christians in the political world are now inclined

---

22 Not all evangelicals use "orientation" language. Other terms like "proclivity," "urge," and "tendency" are frequently substituted. Jared Moore traces some of this among conservative evangelical leaders. See: Jared Moore, *The Lust of the Flesh: Thinking Biblically About "Sexual Orientation," Attraction, and Temptation* (Free Grace Press, 2023), 56.

23 George Marsden, *The Twilight of the American Enlightenment: The 1950s and the Crisis of Liberal Belief* (Basic Books, 2014), 166.

24 J.D. Greear, "How the Fall Affects Us All" (Sermon, Summit Church, January 27, 2019), https://summitchurch.com/message/how-the-fall-affects-us-all/.

to support access to public resources and privileges for LGBTQ+ people and groups in the promotion of their sexual views.

When Uganda passed a bill penalizing "aggravated homosexuality," which involves children, the handicapped, or knowingly spreading HIV, Senator Ted Cruz called it "grotesque & an abomination."[25] After the Florida Senate voted to strip Disney of its self-governing status when the company opposed the *Parental Rights in Education* law, outspoken evangelical lawyer Jenna Ellis offered to represent Disney to "defend [their] right to constitutionally protected speech."[26] In 2023, eighteen Republican Congressional Representatives, half of whom were Protestant, voted to continue funding Pride Month celebrations through the Department of Defense. Marcus Molinaro, one of the evangelical representatives, justified his vote by saying that defunding such activities could be "used to infringe on individual rights."[27]

UNDERSTANDING LIBERALISM

Although the modern Right, and the evangelicals who morally anchor it, are increasingly willing to adopt the language and conclusions of liberalism, a previous generation of conservative thinkers would have disagreed. Russell Kirk, perhaps the most important American conservative intellectual of the mid-twentieth century, released an article in 1956 critiquing the Classical Liberalism of nineteenth century English philosopher John Stuart Mill. Mill believed "that the only purpose for which power can be rightfully exercised over any member of a civilized community, against his will, is to prevent harm to others." Kirk argued experience showed that

[25] Ted Cruz [@tedcruz], "This Uganda Law Is Horrific & Wrong. Any Law Criminalizing Homosexuality or Imposing the Death Penalty for 'Aggravated Homosexuality' Is Grotesque & an Abomination. ALL Civilized Nations Should Join Together in Condemning This Human Rights Abuse. #LGBTQ," *Twitter*, May 29, 2023, https://twitter.com/tedcruz/status/1663200925018726407.

[26] Jenna Ellis [@JennaEllisEsq], "Hi @Disney. Open Offer to Help Defend Your Right to Constitutionally Protected Speech against Florida's Illegal Retaliation. Https://Newsweek.Com/Former-Trump-Lawyer-Breaks-Desantis-over-Disney-Hes-over-Line-1699730," *Twitter*, April 22, 2022, https://twitter.com/JennaEllisEsq/status/1517552285492068353.

[27] Sarah Weaver, "Here Are The Republicans Who Helped Defeat A Measure To Defund Taxpayer-Funded Pride Events," September 29, 2023, https://dailycaller.com/2023/09/29/republicans-defeat-measure-defund-state-department-drag-shows/.

allowing this kind of liberty only worked under certain conditions, namely accompanying a high level of public virtue. Otherwise, it would accelerate immorality as the twentieth century had shown.

Mill's delusion was easy to believe so long as material progress, representative government, and humanitarian reform worked to "subdue the dark passions of the human heart." Unfortunately, dark hearts used these very mechanisms to promote destructive behaviors like pornography, generational welfare, and drug dependency. Mill argued against "unthinking obedience to the dictates of custom," yet it was the obligations embedded in customs that effectively stalled debased passions. Mill's ideology failed to accurately assess real world human behavior. When given almost unlimited access to vice, most people should not be expected to choose it over virtue.[28] Unfortunately, classical liberals are generally blind to the connection that exists between their philosophy of unbridled personal freedom and social moral degradation.

There are two primary reasons for this. One is related to an undeterred faith in the eventual triumph of human reason. The 18th century philosopher Immanuel Kant assumed "if only freedom is granted enlightenment is almost sure to follow."[29] The other is because liberals do not tend to categorize public promotion of immorality as a public evil. Instead, they understand a public evil to be that which hinders human choice. In Ayan Rand's 1943 novel *The Fountainhead*, the libertarian philosopher sums up this sentiment with the statement that "all that which proceeds from man's dependence upon man is evil."[30] Although John Locke, the 17th century philosopher, would certainly not have agreed with many of Rand's conclusions, his views did provide a rational basis for this kind of thinking.

Locke believed people lived in perfect equality in a state of nature until they consented to "make themselves members of some politic society."[31] This set the tone for conceiving of political unions as

---

28 Russell Kirk, "Mill's 'On Liberty' Reconsidered," *National Review*, January 25, 1956.
29 Immanuel Kant, "What Is Enlightenment?" (1784). https://sourcebooks.fordham.edu/mod/kant-whatis.asp.
30 Ayn Rand, *The Fountainhead* (The New American Library, 1971), 682.
31 John Locke, "Of the State of Nature," in *Second Treatise Of Government* (Project Gutenberg, 2021).

contractual arrangements between individuals instead of organic relationships with those with whom one shares life. In this framework, traditional attachments to things like land, religion, and nationality can pose a threat to the liberal order, since they claim people's allegiances in ways that transcend personal choice and are thus capable of challenging social contracts. One only needs to consider the wars of religion that proceeded the Protestant Reformation to understand this fear. In response, Enlightenment thinkers provided a basis for demoting the binding influence of these attachments through the imposition of certain universal principles.

For John Locke, the civil magistrate's role was established in the defense of life, liberty, and property to ensure that no man was "subjected to the will or authority of any other man" without consent.[32] Thomas Hobbes believed that seeking peace and defending oneself against the claims of others were fundamental laws of nature that legitimized the formation of a "leviathan" state to preserve order.[33] Jean-Jacques Rousseau argued for a "social contract" based upon mutual choice that protected people from threats to their individual freedom.

Although each philosopher sought to preserve elements of Christian civilization to varying degrees, they all deviated from the previous Christian assumptions that the ultimate purpose of civil organization was not to protect individual choice, but to enable people to fulfill earthly roles and prepare them for eternity.[34] Humans did not associate with each other out of necessity so they could pursue their own interests more efficiently. God created them as social creatures to function within a community. The basis for society did not arise from below, within the heart of man, but from above, in the providence of God.

Whether they knew it or not, liberals rejected this understanding of divine order and replaced it with more democratic systems that

---

[32] John Locke, "Of Paternal Power," in *Second Treatise Of Government* (Project Gutenberg, 2021).

[33] Thomas Hobbes, *Leviathan, Parts I and II–Revised Edition* (Broadview Press, 2010), 127.

[34] Augustine thought God gave man things that made for "temporal peace" such as "health and safety and human fellowship." He said that "every man who made a good use of these advantages suited to the peace of this mortal condition, should receive ampler and better blessings, namely, the peace of immortality." See: Augustine, *The City of God*, trans. Marcus Dods (Jazzybee Verlag, 2015), 466.

prized autonomy. They followed on the heels of the scientific revolution which mathematized nature. So too, society operated according to laws that if identified could be expressed in a final arrangement which would ensure social harmony. All of society would need to be reshaped to conform to liberal principles.

There was little use in all of this for traditional conservative minds who sought to prudentially restrain human hearts and challenge the different, various, and changing threats to their civilization. Establishments that traditionally reinforced natural duties such as families, churches, and aristocracies were likewise downgraded and made subject to the general will. For classical liberals, the greater threat did not come from sinful hearts, but from forces that placed obligations on them and inhibited their ability to choose freely. Since these impediments were part of an unchosen environment that violated human freedom and produced conflict, traditions that reinforced them were seen as non-binding. Only freely chosen associations could be considered legitimate.

From Liberalism to Wokeness

In this scenario, the basis for social relationships is reduced to personal desire. We see this today in slogans like "love is love" and "my body, my choice." People are no more than atomistic consumers, and their individuality is based on preferences for different things the market provides. Some people want to attend church, while others want to attend strip clubs. As long as no one is harmed during a particular activity, presumably meaning their sovereign choice is not violated, that activity is morally acceptable. This is why the only sexual boundary left for conservatives is "consent," which of course we are now finding cannot even effectively protect children from predators.

In this milieu of forces that threaten choice, the modern state takes on the role of protecting and expanding the freedom to choose as an end in itself. It emancipates individuals from natural attachments and traditional restraints while empowering them to challenge the limitations upon their will that exist in labor, education, government, healthcare, religion, and other public institutions. A major way it achieves this is by introducing market forces where traditional societies forbade them. The modern state thus promotes individual interests over local communities through policies like open borders, subsidized access to schools, medical services, and housing, as well as loosening sexual morals through no-fault divorce, legalized adultery, and same-sex marriage ceremonies. In liberal societies, the open market is the sacred mechanism for individual achievement and full participation is a fundamental right.

Unlike John Locke's conception of the inalienable rights to life, liberty, and property, which were guided by a responsibility to honor God's will in the preservation of mankind, today's civil rights undermine human society by attacking personal responsibility and social order.[35] Christopher Caldwell writes about this in *The Age of Enlightenment*, where he claims affirmative action and political correctness actually destroyed freedom of association and private property rights, effectively ushering in a new constitution. This is where the waters of liberalism and social justice blend.

To illustrate, in 1963, the Chairman of the Educational Policies Commission of the National Education Association testified that America's "traditional system" had failed "to provide that equality of opportunity that should be the condition of all our people." To remedy the situation, he proposed offering black children "educational services beyond the level of what might be called standard equality."[36] The forced busing, less rigorous education standards, and relaxed discipline that followed only exacerbated previously existing problems, while costing taxpayers more. Schools became less interested in conditioning students to manage liberty and more interested in assisting them to express liberty in any unrestrained form. They now provide free contraception, access to abortion, and sex-change therapy.

---

35 John Locke, *Second Treatise Of Government* (Project Gutenberg, 2021), https://www.gutenberg.org/files/7370/7370-h/7370-h.htm.
36 John Fischer, "Educational Problems of Segregation and Desegregation," in *Education In Depressed Areas* (Teachers College Press, 1963), 295-297.

Private businesses are also prevented from choosing whom they hire and do business with if external qualities like race, sex, and sexual orientation factor into their decision. Bakers, photographers, and wedding venues must provide services for LGBTQ+ related celebrations or suffer the legal consequences. Even Christian institutions and churches feel increasing pressure to comply with non-discrimination policies that contradict their religious beliefs.

The initial transformations that led to the current state of affairs took place under the liberal goal of achieving "equality of opportunity." However, this logic soon gave way to the social justice goal of achieving "equality of outcome." This transition naturally took place as people realized liberalism would not deliver the social equality they expected. For example, Derrick Bell, who some consider the father of Critical Race Theory, said the *Brown v. the Board of Education* Supreme Court decision promised equality but failed to change conditions for black people who lacked good jobs and housing. He glumly observed, "Throughout our history, while the idea of equality causes our hopes to soar, the economic reality of our capitalist system keeps our chances low."[37]

One of President Lyndon Johnson's economic consultants, Otto Eckstein, was wrong when he declared in 1968 that the United States had "entered a new era of equality" in which government facilitated employment and education opportunities would lead to black people's "full equality."[38] What he meant was that black people were on the path to proportional representation in various professions and education levels. Of course, this mechanism did not produce the desired goal. A 2018 study maintained that "no progress has been made in reducing income and wealth inequalities between black and white households over the past 70 years."[39]

Despite whatever good intentions the liberal architects of today's

[37] Derrick Bell, *The Derrick Bell Reader*, ed. Richard Delgado and Jean Stefancic, Critical America (NYU Press, 2005), 121.
[38] Otto Eckstein, *Education, Employment, and Negro Equality* (U.S. Department of Labor, Manpower Administration, 1968), 3-13.
[39] Moritz Kuhn, Moritz Schularick, and Ulrike Steins, "Income and Wealth Inequality in America, 1949-2016" (Opportunity & Inclusive Growth Institute, June 14, 2018), https://www.minneapolisfed.org/research/institute-working-papers/income-and-wealth-inequality-in-america-1949-2016.

world harbored, the egalitarian impulses they set in motion have only resulted in less responsibility, less security, and widening economic disparities. In the minds of many, liberalism promised equality but failed to deliver it. This has inevitably led to the system's destruction, which social justice advocates, who exploit the tension between the ideal and reality, are happy to further. They believe "America must live up to her promises" of equality. This is the motive behind things like the 1619 Project.[40]

Meanwhile, liberal loyalists propose more liberalism as their solution to the problem. The 1776 Report maintained that Americans should return to the principles of the Civil Rights Movement which achieved, for a brief moment, America's promise of equality.[41] Conservative talk-show hosts regularly reinforce liberal sentiments with slogans like "Diversity is our strength!" "In America you can be anything you want," and "No one can tell you what to do with your body." For all the positive contributions Christopher Rufo has made against DEI, he still sees his counterrevolution as ultimately a way to help "the common citizen . . . have the space for inhabiting and passing down his own virtues, sentiments, and beliefs, free from the imposition of values from above."[42] The ultimate goal is to ensure individual freedom. The assumption is that this freedom will ultimately produce greater levels of prosperity and equality.

Because of this commitment, today's political Right is incapable of fending off social justice long term. Without a moral vision and particular expectations to guide human choice, there is no reason to assume a positive result from those choices. There is also no way to compete with Leftist dreams of utopia. Moreover, similar to the Left's delusional world, the liberal society the mainstream Right increasingly defends only exists in the imagination. Certain norms, symbols, and rituals are inescapable features that will be imposed whether through social pressure or force. Yet many American

[40] Nikole Hannah-Jones, *The 1619 Project: A New Origin Story* (Random House Publishing Group, 2021), 353.
[41] "The 1776 Report" (The White House, January 2021), 15-16.
[42] Christopher Rufo, *America's Cultural Revolution: How the Radical Left Conquered Everything* (HarperCollins, 2023), 282.

conservatives, who still remember a time when cultural Christianity held the social order together, think things like religious neutrality will solve their dilemma. In reality, they maintain neutral institutions that were never neutral in the first place.

Conservatives may be able to use the free market or democracy to their advantage in varying degrees when they are in control, but when they are not, these tools are used against them. Most examples of "cancel culture" came from the private sector. If experience is any guide, the arc of history bends toward mankind's corruption. Without an imposed moral vision, democracy makes vice more common and achievable. When enough people fail to make good choices, their choices must be limited for the good of society. Instead, the Great American Empire prevents this from happening because it imperialistically imposes liberalism, along with fashionable American decadence, upon more traditional cultures. Nevertheless, this does present an opportunity for Christians to resist modern "woke" ideology as well as liberalism. Christians can provide the alternative solution for reinvigorating society with a conscience while laying the groundwork needed for a possible return to self-government.

A Better Approach

For any society to exist, there must be a baseline of shared trust. People need assurance that those they participate with in civil life will be accountable for their actions. Otherwise, there can be no civic ritual, trade, or common defense. This is why Roger Scruton wrote that even the "economic order depends on moral order."[43] Unfortunately, liberalism eventually destroys this order by imposing a neutral framework that values autonomy and erodes qualities that bind people together. What is good for the market in the short term is not always good for social stability in the long term.

The evidence for this dismal state of affairs surrounds us: the importation of illegal migrants who do jobs Americans allegedly

---

[43] Roger Scruton, *How to Be a Conservative* (A&C Black, 2014), 19.

will not, increasingly complicated business contracts and terms of service, a massive withdrawal from voluntary associations and public institutions, addictions and family breakdown, the unhealthy effects of processed foods, and the list goes on. Films from the golden age of cinema that depict a high-trust society where people knew their neighbors and children could walk to town unaccompanied are gone with the wind. Nevertheless, there are holdouts, and they tend to be in the Bible Belt.

People from liberal strongholds in major cities and more progressive areas are often surprised when they encounter places where residents still leave their keys in the car without worrying about the possibility of theft. Regions strongly influenced by European Protestantism don't tend to experience high levels of crime. This is precisely because they are restrained by internal moral codes, social pressure, and the shared experience that comes from intact families, generational thinking, and interconnectedness. Even without explicit laws, they are governed by mediating institutions like church, family, and voluntary associations.

For Christians who live in these areas, their first social priority ought to be maintaining what makes their regions unique in these respects. There will always be internal threats from corruption, along with external threats from the top-down conglomerations like the Great American Empire with its stranglehold on media, trade, the general government, and the education system's ideologies. However, through localist approaches, Christians can help protect their communities.

A RETURN TO COMMUNITY

In his book *Why Liberalism Failed*, Patrick Deneen observed that "a population seeking to fill the void left by the weakening of more local memberships and associations was susceptible to a fanatical willingness to identify completely with a distant and abstract state."[44] Some

---

[44] Patrick Deneen, *Why Liberalism Failed* (Yale University Press, 2019), 59.

political thinkers believed this in part explained the rise of communism and Nazism, yet it also applies just as much to the liberal state. People fulfilled in their concern for each other are more content and less likely to seek meaning and belonging through regime approval. Christians tasked with loving their neighbor are poised to effectively resist this urge toward deifying the secular state.

The greater the influence of the church and other voluntary associations that emphasize moral responsibility, the better. Organizations for child development, veterans' groups, institutions for the preservation of history, gun clubs, charities, and other local endeavors function in part to set good examples and keep people morally accountable. They reinforce social stigma surrounding vice and identify participants who need moral assistance. They create stronger communities capable of successfully resisting outside pressure to conform. In short, cultivating the prominence of local associations implements a hierarchy of trustworthy leaders, channels social priorities toward positive ends, and limits the choices people make to engage in destructive behaviors that poison society.

A localist approach can also protect a community from global market forces by producing networks of self-sufficiency. Locally sourced food is healthier and avoids supply-chain issues. Local utilities and craftsman generally provide higher quality services and allow communities to be less dependent on things like the power grid or furniture made from pressboard. Small businesses have more latitude to hire employees out of step with corporate DEI requirements. There are still ways within the liberal framework to shield oneself from some of its consequences. The more Christians choose to go to the hardware store rather than Amazon, the stronger their local community becomes at the expense of global corporations unbound by local moral taboos. There are, however, some dangers to avoid while thinking locally.

The first concerns building arrangements that channel resources away from the community. It is important to emphasize the necessity of forming groups and networks around shared loves. Even Rousseau recognized that "the family. . . [was] the first model of political societies" although he incorrectly reduced its purpose to expediency and personal advantage.[45] In reality, God ordered families and the civilizations that sprang from them to demonstrate love within themselves. The special manifestations of this love are found in His laws concerning household, generational, and national relationships. Things like commonly shared religion, region, lineage, and tradition are foundational for establishing healthy identity, loyalty, and defense.

In contrast, residents of liberal societies, aided by technology, increasingly form groups and networks around specific forms of entertainment. Video game forums, Comic Con events, and shared allegiance to various performers fill a void left in the wake of broken families and ruined cultures. Many Zoomers seem to know more about the history and happenings of the Marvel Universe than they do their own. What loyalty they have is directed toward the glory of fantasy worlds and the band of acquaintances who share their preoccupation.

There is certainly a place for art and leisure to aid in strengthening shared commitments. Yet, such art reflects true and valuable things about the world that birthed it. It cannot provide a basis for mutual obligation in itself. The kind of shallow entertainment offered by liberal societies flows more from hormonal urges. The inevitable result is further degradation toward bombast and pornography, not the rebuilding of society. The strength to band together against the Great American Empire requires deeper bonds oriented around God's natural order.

The second danger when thinking locally concerns cultivating a separatistic mindset where one association becomes the only important one in the minds of its members. This can inhibit the formation of local identity, trust, and cooperation. A good example would be cults and ecclesiocentric churches which absorb familial loyalty and impose overbearing authority on personal decisions. Schools, sport leagues, and other institutions are capable of functioning in similar

[45] Jean Jacques Rousseau, *The Social Contract*, trans. G. D. H. Cole (ETH Zurich, 1762), 2.

ways. While they may limit many negative personal choices, they also prevent society from reaching its full potential, since members cannot express the full range of their loves, abilities, and service. Social institutions should grant members the latitude to participate in wholesome community activities. Otherwise there is no community.

RETURN TO THE POLITICAL

Of course, many of the local solutions, such as engaging in regional commerce, building alternative institutions, and joining voluntary associations, presuppose the ability of its members to make wise decisions. This in turn requires a virtuous people who are interested in choosing the good despite the range of evil options available to them. This is one reason why, even from a social perspective, it is important for believers to share the gospel message which regenerates hearts and makes them desire Christian obedience. Even when institutions establish righteous standards and the social pressure that comes from them, those standards must be maintained by those who desire virtue. Under these conditions, limited governments are possible, since self-governing societies are composed of people who choose wisely. Unfortunately, most societies are not this way, and the ones that have taken time to develop. This is where Christians can collectively band together to wield power and suppress vice through corporate political action.

This is ironically controversial today within Christianity itself. Voices influential in mainstream evangelicalism regularly speak against efforts to use governmental force toward Christian ends. The late pastor Tim Keller said Christians who pursued political power against gay activists and Democrats operated on fear and resentment and were out of step with Jesus' example to serve instead of rule.[46] Of course this position must ignore Christ's physical reign, as well as the many examples of patriarchs, judges, kings, and prophets who wielded political power to suppress threats to their civilization.

---

[46] *Timothy Keller: How to Know If You Are a Christian Nationalist*, 2021, https://www.youtube.com/watch?v=o4M_K5vmDc8, 17:30, 19:00.

The fact of the matter is that politics by its very nature prohibits morally neutral approaches. Civil magistrates must impose what they believe the standards of acceptability to be. When Christians are not involved in this process, competing moral visions gain ascendence and force believers into compliance. Many Christian wedding photographers and bakers can attest to this. When believers ignore the political realm, they do so to their own peril as well as the peril of everyone else.

Strategies to engage politically range. Some Christians think mainly in terms of operating within conventional boundaries. The old guard of the religious Right continues to enjoy a seat at the table in national Republican politics, even if it is a diminishing one. Some Christians who desire a greater moral presence part ways with the religious Right. For example, abortion abolitionists pursue a more hard-line approach and criticize more established organizations for compromise. Dusty Deevers, a pastor turned state senator from Oklahoma, represents this strategy. On the other hand, pastors like John MacArthur see a place for Christian political involvement in upholding righteousness, but deviate from the motivations and expectations of the religious Right to make America more Christian.[47]

Other Christians propose unconventional approaches. Author Rod Dreher wrote that "losing political power" and confining Christian efforts to "our own little shires" is the best hope for recovering social influence.[48] His suggestion can hardly be considered political, except for the fact that he hopes for an eventual return to Christian involvement. Political philosopher Stephen Wolfe disagrees with this and thinks a "strong-willed and resolute minority" of cultural Christians is enough to impose institutional Christian identity and morals in the areas they live in.[49] Stephen does not elaborate on whether this must be accomplished through a democratic process. Pastor Joel Webbon may sound like Dreher because he suggests Christians should temporarily leave heavily progressive areas

---

[47] *John MacArthur on Christian Politics, Nations, and Nationalism* (Conversations That Matter, 2024), https://www.youtube.com/watch?v=HkDwTeUC3h4.
[48] Rod Dreher, *The Benedict Option: A Strategy for Christians in a Post-Christian Nation* (Penguin, 2018), 99.
[49] Stephen Wolfe [@PerfInjust], "@stainedglasscap Cultural Christianity Is Enough," Tweet, *X*, April 23, 2023, https://twitter.com/PerfInjust/status/1650238189649506313.

and flee to more culturally Christian ones. But he is actually closer to Wolfe in that he wants Christians to rule locally for a few generations before returning to more progressive areas.[50] His is a strategic withdrawal, not a wholesale retreat.

There are also Christians who envision coming changes to the current political order. Josh Abbotoy, the Executive Director of American Reformer, invited a firestorm of criticism when he suggested America needed a "Protestant Franco."[51] Timon Cline, the Editor in Chief for the same outlet, believes there are reasons to favor a monarchy.[52] Congresswoman Marjorie Taylor Green called for a "national divorce."[53] Conversely, some Christians are involved in projects like the Greater Idaho and the Texas Nationalist movements which aim to redraw geographic lines in order to escape the influence of more progressive areas. Perhaps in a crisis of legitimacy, such notions are not far-fetched, although believers would likely need to gain power to be ready for such a time.

While an entire chapter can be written on all the various opinions regarding how Christians should approach, gain, and keep political power, whatever the current strategy, the mission must include rolling back liberal assumptions about the state and replacing them with Christian ones. The ultimate purpose of government is not to protect or expand the individual's rights to choose, or to spread the democratic process, or to ensure a certain level of social equality. There are moral, prudential, and procedural reasons to maintain certain social arrangements and different forms of government, but they are the means to a higher end. This means that involvement in governmental affairs, whether through prayer or direct action, should be more important to believers than to other groups.

---

[50] Joel Webbon, *Fight by Flight: Why Leaving Godless Places Is Loving Godless Places* (Right Response Ministries, 2023). 40.

[51] Joshua Abbotoy [@Byzness], "Basically, America Is Going to Need a Protestant Franco," Tweet, *X*, May 23, 2023, https://twitter.com/Byzness/status/1660851914429411328.

[52] Timon Cline, "Monarchy in America," *American Reformer*, April 19, 2023, https://americanreformer.org/2023/04/monarchy-america/.

[53] Marjorie Taylor Greene [@mtgreenee], "We Need a National Divorce. We Need to Separate by Red States and Blue States and Shrink the Federal Government. Everyone I Talk to Says This. From the Sick and Disgusting Woke Culture Issues Shoved down Our Throats to the Democrat's Traitorous America Last Policies, We Are...," Tweet, *X*, February 20, 2023, https://twitter.com/mtgreenee/status/1627665203398688768.

During the age of Christendom, people agreed with Jesus' and Paul's teaching that civil magistrates represented the rule of God.[54] Legal documents commonly used the title "Christian prince" to describe the ideal ruler.[55] This meant government was chiefly concerned with applying God's order in society. John Calvin wrote that "no polity can be successfully established unless piety be its first care, and that those laws are absurd which disregard the rights of God, and consult only for men." Civil government was first to assert and defend the honor of God and then to guard and vindicate "public innocence, modesty, honour, and tranquillity" in order to "provide for the common peace and safety."[56]

The implications of this are both far-reaching and controversial in the modern age. There is no moral reason preventing Christians from reinstating laws against actual blasphemy, Sabbath-breaking, and obscenity. Such laws do nothing to trample the rights of citizens as understood in the pre-modern West, yet these practices do undermine the foundation for law itself by trampling on God's rights.

The Founding generation's conception of civil liberty did not resemble the personal "license" of today. Legal expert Daniel Driesbach points out that "civil liberty typically deferred to the needs of the community" and accompanied responsibility.[57] In 1779, Samuel Adams warned, "A general dissolution of principles and manners will more surely overthrow the liberties of America than the whole force of the common enemy."[58] Christians in the United States are watching this prediction unfold in real time.

Christians of course believe that God's universal law is good and ought to be mediated through culture in order to suit all people. Proverbs 29:2 states: "When the righteous increase, the people rejoice, but when a wicked man rules, people groan." People in the

---

54 John 10:34, Rom 13:4.
55 For example, the First Charter of Virginia (1606) states: "We would vouchsafe unto them our Licence, to make Habitation, Plantation, and to deduce a colony of sundry of our People into that part of America commonly called Virginia, and other parts and Territories in America, either appertaining unto us, or which are not now actually possessed by any Christian Prince or People."
56 John Calvin, *Institutes of the Christian Religion*, trans. Henry Beveridge (T.&T. Clark, 1863), 658-659.
57 Daniel Dreisbach, *Reading the Bible with the Founding Fathers* (Oxford University Press, 2017), 202-203.
58 Ralph Volney Harlow, *Samuel Adams, Promoter of the American Revolution: A Study in Psychology and Politics* (H. Holt, 1923), 298.

United States are groaning today over many social and political issues. This presents an opportunity for believers, whether they live in the Bible Belt or not, to practice being salt and light in various ways. As the Great American Empire continues to impose the negative effects of the liberal order, many are horrified by the world that is emerging. Some of these changes have motivated public figures like JP Sears, Kat Von D, Nala Ray, Russell Brand, and others to question their former assumptions and has led them to professing faith in Christ. Perhaps if these conditions continue and God works in the hearts of men, we will live to see the return of the Christian prince, the rebuilding of a civil society, and the downfall of liberalism.

6

THE
PROPOSITION
NATION

It is our duty to teach the workers to be indifferent to
national distinctions. There is no doubt about that... To
be an internationalist Social-Democrat one must not think
only of one's own nation, but place above it the interests
of all nations, their common liberty and equality.

Vladimir Lenin

It is easy to forget that today's accepted ideas were once debated. Opponents of social equality who challenged things like universal suffrage, public education, and same-sex marriage are now seen as bigots. But how did society reach these modern and rather novel conclusions? Despite current debates over immigration and gender identity, most public figures avoid questioning our views on equality, which has opened the way for lesser-known truth-seekers to gain traction online.

Critics of feminism, multiculturalism, and pluralism blame concepts like the "post-war consensus" or "the longhouse" for weakening

71

civilization.[1] But it is the revolutionary language of the "proposition nation" which Progressives most often use to justify their policies. The Modern Left views America as a symbol of universal social equality, and surprisingly the modern Right does as well. Harry Jaffa is a key figure in shifting the Right to embrace the Left's revolutionary ideas, and it is important to know how he accomplished this.

THE REVOLUTIONARY FOUNDING MYTH

Harry Jaffa was an influential force in political conservative circles before his death in 2015. He had studied political philosophy under Leo Strauss, published for outlets like *National Review*, and wrote most notably on Abraham Lincoln and Constitutional law. His students formed the Claremont Institute, which is one of the most popular conservative think tanks to this day. It is easy to see the impact his ideas have had on influential voices on the Right.

Jaffa believed that the "rights to which the Americans appealed to justify their independence were rights which they shared with all human beings everywhere." America was both exceptional and great because it "indentif[ied] itself with a universal humanity."[2] This meant the pluralistic society that came to dominate America was a positive, and even a conservative, development.[3]

Jaffa believed modern Conservatism was actually a form of Radicalism because it sought to realize ideals of the Founding "rooted in revolution." The Founding, Jaffa thought, was based on social equality and represented a "radical break with tradition" in an "attempt to establish a regime of liberty" previously unseen by the world.[4] This version of the Founding was supposed to contradict

---

[1] The concept of the longhouse was popularized by Bronze Age Pervert, an anonymous name for the author of *Bronze Age Mindset*, a popular book on the Pagan Right. He described it as "the return of a very ancient subjection [of] . . . young men dominated and broken by the old and sclerotic, by the matriarchs, the blob and yeast mode in human life overtaking and subjecting all higher aspiration." See: Bronze Age Pervert, *Bronze Age Mindset*, 2018, 42.

[2] Harry Jaffa, *Crisis of the Strauss Divided: Essays on Leo Strauss and Straussianism, East and West* (Rowman & Littlefield Publishers, 2012), 280, 292.

[3] Ibid., 24.

[4] Harry Jaffa, "Kendall & Carey: The Basic Symbols of the American Political Tradition," *Loyola of Los Angeles Law Review 8*, no. 2 (June 1, 1975), 473-474.

modern Progressives who saw rights as evolving instead of rooted in nature.[5] Yet Progressives on both sides of the aisle remain unmoored as they justify new rights and privileges and, like Jaffa, connect their rhetoric of equality to the Founding.

The Founding narrative they embrace, along with Jaffa, is actually filtered through an interpretation of the Declaration of Independence found in Abraham Lincoln's thinking, especially the Gettysburg Address. The Declaration's claim that "all men are created equal" was used by Lincoln to expand American identity to include new European immigrants, making individual ancestry less important than shared equality. Jaffa said this paralleled Christ's teaching that whoever did the will of His Father was His "brother and sister and mother."[6] It also filtered into the Constitution in places like the No Religious Test clause which Jaffa claimed fulfilled Jesus' instruction to "render to Caesar the things that are Caesar's, and to God the things that are God's."[7] In other words, sound reason, major Founding documents, and seemingly Jesus Himself all agreed that America was to be multicultural and treat social differences, including nationality and religion, the same.

Essentially, Jaffa spiritualized the Declaration of Independence in a manner similar to how John Winthrop likened Puritan settlers to a "city set on a hill," charged before the "eyes of all people" to create an exemplary society.[8] Jesus' teachings about the spiritual nature and mission of His followers are not about the United States, but politicians continue to mingle this language with America's purpose, christening the country with a revolutionary campaign. Of course, this campaign is constantly threatened. From the start, even the Founding Fathers seemed to endanger their own purpose.

According to Jaffa, Lincoln himself had to "[correct] the work of the Founders" and "put the nation on a sounder footing than

---

5 Jaffa, *Crisis of the Strauss Divided*, 12.
6 Ibid., 11; Matt 12:50.
7 Jaffa, *Crisis of the Strauss Divided*, 12; Mark 12:17.
8 Matt 5:30; John Winthrop, "City Upon a Hill Speech" (Gilder Lehrman Institute of American History, 1630); For a more complete study of this analogy in American political life see: Richard Gamble, *In Search of the City on a Hill: The Making and Unmaking of an American Myth* (A&C Black, 2012), 4.

the Founders themselves had left it."[9] Despite Lincoln's denial of wanting social equality between races, Jaffa argued that Lincoln actually was committed to "complete equality" and took the first step by ending slavery.[10] Jaffa admitted Lincoln "had no present or immediate intention to make voters or jurors of Negroes," but this was just to accommodate "the racism of Illinois voters."[11]

In the Gettysburg Address, "Lincoln's interpretation of 'all men are created equal' transform[ed] that proposition from a . . . norm which prescribes what civil society ought not to be, into a transcendental affirmation of what it ought to be."[12] America was based upon and characterized by an ultimate pursuit of social equality which in the minds of many, including the *1619 Project* contributors, has yet to be achieved.[13] This meant that even Lincoln's measures failed to defeat the forces of inequality.

Harry Jaffa said the "principles of the Declaration of Independence, celebrated in The Gettysburg Address, were eclipsed almost immediately."[14] Governments were constantly in danger of abandoning social equality and in so doing embracing moral relativism and totalitarianism.[15] This is what led to the Jewish Holocaust, and it continues to threaten America if the opposing political Party, depending on which perspective someone brings, gains control.

This describes much of our modern political situation. Both sides seek the interests of their particular constituencies but frame their struggle as the pursuit of universal equality. The Democrat Party Platform says that America is "built on an idea: that all people are

---

[9] Harry Jaffa, *Lincoln with Harry Jaffa*, interview by Peter Robinson, July 22, 2009, 19:00, https://www.youtube.com/watch?v=lbjCAeStpP0.

[10] In 1858 Lincoln said: "I am not, nor ever have been in favor of bringing about in any way the social and political equality of the white and black races . . . [I] am in favor of having the superior position assigned to the white race." See: Abraham Lincoln, *Abraham Lincoln: Speeches and Writings* Vol. 1 1832-1858 (Library of America, 1989), 636; Lincoln also supported the Corwin Amendment, which would have prohibited Congress from abolishing or interfering with slavery. See: "Corwin Amendment" (University of Maryland, 1860), https://blog.umd.edu/slaverylawandpower/corwin-amendment-1860/; Jaffa, *Crisis of the Strauss Divided*, 21.

[11] Ibid., 22.

[12] Harry Jaffa, *Crisis of the House Divided: An Interpretation of the Issues in the Lincoln-Douglas Debates*, 50th Anniversary Edition (University of Chicago Press, 2012), 321.

[13] Jaffa went so far as to say the "Constitution had no ultimate justification apart from that principle [of equality]." See: Jaffa, *Crisis of the Strauss Divided*, 25.

[14] Ibid., 13.

[15] Jaffa, "Kendall & Carey," 477.

created equal." This is the basis of their disagreement with "Donald Trump and MAGA Republicans."[16] Republican Platforms have typically sounded similar, claiming things like "the American Dream" of "equal opportunity for all" is threatened by the Democrats.[17] However, as Republicans have moved toward populism under Donald Trump, there does seem to be a shift.

The 2024 Republican Platform mentioned equality before the law but mostly focused on more tangible things like the "stories of brave men and women who gave everything they had to build America."[18] In this framework, America is more of a unique place and less of a universal abstraction. Vice President J.D. Vance even said during his 2024 convention speech that "America is not just an idea. It is a group of people, with a shared history and a common future."[19] These developments suggest the Conservative movement may be starting to return to older notions of what America is.

Harry Jaffa's Dilemma

Mel Bradford, a literature professor and traditional Southern Conservative, was one of Harry Jaffa's chief critics. As a Christian, Bradford agreed with "Jaffa concerning the danger of relativism." But he saw Jaffa's argument that Americans must choose between equality or relativism as a false dilemma. To remain free, Bradford thought Americans should reject equality as an unbounded abstract right, which tyrants used to oppress, and instead embrace an ordered freedom "embodied somewhere, rooted in a history, located in space, sanctioned by a genealogy, and blessed by a religious establishment."[20] The Founding did not invent or discover rights from scratch using

16 "2024 Democratic Party Platform," August 19, 2024, https://www.presidency.ucsb.edu/documents/2024-democratic-party-platform.

17 "2012 Republican Party Platform," August 27, 2012, https://www.presidency.ucsb.edu/documents/2012-republican-party-platform; Also see equality language in 2008, 2012, and 2016 Platforms.

18 "2024 Democratic Party Platform," August 19, 2024, https://www.presidency.ucsb.edu/documents/2024-democratic-party-platform.

19 *The American Conservative* [@amconmag], "JD Vance: 'America Is Not Just an Idea. It Is a Group of People, with a Shared History and a Common Future.' Https://T.Co/K0tlIJzi8b," Tweet, *X*, July 18, 2024, https://x.com/amconmag/status/1813775880071823395.

20 Mel Bradford, *A Better Guide Than Reason: Federalists and Anti-Federalists* (Routledge, 2017), 35, 32, xvii.

reason, but preserved what Americans had already inherited through centuries of development in England.

Bradford believed that the moral scaffolding needed for mutual social trust was normally built through common experience, not imposed theories detached from experience. For example, society allows people to drive, marry, and buy alcohol at different ages to ensure safety and order. These rights and restrictions are not determined by simply contemplating equality or even justice. They are particular to a certain set of circumstances with their own histories. It takes experience to understand the universal principles that apply and wisdom to know how to apply them. This reverence for "national experience" as it mediates the "wisdom of the ages" is the essence of authentic Conservatism.[21]

In contrast, Harry Jaffa championed "equality as a moral or political imperative, pursued as an end in itself," which Bradford argued was fundamentally opposed to Conservatism. It was a modern ideology that reduced politics to a "science" and appealed to people's envy. It encouraged "arrant individualism," "rationalized cowardice, shame, and ingratitude," destroyed the "interdependence" and "communal bond" that extended from the family, and hated "providential distinctions."[22]

It is interesting to think in an age of effeminate men, entitled attitudes, dysfunctional families, broken communities, and gender confusion that Bradford made his observations on the consequences of pursuing social equality in 1976. It seems history itself has vindicated his reading of it. Nevertheless, Harry Jaffa's interpretation of the Founding, read through Lincoln's appropriation of the Declaration's reference to equality, appeals to us because it aligns with how we are accustomed to seeing ourselves. A certain class of Americans claims the moral high ground to invade most every area of existence by divine right. Whether it be the "Puritan dream of a New Jerusalem governed by an elect" or "the manifest destiny of American democracy led by keepers of the popular faith," Americans are "authorized from on High to reform the world into an imitation

---

[21] Ibid., 34, 31.
[22] Ibid., 30.

of themselves."[23] However, our major founding documents, including the Declaration, do not reinforce this holy mission.

THE CONSERVATIVE DECLARATION

Mel Bradford argued that neither the War for Independence, the Declaration, nor the Constitution were "very revolutionary." The Declaration's focus was equality between formerly American British subjects and those born and living in Britain, not universal social equality.[24] From the colonial perspective, they had been under King George III by blood and law, but Britain severed this connection through "a long train of abuses and usurpations."[25] The Declaration thus confirmed and justified, to an international audience, the reasons for initiating a national divorce. Congress did not intend for it to be an innovative piece of political philosophy. It was always a legal brief.

When it said "we hold these truths," "we" referred back to "thirteen united States of America" altering a corporate relationship, not individuals concerned with domestic arrangements. The Continental Congress made this clear on June 30, 1777, in response to land grantees who sought independence from New York for violating their rights. Congress declared: "Congress is composed of delegates chosen by, and representing the communities [of 13 separate colonies], as they respectively stood at the time of its first institution; that it was instituted for the purposes of securing and defending the communities aforesaid against [Britain]."[26]

Of course, Congress did remind their audience that, like all people, they naturally possessed individual and corporate rights to self-preservation (Life, Liberty, and the Pursuit of Happiness).[27] In the 18th

---

23 Ibid., 43.
24 Ibid., 36, 38; Barry Shain, "The Declaration Of Independence: Founding Narratives, Contested Understandings, And Slavery's Challenge" in *Virginia First: The 1607 Project* (Abbeville Institute, 2024), 142.
25 "Declaration of Independence: A Transcription," July 4, 1776, https://www.archives.gov/founding-docs/declaration-transcript.
26 See: Edmund Bailey O'Callaghan, *The Documentary History of the State of New York* (Charles Van Benthuysen, public printer, 1851), 945.
27 Historian Caroline Roberts maintains that "happiness meant public happiness . . . achieved by satisfaction of the aspirations of the majority of the people living together." See: Caroline Robbins, *Absolute Liberty: A Selection from the Articles and Papers of Caroline Robbins* (Conference on British Studies and Wittenberg University, 1982).

century, it was believed that people with equal natural rights in a
pre-social state consented to abridge or modify these rights upon
entering society in order to achieve greater security and happiness.
In return, society granted them civil rights suited to their unique
situation.[28] Unlike natural rights, which were universal, abstract,
and based on an equal status granted by God in a theoretical state
of nature, civil rights were particular, tangible, and based on social
conditions with their hierarchies, traditions, and exceptions. The
Declaration addressed Parliament violating, and the King failing to
defend, American's common law arrangement which secured their
natural "inalienable rights" (rights that cannot be given up). Simply
put, the phrase "all men are created equal . . . with certain unalien-
able Rights" referred to a basic self-preservation that political communities have a "duty" to secure.[29]

Thus, the significance of the Declaration's language on rights was
not its assertion of natural equality but its accusation that Britain
violated their civil rights, and more importantly, that they possessed
a corporate right to self-government so as "to effect their Safety and
Happiness." Historian Pauline Maier said the equality and inalienable rights language initially "went unnoticed because . . . their statement seemed commonplace, even a kind of 'boilerplate.'"[30] Thomas
Jefferson himself wrote that the document's object was "not to find
out new principles . . . never before thought of . . . but to place before

---

[28] Supreme Court justice and *Declaration* signer James Wilson said: "Civil liberty is nothing else but
natural liberty, divested of that part which constituted the independence of individuals, by the authority,
which it confers on sovereigns, attended with a right of insisting upon their making a good use of their
authority." See: James Wilson, *The Works of James Wilson*, ed. James Andrews, vol. II (Chicago: Callaghan
And Company, 1896), 508; Thomas Jefferson said "natural rights, may be abridged or modified in [their]
exercise" according to the consent of the majority. See: Thomas Jefferson, *The Writings of Thomas Jefferson*,
vol. VII (J. B. Lippincott & Company, 1869), 496. George Washington said: "Individuals entering into
Society must give up a Share of Liberty to preserve the Rest." See: From George Washington to the President
of Congress, 17 September 1787," *Founders Online*, National Archives, https://founders.archives.gov/
documents/Washington/04-05-02-0306; Gouverneur Morris said: "Natural Liberty absolutely excludes
the Idea of political Liberty since it implies in every man the Right to do what he pleases. . . He who wishes
to enjoy natural Rights must establish himself where natural Rights are admitted. He must live alone." See:
"Political Enquiries [1776], Americastudien 21, 330; Constitutional Law expert Benjamin Wright said
natural rights language was "invariably combined with a theory of the British constitution" before Thomas
Paine. See: Benjamin Fletcher Wright, *American Interpretations of Natural Law: A Study in the History of
Political Thought* (Routledge, 2017), 54.

[29] Bradford, 40, 104.

[30] Pauline Maier, "The Strange History of All Men Are Created Equal," *Washington and Lee Law Review* 56,
no. 3 (Summer 1999): 873-890, 877.

mankind the common sense of the subject."[31] Hence, Congress could assume a metaphysical equality between people while maintaining unequal civil arrangements. The Declaration makes this crystal clear as it blames the King for violating uniquely British rights, including offenses that directly contradict notions of social equality.

For example, it charges King George III with "excit[ing] domestic insurrections" which signals opposition to Virginia's Royal Governor, Lord Dunmore, who issued an emancipation proclamation long before Abraham Lincoln and for similar reasons.[32] Slaves who joined the British Army to fight their rebel masters were granted freedom. The colonists also complained that the British hired "foreign Mercenaries" and stirred up "merciless Indian Savages" to fight them. They also emphasized blood ties to "common kindred" and clarified that their issues with the King were connected to his abuses, not the nature of monarchy itself. So much for valuing diverse cultures and rejecting hierarchy, which is how the preamble is often used today.[33]

Bradford observed that Lincoln's "refound[ing] of the Union" as a proposition nation which "the gates of hell shall not prevail against" initiated "an endless series of turmoils and revolutions, all dedicated to freshly discovered meanings of equality." If, as Lincoln said, the purpose of the equality phrase did not relate to British separation but was "for future use" to be a "constantly labored for . . . though never perfectly attained" to achieve "happiness" for "all people, of all colors, everywhere," it could be used against "the tyranny of husbands, factory owners, and other supposed agents of oppression." Today, we often hear this language attached to the normalization of sexual deviancies.[34]

However, Lincoln and especially Jaffa were wrong on this point.

---

31 Jefferson, 407.

32 Lincoln's *Proclamation* specifically withheld freedom from slaves in his own jurisdiction and symbolically granted it to slaves in his enemy's jurisdiction. Many journalists and statesman interpreted this as an attempt to foment slave insurrections in the South.

33 Ibid., 40.

34 Ibid., 43-44; Abraham Lincoln, "Speech on the Dred Scott Decision," June 26, 1857; Abraham Lincoln and Stephen Arnold Douglas, *The Lincoln-Douglas Debates of 1858* (Trustees of the Illinois State Historical Library, 1908), 469; Maier, 883.

As political theorist Barry Shain summarized: The *Declaration* was not "an individualistic vision with a domestic focus, [with] rights claims that are distinctly abstract and universal (and untied to any correlative duties) . . . [but] majoritarian democratic and communally inspired . . . its goals preeminently international, and its rights claims derived from norms associated with America's British constitutional and Protestant inheritances.[35] Understanding this truth is helpful in navigating many current issues.

Unfortunately, many Christians and members of the Right seem to base their understanding of nationality more on the "proposition nation" theory than on their own Bibles or heritage. But to truly grasp what is at stake in the immigration debate, we must first understand what we mean when we talk about nations. If nations are merely abstract, universal concepts without any unique identity, then there is little reason to care about things like borders. For decades, the United States has been run by people who seem at best indifferent and at worst encouraging a massive transformation of the country. However, a growing resistance is emerging from newer groups on the Right who reject the proposition nation theory. Self-proclaimed Christian Nationalists, who have received significant media attention, have become a primary target in this and other related debates, which is the focus of the next chapter.

---

[35] Shain, 133.

7

THE SOUL
OF AMERICA

*Whatever may be conceded to the influence of refined
education on minds of peculiar structure, reason and
experience both forbid us to expect that national morality
can prevail in exclusion of religious principle.*

George Washington–*Farewell Address*

The debate over so-called Christian nationalism is becoming the definitive political boundary of our time in the United States. Unfortunately, competing definitions, most of which are not rooted in previous uses of the term, create a cloud of confusion over what Christian nationalism is.[1] In general, proponents see it as a self-aware attempt to conform the nation to Christian standards for the common good, while opponents use it as a pejorative representing state-supported bigotry toward non-Christians.[2]

---

[1] For a short historical survey on how the term "Christian nationalism" was used in the United States see: Jon Harris, *Christianity and Social Justice: Religions in Conflict* (Reformation Zion Publishing, LLC, 2021), 155.
[2] Andrew Torba and Andrew Isker, *Christian Nationalism: A Biblical Guide For Taking Dominion And Discipling Nations* (Independently published, 2022), Kindle Locations 94-95; Stephen Wolfe, *The Case for Christian Nationalism*, (Moscow, Idaho: Canon Press, 2022), 9, 105; "Christians Against Christian

MSNBC columnist Anthea Butler blamed Christian nationalism for Florida Governor Ron Desantis's policies "against Trans kids and the don't say gay bill." She stated bluntly that "people who believe in Christian nationalism . . . believe that God has given them dominion and that dominion means they have dominion over everybody who doesn't believe in God, who doesn't think like they do, and that God created this nation for them."[3] Thus, Butler's major problem with Desantis concerns his willingness to conform civil society to Christian, instead of cosmopolitan, standards.

This focus on Christian concerns contradicts a national identity based on universal secular principles which remains neutral among religions. Regardless of how one defines Christian nationalism, the battle over whether national character includes a religious element lies at the root of the conflict. This is mainly because elites on both sides of the political aisle pledged themselves to an America fundamentally reducible to an abstract idea of equality.

The Irish rock star Bono articulated this well in an interview for the Rock and Roll Hall of Fame when he stated: "America is not just a country. It's an idea. Ireland is a great country, I'm very proud to be Irish. It's not an idea. Great Britain is a great country but it's not an idea. America is an idea. And that idea sort of belongs to everybody who wishes to serve it."[4] Bono's commonly held belief means that the United States can belong to anyone whether citizen or not. Conversely, the United States does not necessarily belong to citizens unless they share this idea. Appeals to this "propositional nation" justify causes for both political parties.

Consider what George W. Bush told a Morgantown, West Virginia crowd on Independence Day in 2005. After opening his

---

Nationalism Statement," July 29, 2019, https://www.christiansagainstchristiannationalism.org/statement; Andrew Whitehead, Joseph Baker, and Samuel Perry, "Despite Porn Stars and Playboy Models, White Evangelicals Aren't Rejecting Trump. This Is Why.," *Washington Post*, December 7, 2021, https://www.washingtonpost.com/news/monkey-cage/wp/2018/03/26/despite-porn-stars-and-playboy-models-white-evangelicals-arent-rejecting-trump-this-is-why/.

3   American Voices with Alicia Menendez [@AliciaOnMSNBC], "'It's Very Important to Understand with the People Who Believe in Christian Nationalism like Ron DeSantis or Others. They Believe God Has given Them Dominion... and That God Created This Nation for Them and Specifically for *white Men*.' @AntheaButler Https://T.Co/Lvgqfxmj4c," Tweet, *Twitter*, November 14, 2022, https://twitter.com/AliciaOnMSNBC/status/1591953189493940224.

4   Bono: "America is an Idea," July 22, 2016, https://www.youtube.com/watch?v=O8aLAZ8SnvI.

speech by quoting Lincoln's proposition, the President argued for continued military involvement in the Middle East to secure the "ideal of human freedom." He encouraged his audience with the hope that the terrorists would inevitably fail as the world entered a "new age" called the "liberty century." He closed stating: "We know that the freedom we defend is meant for all men and women, and for all times." It is clear that for Bush, "defending America" actually meant defending a universal "ideal of liberty."[5]

In a similar way, President Barack Obama during his second inaugural address pushed for policies like regulating health insurance, combating climate change, and recognizing same-sex marriage by appealing to the nation's universal and "never-ending quest" to secure the "bedrock principle that we are all created equal."[6] The drive to realize certain dreams by appealing to a nebulous liberty or equality serves as an easy way to rationalize almost any set of policies. The reasons are simple:

First, this basic conflation between the purpose or function of a nation and the definition of a nation inspires conformity. Those who fail to participate in a national cause, whether it be going to war or the elimination of a virus, are suspected of not being true Americans. Their very identity hangs in the balance contingent on their compliance. Practically speaking, an American is thus someone who values equality and obeys orders.

Second, these innovators can discard the importance of true national traits like lineage, tradition, and religion, when these conflict with their alleged national purpose. If actions like attacking American institutions, destroying monuments, and importing large groups of foreigners are done in the name of equality, innovators can spin them as truly American objectives. Legitimate concerns from decent ordinary Americans are thus neutralized. President Donald Trump represents many who rejected this view.

James Carville, a Democrat strategist, defined "Trumpism" as the

---

5 George W. Bush, "President Celebrates Independence Day in West Virginia," https://georgewbush-whitehouse.archives.gov/news/releases/2005/07/20050704.html.

6 Barack Obama, "Inaugural Address by President Barack Obama," https://obamawhitehouse.archives.gov/the-press-office/2013/01/21/inaugural-address-president-barack-obama.

belief that "the United States of America is a place and not an idea."[7] Trump's slogan, "Make America Great Again," signals a recognition that the nation does not need fundamental restructuring in order to achieve an ideal realized in a glorious future. Nor does the United States suffer from an identity crisis separating what it was and what it should be. Rather, America is a particular people in a particular place being kept from pursuing its own national interest by elites in both parties. Trump made this clear in almost every campaign speech when he cited tangible ways citizens suffered and elites prospered. The belief that the nation and people were synonymous, and that America was not an ideal belonging to the world, motivates his mission to transfer power back to the people and ensure the government worked for their benefit alone. Trump's instinctual rejection of the proposition nation offended elite sensibilities and eventually tied him to Christian nationalism.

Christian Nationalism Threatens Political Orthodoxy

Opposition to Trump as a proto-Christian nationalist increased as he recognized the importance of Christian practices and symbols to American identity. It started during his first campaign when Trump promised supporters that if he were President, people would see "Merry Christmas" displayed at shopping centers again. A professor from King's College claimed this was "part of [Trump's] coming war on free speech."[8] During the 2017 refugee crisis the *New York Times* reported that Trump's intention to favor previously neglected Christian refugees was a violation of the First Amendment's establishment clause.[9] In 2020, Trump famously received criticism

---

7 John Melendez [@stutteringjohnm], 2020, "@realDonaldTrump I was just talking to @JamesCarville and he said you are going to get your fat ass beat. #Biden2020 @CaslerNoel," May 21, 2020, 6:15 p.m., https://twitter.com/stutteringjohnm/status/1263594299985281030.

8 David Johnson, "Trump's War on Christmas Is Just One Part of His Coming War on Free Speech | USAPP," December 23, 2016, https://blogs.lse.ac.uk/usappblog/2016/12/23/trumps-war-on-christmas-is-just-one-part-of-his-coming-war-on-free-speech/.

9 Adam Liptak, "President Trump's Immigration Order, Annotated," *New York Times*, January 28, 2017, https://www.nytimes.com/2017/01/28/us/politics/annotating-trump-immigration-refugee-order.html.

for posing with a Bible in front of St. John's Episcopal Church in Washington D.C. after protestors damaged the building. The *Washington Post* ran a story claiming Trump used the Bible to signal "his Christian nationalist followers."[10] The recent attacks on Christian nationalism can thus be understood as part of a broader effort to divorce American identity from the traditional American character defended by people like Donald Trump.

Paul Miller's popular critique of Christian nationalism typifies this approach. In Miller's book *The Religion of American Greatness: What's Wrong with Christian Nationalism*, the Georgetown University professor promotes an America not "defined by language, ethnicity, religion or culture," but instead by a "set of ideas" that are "universal."[11] When citizens love these ideas they are able to love humanity more generally and reach a truer love for their homeland.[12] Barriers to this love, put simply, include Donald Trump and Christian nationalists.

According to Miller, Trump failed to "encourage democracy abroad" because he mistakenly thought American "culture, faith, and tradition" were uniquely "the source of liberal values." Consequently, some people missed opportunities as the forty-fifth President pursued "National power" instead of their "freedom."[13] This is one reason Miller calls "Nationalism . . . Jim Crow on a global scale."[14]

Many Christians supported Trump's agenda, according to Miller, because they were shaped more by racial identity than religion.[15] Their desire to "assert ownership over American identity" by codifying Christianity into "public symbolism," the teaching of American history, and political rhetoric was actually just an extension of their Anglo-Protestantism.[16] Thus Miller delegitimizes a specific Christian

---

10 William Barber and Jonathan Wilson-Hartgrove, "Trump's Use of the Bible Was Obscene. He Should Try Reading the Words Inside It.," *Washington Post*, June 2, 2020, https://www.washingtonpost.com/opinions/2020/06/02/trumps-use-bible-was-obscene-he-should-try-reading-words-inside-it/.
11 Paul D. Miller, *The Religion of American Greatness: What's Wrong with Christian Nationalism* (IVP Academic, 2022), 37, 18, 29.
12 Ibid., 29.
13 Ibid., 39-40,
14 Ibid., 75.
15 Ibid., 224.
16 Ibid., 162, 261.

tradition because of its cultural embeddedness and instead encourages Americans to "grow beyond our Anglo-Protestant past" to "incorporate universal ideals."[17] The creed of "liberty and equality," once again becomes the barometers by which to measure all national action.[18] This is how Miller, although a Southern Baptist, can defend allowing Drag Queen Story Hour at a public library while blasting "white American Christians" for rejecting their obligation to eliminate racial disparities.[19]

In contrast, Stephen Wolfe's best-selling book *The Case for Christian Nationalism* argues for a nation based upon natural affection, similarity, and fellowship. This includes a "common language, manners, customs, stories, taboos, rituals, calendars, social expectations, duties, loves and religion."[20] Stephen sees the nation as an extension of the family and just as families "can be Christian, then so too can the nation."[21] In contradiction to prevailing stereotypes, love rather than hate motivates this preference for one's own people even over abstract notions of liberty and equality.

Wolfe sees the normalization of Christian customs as a way to order earthly life to heavenly life as society encourages citizens toward conversion, faithfulness, and "a commodious social life."[22] The final result is a citizenry oriented toward worshiping God and loving their neighbor.[23] Conserving differences and excluding "foreigners in mass" is a "universal good" meant to protect "civil fellowship and symbiosis."[24] Wolfe states: "A Christian should love his children over other children, his parents over other parents, his kin over other kin, his nation over other nations."[25] This of course directly contradicts the proposition nation idea.

Wolfe acknowledges that the "intimate connection of people

---

[17] Ibid, 242.
[18] Ibid., 28.
[19] Ibid., 90, 99, 193.
[20] Stephen Wolfe, *The Case for Christian Nationalism,* Kindle Edition (Moscow, Idaho: Canon Press, 2022), 135.
[21] Ibid., 180.
[22] Ibid., 206-207.
[23] Ibid., 2010.
[24] Ibid., 145.
[25] Ibid., 101.

and place" he argues for "undermines the so-called 'creedal' nation concept" popular "among neo-conservatives, mainstream Republicans, and left-liberals." In fact, Wolfe declares that "propositions do not and cannot serve as the foundation for nations." The reason is simple. A sense of familiarity, attachment, and ownership of a place is "rooted in a pre-reflective, pre-propositional love for one's own, generated from intergenerational affections, daily life, and productive activity that link a society of the dead, living, and unborn." This does not mean that political creeds are useless or unimportant, but they are not "what grounds the nation."[26] Although this is the rock of offense modern elites find so disturbing about modern nationalism, it is not unique in the history of the world.

Virtually all pre-modern societies and most nations today think of themselves in organically rooted ways and self-consciously pursue their own interests. Plato observed "an element of friendship in the community of race, language, and laws . . . and rites of worship" that precluded different laws and forms.[27] Augustine believed that "difference of race or condition or sex" were "imbedded in our mortal interactions" and "to be respected."[28] If anything is universal, it is the way nations prefer themselves. The Bible is no exception.

After God created distinct languages by which to separate the people of the world, He made Abraham's descendants into what Genesis calls a "great nation." For them He established special rituals, laws, a homeland, a shared history, and kept them distinct even when living in captivity to other nations.[29] Walls surrounded their major cities, foreigners were identifiable, and children were to speak the language of their parents.[30] The coming of Christ fulfilled the ceremonial law and instituted a "holy nation" called the church, but it did not erase the tangible realty of earthly nations.[31] The Great Commission, as well as Luke's, Paul's, and John's writings,

---

[26] Ibid., 118-120.
[27] Plato, *The Dialogues of Plato*, trans. B. Jowett, Third (London: Oxford University Press, American branch, 1892), 90.
[28] Mark Edwards and Thomas Oden, *Galatians, Ephesians, Philippians* (InterVarsity Press, 2014), 49.
[29] Gen 12:2, Ex 12:14.
[30] 2 Chron 2:17-18, Neh 13:23-26.
[31] I Pet 2:9.

all use the concept of nation to organize humanity.[32] Paul even desired to sacrifice himself spiritually on behalf of his "kinsmen according to the flesh."[33] Clearly, the Kingdom of God did not erase natural relationships.

The question before us today is not whether Americans will follow a new Christian nationalist movement to either victory or perdition. If anything is new, it is the proposition nation that belongs to everyone and no one simultaneously. The question is whether Americans will cast off modern innovations that contradict human nature and thereby pave the way for globalism. Today's Christian nationalism should be seen as a resistance movement. In that sense it is both populist and aligned with an America First agenda. It is resistance against a century of elites foisting upon the American public an idea meant to neutralize their natural inclinations toward self-preservation. All Americans, whether they object to the terminology or certain features advocated by some proponents, should wish Christian nationalism a measure of success if they are to truly stay American. So far, their agenda has started to make some inroads. Not long ago, the issue of religions role in the country's identity came to a head in debates over the display of Satanic imagery in public spaces, an issue Christian nationalist types seem to be winning on.

FOUNDING FATHERS, MEET THE PLURALIST SATAN

In December 2023, fault lines emerged within the ranks of both conservative and evangelical leadership after a Navy pilot destroyed a Baphomet statue depicting Satan in the Iowa State Capitol building. The Iowa Legislature approved a request from the Satanic Temple to admit the figure in their holiday display under a commitment to include all religions. Jon Dunwell, a Christian and Missionary Alliance pastor as well as an Iowa State Representative, became one of the first to publicly use the logic of religious neutrality to support

---

[32] Matt 28:19, Acts 17:26, Eph 3:14, Rev 7:9.
[33] Rom 9:3.

the statue's presence. Although he found the depiction personally objectionable, he did not want the "state evaluating and making determinations about religions."[34] Soon voices influential in evangelicalism echoed Dunwell's sentiment.

Former Trump administration lawyer and radio host Jenna Ellis wrote, "Destruction of property is not okay for the Christian who hates a satanic statue any more than it's okay for the satanist who hates a nativity scene."[35] Author and speaker James Lindsay who, although an atheist, is frequently featured at Christian gatherings, posted a picture of the broken-down Baphomet, blaming the rejection of "a Classically Liberal Society" in favor of "a Fascist Society" for its demise.[36] Presbyterian pastor and theologian R. Scott Clark stated Christians should not engage in iconoclasm and reasoned that since the Iowa State Capitol is a secular building no religious displays of any kind should be present there, including Nativity scenes.[37]

Other prominent conservatives such as Michael Knowles, Charlie Kirk, and Ron Desantis argued that knocking the statue down was right since Satan was evil and religious protections should not apply to those who claim to follow him. Just as issues like same-sex marriage, preferred pronouns, and drag queen story hour challenged the political Right's commitment to neutrality in areas of speech and social arrangement, the Satan display forced conservatives to decide the limits of religious liberty. According to the Satanic Temple, this was their purpose in the first place.

In *Hail Satan*, a 2019 documentary about the Satanic Temple,

---

[34] Rep. Jon Dunwell [@jdunwell], 'As Many of You Have Become Aware, Last Week a Display Was Erected at the Iowa Capitol by the Satanic Temple of Iowa. . ." Tweet, *X*, December 8, 2023, https://twitter.com/jdunwell/status/1733191110858559506.

[35] Jenna Ellis [@JennaEllisEsq], "I Respectfully Disagree. This Is Not the Way. . ." Tweet, *X*, December 15, 2023, https://twitter.com/JennaEllisEsq/status/1735716512885813587.

[36] James Lindsay is frequently a speaker at Turning Point Pastor's Conferences. He has also spoken at events with Christian audiences and dominated by Christian speakers from ministries like G3 and Founders; James Lindsay, epic manspreader [@ConceptualJames], "A Moment Is Likely Coming, and May Have Already Passed, Where the Woke Winning Is Not a Thing That's Going to Happen, in Which Case Our Possible Paths Diverge into a Classically Liberal Society or a Fascist Society That Destroys Them All, Root and Branch, without Apology," Tweet, *X*, December 14, 2023, https://twitter.com/ConceptualJames/status/1735419179057004697.

[37] R. Scott Clark, "Heidelminicast Special: On Smashing Satanic Statues," *Heidelcast*, December 16, 2023, https://heidelblog.net/2023/12/heidelminicast-special-on-smashing-satanic-statues/.

leaders in the movement explain their goal to use Satanism as a tool
to fight for social justice and to challenge "Christian privilege" in the
culture wars. Many of their adherents are atheists who view Satan
as a symbol of rebellion against God. Their requests to participate
in public displays of worship helped place a satanic holiday exhibit
in the Florida State Capitol, shut down invocations at the City of
Phoenix Council meetings, and challenged the Oklahoma Ten
Commandments statue in Federal Court. They sponsor multiple
after-school Satan clubs in public high schools and object to state-
imposed abortion restrictions on religious grounds. Their strategy
is to make civil magistrates choose between accommodating them
or refusing to accommodate any religion. Municipalities that deny
them access will likely face legal action.

The Satanic Temple essentially exploits America's tradition of religious toleration while exposing the weakness of Republicans to do
anything about it. Even though over three-quarters of Iowans identify as Christian and the State government is overwhelmingly controlled by Republicans, Governor Kim Reynolds signaled that the
only acceptable recourse they had was to focus on the Nativity scene
and pray over the Capitol.[38] According to Franklin Graham, this
was enough to count as "opposing a satanic display."[39] Yet, the Iowa
Legislature is able to "set the rules and standards for any display" and
succeeded in prohibiting the Satanic Temple from using an actual
goat head in theirs.[40] Some opponents of the exhibit also pointed
to the fact that the Iowa State Constitution's primary purpose for
the government was the furtherance of God-ordained blessing.[41]

---

[38] "Religious Landscape Study," *Pew Research Center's Religion & Public Life Project* , June 13, 2022,
https://www.pewresearch.org/religion/religious-landscape-study/; Stephen Gruber-Miller, "Kim Reynolds
Calls Iowa Capitol Satanic Display 'objectionable,' Encourages Iowans to Pray," *The Des Moines Register*,
13 2023, https://www.desmoinesregister.com/story/news/politics/2023/12/12/governor-kim-reynolds-
criticizes-satanic-altar-at-iowa-capitol-asks-for-prayer/71891969007/.

[39] Franklin Graham [@Franklin_Graham], 'I Applaud @IAGovernor Kim Reynolds for Opposing a Satanic
Display in Her State's Capitol. Her Response Was to Hold a Nativity Prayer Meeting! I like It! The Nativity
Represents the Greatest News the World Has Ever Known." Tweet, *X*, December 16, 2023, https://twitter.
com/Franklin_Graham/status/1736087773994435020.

[40] Jon Dunwell

[41] The preamble states: "We the people of the State of Iowa, grateful to the Supreme Being for the blessings
hitherto enjoyed, and feeling our dependence on Him for a continuation of those blessings, do ordain and
establish a free and independent government . . ."

A satanic symbol thus stood opposed to more than Christianity as a religion, but also the foundation of Iowa law. Republicans who favored religious neutrality were able to ignore these elements by deferring to a higher principle of religious freedom they believed was enshrined in the Establishment Clause of the First Amendment.

For example, Jenna Ellis lashed out against Christian nationalists for violating the First Amendment in order to "create a theocracy that doesn't allow religious freedom."[42] However, this understanding of the Founders' purpose is relatively recent. In 1787, when the Federal Constitution was ratified, nine state constitutions included Christian religious test requirements for officeholders including adherence to doctrines such as the Trinity and the inspiration of Scripture.[43] The four remaining states were governed by explicitly Christian Royal Charters or constitutions.[44]

New York, one of the states without a religious test, stated in her Constitution of 1777 that "free exercise . . . [of] worship" and "liberty of conscience . . . shall not be so construed as to excuse acts of licentiousness." The document limits its religious conception to Christian "ministers of the gospel" and priests "of any denomination."[45] Ten years later, Virginia, which also precluded a religious test, stated in its Constitution that "the free exercise of religion" was governed by "the mutual duty of all to practice Christian forebearance, love, and charity towards each other."[46] Not only did all thirteen states recognize God, but they exclusively preferred Christianity.

Even those advocating the freedom to worship God according to the dictates of conscience intended its application for a broadly

---

[42] Jenna Ellis [@JennaEllisEsq], "@njhochman @Newsweek The History of the First Amendment Says Otherwise. You're Purposefully Confusing the Issue by Invoking Liberty vs License, While Ignoring the CN's Intent to Create a Theocracy That Doesn't Allow Religious Freedom.," Tweet, X, December 17, 2023, https://twitter.com/JennaEllisEsq/status/1736473188261933411.

[43] "Religious Tests and Oaths in State Constitutions, 1776-1784," *Center for the Study of the American Constitution*, accessed December 20, 2023, https://csac.history.wisc.edu/document-collections/religion-and-the-ratification/religious-test-clause/religious-tests-and-oaths-in-state-constitutions-1776-1784/, Also: "Constitution of South Carolina," March 19, 1778, https://avalon.law.yale.edu/18th_century/sc02.asp#1.

[44] Rhode Island and Connecticut were the only two states still governed by their Royal Charters.

[45] "The Constitution of New York," April 20, 1787, https://avalon.law.yale.edu/18th_century/ny01.asp.

[46] "The Constitution of Virginia," 1776, https://encyclopediavirginia.org/entries/the-constitution-of-virginia-1776/.

Christian conception of God.[47] In pursuing the disestablishment of the Church of England in Virginia, James Madison appealed to this principle yet invoked a duty to "the Supreme Lawgiver of the Universe" who guided lawgivers according to His plan, trust, and blessing.[48] In 1786, the Virginia Statute for Religious Freedom, authored by Thomas Jefferson, passed the Virginia General Assembly. Although there were those like Jefferson and Richard Henry Lee before him who extended freedom of conscience to non-Christian religions, the statute's immediate impact was to foster greater peace between competing Christian denominations by ending compelled worship in the name of Almighty God. That same year, James Madison also introduced another bill authored by Thomas Jefferson that punished Sabbath breakers. This showed that even the Founding generation's greatest champions for religious liberty did not see a conflict between freedom to worship and a legally upheld Christian civilization.[49]

This broad support for Christianity often manifested itself on the state level against undermining influences such as witchcraft, blasphemy, and Sabbath breaking.[50] Even if one assumes the Federal Constitution promoted secularism, it could do nothing to suppress these precedents, since the First Amendment only prevented Congress, not states, from making laws "respecting an establishment of religion."

However, it is worth noting that even Congress did not think they were in violation of this principle when in 1789 they appointed

---

[47] This principle is reflected in early documents such as the Pennsylvania Constitution of 1776 and the New Hampshire Constitution of 1784. See: "Constitution of the Commonwealth of Pennsylvania," PA Constitution (blog), September 28, 1777, https://www.paconstitution.org/texts-of-the-constitution/1776-2/; "New Hampshire State Constitution–Bill of Rights," June 2, 1784, https://www.nh.gov/glance/bill-of-rights.htm.

[48] James Madison, "Founders Online: Memorial and Remonstrance against Religious Assessments" (University of Virginia Press, 1785), http://founders.archives.gov/documents/Madison/01-08-02-0163.

[49] Thomas Jefferson, "A Bill for Punishing Disturbers of Religious Worship and Sabbath Breakers" (University of Virginia Press, June 18, 1779), http://founders.archives.gov/documents/Jefferson/01-02-02-0132-0004-0084.

[50] Here are a few examples: The English 1604 Act against Witchcraft and Conjuration, which prescribed the death penalty, was adopted by South Carolina, Pennsylvania, and Rhode Island between 1718 and 1728. See: Owen Davies, *America Bewitched: The Story of Witchcraft After Salem* (OUP Oxford, 2013), 45; Massachusetts, New Hampshire, and New Jersey passed blasphemy laws in the 1780s-1790s though their State Constitutions contained religious freedom protections. See: Anna Price, "A History of Blasphemy Laws in the United States," *The Library of Congress* (blog), December 19, 2023, //blogs.loc.gov/law/2023/12/a-history-of-blasphemy-laws-in-the-united-states.

publicly-funded Protestant chaplains, passed the Judiciary Act which required Supreme Court justices to acknowledge God in their oath of office, renewed the Northwest Ordinance which encouraged "religion" in schools as "necessary to good government," and issued overtly Christian Thanksgiving resolutions.[51] The Establishment Clause prevented the United States from erecting an official ecclesiastical body similar to the Church of England, but it did not prevent Congress from recognizing God or Christianity.

It was commonly acknowledged that religion in general, and Christianity in particular, was necessary for public morality, and public morality was necessary for self-government. George Washington represented this sentiment well in his Farewell Address when he stated: "Of all the dispositions and habits, which lead to political prosperity, Religion and Morality are indispensable supports."[52] While the Founders tolerated a small Jewish population which shared much in common with Christians, Judaism did not enjoy the same public accommodation as Christianity did. Outside of Christendom there were no significant religions within the early American body politic. There is no evidence to suggest the men who crafted the Federal Constitution intended to accommodate something like a future image of Satan in the United States Capitol, let alone a state capitol, yet this is what some conservative leaders want us to believe.

One reason many modern conservatives are confused on this issue is because of the way courts contrived and applied the "incorporation doctrine" which, starting in the 1920s especially, used the "due process" clause in the Fourteenth Amendment to apply certain aspects of the Bill of Rights to the States. It was not until 1947 that the Supreme Court applied the Establishment Clause to a state in the *Everson v. Board of Education* decision. Chief Justice Hugo Black

---

51 Barry Adamson, *Freedom of Religion, the First Amendment, and the Supreme Court: How the Court Flunked History* (Pelican Publishing, 2008), 139-148.
52 George Washington, "Washington's Farewell Address," 1796, https://www.mountvernon.org/education/primary-source-collections/primary-source-collections/article/washington-s-farewell-address-1796/.

maintained in his majority opinion that states could not participate in or use tax revenue to support religious activities.[53]

In the 1980s, the Supreme Court began to handle religious displays using this logic, culminating in the *County of Allegheny v. American Civil Liberties Union* decision which disqualified a Nativity scene that included a banner which read: "Glory to God for the birth of Jesus Christ." Local holiday displays were now unconstitutional if they endorsed religion, made someone feel like an outsider, or entangled the state in religious activities.

In recent years, more conservative Supreme Court justices have utilized a competing standard that allows for religious displays if they are consistent with "historical practices and understandings."[54] Though the dust has not yet settled on this issue in modern legal terms, the fact of the matter is that a historically rooted understanding of civics which separates original intent from innovations of the Court would go a long way to clarify the issues concerning the Baphomet statue in Iowa.

Unfortunately, fidelity to a misunderstanding of the Founders is not the only thing motivating those who support religious neutrality. For years, elites on the Right developed a commitment to pluralistic democracy. Under this philosophy, things like blasphemy laws, sexual norms, and Confederate imagery conflict with the new America leaders in both parties are working to realize. As I type these words, a crew is removing the Arlington Reconciliation Monument with little fanfare from conservative media, who also largely ignored the recent vandalizing and destruction of hundreds of similar statues.

It stands to reason that if actions like these are acceptable, then tearing down a statue of Satan would also be viewed favorably. Today's political Right praises examples of civil disobedience from the past like the Boston Tea Party or Civil Rights' "sit-ins." These examples are conceived as helping evolve society toward greater

---

[53] Hugo Black, *Everson v. Board of Education*, 330 U.S. 1 (1947). (Supreme Court of the United States October 1946), 15.

[54] Scott Bomboy, "Did a Supreme Court Decision Change the Rules for Holiday Displays?," *National Constitution Center*, December 7, 2023, https://constitutioncenter.org/blog/did-a-supreme-court-decision-change-the-rules-for-holiday-displays.

levels of freedom and autonomy. The modern conservative disposition increasingly tolerates evil, while failing to defend good with the hope that a more equal society will emerge from the ruins. Yet all around us things seem to be deteriorating. It is important to interpret the Baphomet statue's demise in light of this.

People like Michael Cassidy, the Navy test pilot who knocked down the display, are losing confidence in their leadership. Cassidy was surprised "that the legislature allowed it up and that they didn't do anything to take it down." When he arrived at the Capitol, "it touched a nerve," and in "righteous indignation" he practiced what he believed was "Christian civil disobedience."[55] After turning himself over to Capitol police, it disappointed him that some "professing Christians" disapproved and seemed to want to "give equal time to evil as to good." He told Tucker Carlson: "I love our country and I don't want statues of Satan in our government buildings."[56] This simple display of moral clarity and courage still resonates with many Americans who are not in the leadership class.

It did not take long for Christians who supported Cassidy to compare his actions to Gideon destroying the altar to Baal. Those who disapproved contrasted him with the Apostle Paul who did not rip down idols to pagan deities. Gideon and Paul both serve as positive examples for Christians, yet their contexts, callings, and purposes are distinct. Paul was an "apostle to the Gentiles" who introduced the gospel and built the church within pagan contexts. Gideon did not start out as a political leader, but he rose to the occasion and liberated Israel from a pagan nation in her time of need. If we are entering a time of social breakdown similar to that of Judges, where "everyone did what was right in his own eyes," Christians will likely need more men like Cassidy, not fewer.

It would have been preferable for someone who already held

55 Michael Cassidy, *Man who beheaded satanic statue at state capitol speaks out: "Righteous indignation,"* interview by Jesse Waters, December 15, 2023, https://www.youtube.com/watch?v=ZOkpAR5VHOo.

56 Tucker Carlson [@TuckerCarlson], "Liberal Mobs Have Torn down Countless Statues of Christians in This Country. But Topple a Monument to Satan, and CNN Will Denounce You as Dangerous. Https://T.Co/YboWAQBsXH," Tweet, X, December 20, 2023, https://twitter.com/TuckerCarlson/status/1737265376486891819.

political office in Iowa to destroy the satanic image, but the political will did not exist. Satan worship is perhaps the highest form of blasphemy and a direct attack on Anglo-American law. The reason blasphemy was universally punished until recently is because the laws of a country flow from that country's religion.[57] To attack the religion so aggressively is an attack on the people who live under its laws. In the words of George Washington, "Who, that is a sincere friend to [free government], can look with indifference upon attempts to shake the foundation of the fabric?"[58]

Instead of getting caught up in the minor details of whether Cassidy's actions line up with rigid ideological commitments to free expression, private property, or civil disobedience, it is time for both evangelical and conservative leadership to examine the entire picture. The house is on fire, and if elected officials refuse to put it out, someone else will—whether their bucket is to our liking or not. It would be better for all if civil magistrates under God's authority simply did their job. If they do not, new leaders will be found.

But perhaps this is what the country needs. It would be preferable to have leaders who understand some basics of what their states and country have traditionally been. Every society must justify its laws and mores according to a transcendent moral standard that is then mediated in specific ways through tradition. Without Christianity to guide the United States, another religion will inevitably fill that void. To a large extent, this is already happening, as social justice operates in this manner. What cannot be a viable solution is a neutral public square in a proposition nation. Christians should know better than to fall for that. Perhaps it takes a Satanic statue to drive the point home.

---

57 William Blackstone said: "Blasphemy against the Almighty, by denying his being or providence, or by contumelious reproaches of our Saviour Christ, as well as all profane scoffing at the holy Scripture, or exposing it to contempt and ridicule, are offences punishable at common law by fine and imprisonment, or other infamous corporal punishment; for Christianity is part of the laws of England." See: John Henry Hopkins, *The American Citizen: His Rights and Duties* (Pudney & Russell, 1857), 84.
58 Washington

8

WHAT IS A NATION?

A human life, I think, should be well rooted in some spot of a native land, where it may get the love of tender kinship for the face of the earth, for the labours men go forth to, for the sounds and accents that haunt it, for whatever will give that early home a familiar unmistakable difference amidst the future widening of knowledge.

George Eliot

Conservative thinkers sometimes point out that culture war issues are simply battles over the dictionary. In order to navigate basic questions concerning abortion, same-sex wedding ceremonies, and illegal migration, one must first understand what a baby, a marriage, and a citizen are. Columnist Matt Walsh starred in the documentary *What is a Woman?* to expose Leftist activists' vacuous understandings on gender. The Southern Baptist Convention fragmented over the definition of "pastor" at their 2023 annual meeting. All around us the world is giving up on basic concepts our grandparents took for granted.

Evangelical thinkers have pushed back against some of these new definitions, knowing they undermine the faith. Interestingly though, they have not effectively defended God's good order concerning nations. Instead, they have often embraced the proposition nation, occasionally confusing it with the church and suggesting that Christians who adhere to traditional definitions might be "racist."

Tim Keller, in his influential book *Generous Justice*, taught that "pride and lust for power" led to the formation of separate nations at Babel. God, he claims, is "distressed that the unity of the human family has been broken, and declares his intention to take down the walls of racism and nationalism that human sin and pride have put there." Part of this effort includes "reversing" the "curse of Babel" at Pentecost, when God declared "that the grace of Jesus can heal the wounds of racism." This led to a "community of equal 'fellow-citizens' from all races" in the church. The gospel was thus a mechanism to give people "critical distance from their own culture" and "end all racial division." As a result, Keller interprets passages like Ephesians 2, that describes the now inconsequential barrier of adhering to Jewish ceremonial law for entering the community of faith, as admonitions against racism.

In addition, Keller also charges Christians with the duty to socially overcome national barriers by doing things like diversifying community leadership and providing economic relief in poor communities. This responsibility stems from the biblical teaching that God created humanity from "one blood," the gospel's power to dismantle national divisions, and the belief that diversity reflects the church's role as a living testament to the gospel's truth.[1] Many of today's evangelical pastors drank deeply from Keller's well and subscribe to these teachings, even though they are mostly untrue.

From the beginning of the Bible we find that nations are distinct peoples with ties to particular lands, languages, and ancestry. They develop organically as families grow and settle in different areas to suit their needs.[2] They are, in a real sense, extensions of families, and

---

1   Timothy Keller, *Generous Justice: How God's Grace Makes Us Just* (Penguin Publishing Group, 2012), 120-125, 130-133.
2   "From these the coastlands of the nations were separated into their lands, every one according to his language, according to their families, into their nations." Gen 10:5; "These are the sons of Ham, according to their families, according to their languages, by their lands, by their nations." Gen 10:20; "These are the sons of Shem, according to their families, according to their languages, by their lands, according to their nations. These are the families of the sons of Noah, according to their genealogies, by their nations; and out of these the nations were separated on the earth after the flood." Gen 10:31-32.

Scripture often refers to them this way.[3] God's division of people into different nations at Babel was not a punishment for their pride but rather a fulfillment of His intention for humanity to "fill the earth." The residents of Babel had deliberately resisted dispersing, which led God to intervene by confusing their languages.[4]

The fact that God "made from one man every nation of mankind to live on all the face of the earth," as Paul said in Acts 17, does not erase national distinctions. On the contrary, Paul followed this statement up by pointing out that God also "determined their appointed times and the boundaries of their habitation." According to New Testament scholar David Peterson, this referred to "various areas in which the races live . . . [and] the periods in history when those regions are dominated by particular races."[5] In a real sense, God "gave the nations their inheritance . . . separated the sons of man . . . [and] set the boundaries of the peoples" as Deuteronomy 32:8 states.

Neither did the gospel erase national distinctions. God foreshadowed Christ's coming when He promised to bless "all the families of the earth" through Abraham's seed.[6] This is why Christ charged His disciples to "make disciples of all the nations."[7] Through His atonement, Christ fulfilled the Jewish ceremonial law and thus "broke down the [spiritual] barrier" between Jews and Gentiles. This "new man" formed the universal church, figuratively called by Peter "a holy nation," but it did not recategorize "every family in heaven and on earth" into a universal mold.[8] The spiritual reality of the univer-

---

3 "I will bless those who bless you, and him who dishonors you I will curse, and in you all the families of the earth shall be blessed." Gen 12:3 (also quoted in Acts 3:25); "All the ends of the earth will remember and turn to the Lord, and all the families of the nations will worship before You." Psalm 22:7; "You only have I chosen among all the families of the earth; therefore I will punish you for all your iniquities." Amos 3:2; "And it will be that whichever of the families of the earth does not go up to Jerusalem to worship the King, the Lord of hosts, there will be no rain on them." Zech 14:17.

4 "God blessed them; and God said to them, "Be fruitful and multiply, and fill the earth, and subdue it; and rule over the fish of the sea and over the birds of the sky and over every living thing that moves on the earth." Gen 1:28; "They said, 'Come, let us build for ourselves a city, and a tower whose top will reach into heaven, and let us make for ourselves a name, otherwise we will be scattered abroad over the face of the whole earth.'" . . . "So the Lord scattered them abroad from there over the face of the whole earth; and they stopped building the city." Gen 11:4a,8.

5 David Peterson, *The Acts of the Apostles* (Wm. B. Eerdmans Publishing, 2009), 497.

6 Gen 12:2-3.

7 Matthew 28:19.

8 Eph 2:14-16; 1 Pet 2:9; Eph 3:15.

sal church transcends national differences, in the same way it transcends labor and gender differences.[9] Christians do not forfeit their
class, gender, or national identities upon conversion.

Pentecost did not erase national distinctions either. God did
miraculously cause people to "speak with other tongues," but this
was to fulfill the prophecy that He would "pour forth of [His] Spirit
on all mankind."[10] This overcoming of language barriers was not universal and it did not last permanently. Even in a glorified state, the
people of God are still comprised of "a great multitude . . . from
every nation and all tribes and peoples and tongues."[11] The differences that naturally group people together will still be apparent, but
they will not act as barriers to belonging in God's assembly.[12]

One question that often arises in the context of modern life is
whether the definition of a nation has evolved in today's environment, now marked by a global economy, ease of immigration, and
technological networking. Even some Bible study tools signal a
fundamental change in the meaning of the term. For example, *The
Lexham Cultural Ontology Glossary* defines nation as: "A collection of
people under the authority of a government."[13] If this definition were
true, the Jewish people would have ceased to be a nation during the
Babylonian captivity. One of *Webster's* definitions of a nation states
it is "a community of people composed of one or more nationalities
and possessing a more or less defined territory and government." If
the only thing required for nationhood is community, territory, and

---

9 "There is neither Jew nor Greek, there is neither slave nor free man, there is neither male nor female; for you
are all one in Christ Jesus." Gal 3:28.
10 Acts 2:4, 17.
11 Rev 7:9.
12 "Nation" (ἔθνος), from which we get the English term "ethnicity," refers to "a body of persons united by
kinship, culture, and common traditions." See: Matthew Minard, "Gentiles," ed. Douglas Mangum et al.,
Lexham Theological Wordbook, Lexham Bible Reference Series (Bellingham, WA: Lexham Press, 2014); In a
biblical context, "tribe" (φυλή) most illustratively refers to smaller familial groups within the nation of Israel
with distinct roles, duties, lands, and privileges. For example, the Levites occupied the priestly roles. They
fulfilled incumbent duties (Num 1:50-53), managed cities of refuge (Num 35:6), and their priests attended
to lepers (Lev 14), thus fulfilling some of the judicial and medical roles. They also possessed 48 cities (Num
35:7) and were exempted from military service (Num 1:49-50) unlike the other tribes; "People" (λαός) is a
general term for a group of people that can apply to nations, tribes, or other groups. Here it expresses, as if to
leave no stone unturned, the extent to which membership in God's congregation applies to all the redeemed;
"Tongue" (γλῶσσα) refers to language groups.
13 The definition goes on to say: "In ancient times the people of a nation were generally perceived to be from
a common ancestral family" as if this is an archaic feature. See: David Witthoff, ed., *The Lexham Cultural
Ontology Glossary* (Bellingham, WA: Lexham Press, 2014).

government, regardless of whether multiple nationalities share these features, then nations are indistinguishable from cities and empires. Clearly, some of our modern understandings of nationhood are more general and shallow than the picture given in Genesis.

In pre-modern times, concepts like race, ethnicity, and nation were practically indistinguishable.[14] Features associated with them such as homeland, dialect, religion, and culture also corresponded with one another. The English were different from the Turks and the Turks were different from the Chinese, etc. People understood the differences between them were bigger than just one element. Yet, the impulse of modernity is to reduce things to basic parts that scientifically hold the key to understanding the whole. Darwinists reduced people to genetic determinations. Critical race theorists reduced them to power dynamics. These specialized classifications, combined with unprecedented levels of immigration and the erosion of organic culture by mass media, have created the confusing world modern Westerners inhabit.

Today, race is commonly viewed as either a purely genetically determined reality or more often a "social construct," ethnicity more closely approximates cultural patterns, and nationality applies to everything from bloodlines and culture, such as the Navajo Nation, to multicultural empires likes the United States. People also harbor their own definitions depending on different schools of thought, which complicates discussions on this topic. A single misstep can lead to accusations of racism, simply based on word choice.

Modern American Christians often mirror the diluted concept of nationhood prevalent in their surroundings—an idea their ancestors in the faith would have found most unusual. They readily embrace the "nation of immigrants" and "melting pot" slogans intended to reinforce the proposition nation. In reaction to Darwinism, eugenics, and Nazi racial ideology, they also tend to adopt a perspective on race and nationality that minimizes ancestral and, at times, cultural

---

14 Even our English terms were mostly synonymous at one time. Race represented people of common stock, ethnicity a shared nation, and race a common ethnicity and language. See: "Etymology Dictionary," https://www.etymonline.com/.

distinctions. One of the deceptions of life in the information age is the tendency to exchange one reductionist ideology for another, believing it solves a problem, when in reality it often creates new ones.

Creationist organizations do a good job arguing against biological determinists who say things like "Nature" achieved "superior race[s]" through "establish[ing] an evolutionary higher stage of being" and "every historical event in the world is nothing more nor less than a manifestation of the instinct of racial self-preservation."[15] While genetics do influence some behaviors and confer important elements of identity, Christians do not believe that it determines intrinsic worth or explains all human behavior.[16] All people are in a real sense part of a singular human race with universal characteristics, including the *Imago Dei*, sinfulness, a moral sense, an ability to reason, and a need for salvation.[17] This does not mean that ancestral connections are irrelevant or just a "social construct." There can be one human race in an important universal sense, while at the same time different nationalities can exist with their own unique lineages and traditions. Indeed, much of the Bible concerns itself with a specific nation to whom God gave land, laws, and customs that were intended to set them apart from other nations for His special purposes.

The reality is, nations are organic compositions that can develop, die, and even merge with other nations. Israel's boundaries changed over time, as did its government. Yet, throughout all its changes, God continued to identify Israel as a distinct nation with unique characteristics stretching back to its origins. There is no reason to believe the Creator's concept of a nation has changed even though the modern world has. This naturally raises questions about immigration and assimilation in a country where borders have already

---

[15] Adolph Hitler, *Mein Kampf*, trans. James Murphy, 1939, 238, 246.

[16] For examples of genetics influencing behavior, consider something as simple as human size. Goliath was intimidating because of his stature, and his defeat was a triumph that intimidated the Philistines. Zacchaeus's short stature prompted him to climb a tree where Jesus noticed him. See: 1 Sam 17:4 and Luke 19:3. According to Scripture, genetics influence identity by providing a sense of kindredness with ancestors and future generations. See: Gen 12:1-3, Ex 20:5-6, Rom 11:1.

[17] In certain niche Reformed Christian circles, there is skepticism about humanity's ability to reason independently of Christian conversion due to concerns that it may suggest human autonomy. I will not delve into that debate here. My focus is to highlight that humans possess a reasoning faculty that can be used for both good and evil. See: Luke 16:8.

been crossed, multicultural cities have been established, and multi-generational communities are disrupted by market forces and government policies.

WHAT AMERICA IS

Defining America, at this point, is a challenging task. Though it began as a primarily English endeavor, by 1784, a French-born New Yorker described Americans as a "mixture of English, Scotch, Irish, French, Dutch, Germans, and Swedes."[18] Add to this Sephardic Jewish, African, and indigenous populations integrated at various levels into certain aspects of society, and America appears to have been diverse from an early stage. Yet, a closer examination reveals that populations from the British Isles dominated early American life in both size and scope.

Of the 39 signers of the Constitution, all were Protestant except for two who were Catholic—Daniel Carroll and Thomas FitzSimons. All had British ancestry, with the majority being of English descent. They all spoke English, and American institutions were predominantly English in character. It is no wonder that in the award-winning book *Albion's Seed*, historian David Hackett Fischer described four folkways originating in Britain that ultimately defined what America was and became. The Founding generation knew this well.

In *Federalist No. 2*, John Jay stated: "Providence has been pleased to give this one connected country to one united people—a people descended from the same ancestors, speaking the same language, professing the same religion, attached to the same principles of government, very similar in their manners and customs."[19] Other Founders such as George Washington and Thomas Jefferson expressed similar sentiments.

---

[18] John Hector St. John de Crèvecœur, "Letter III–What Is An American," in *Letters From an American Farmer*, 1784, https://avalon.law.yale.edu/18th_century/letter_03.asp.

[19] "The Federalist 2, Independent Journal (New York), 31 October 1787," *Founders Online*, National Archives, https://founders.archives.gov/documents/Jay/01-04-02-0282. [Original source: *The Selected Papers of John Jay*, vol. 4, 1785–1788, ed. Elizabeth M. Nuxoll. Charlottesville: University of Virginia Press, 2015, pp. 585–589.]

Jefferson argued, prior to the American War for Independence, that King George III should uphold the British rights of Americans, since their forebears were, before emigrating to America, "free inhabitants of the British dominions in Europe."[20] He believed American "laws, language, religion, politics, & manners are so deeply laid in English foundations, that [Americans would] never cease to consider their [English] history as a part of [their own]."[21] Yet he also acknowledged significant cultural differences between the North and South and also expressed concern about how mass immigration could turn America into a "heterogeneous, incoherent, distracted mass."[22] He was not the only member of the Founding generation to fear this.

In 1790, Pennsylvania had the highest percentage of citizens without British ancestry, with Germans comprising 33% of the state's population.[23] Today, with millions of immigrants coming from cultures significantly more diverse than those of the British Isles, this might seem like a trivial matter. Yet Benjamin Franklin, who lived in Philadelphia during a significant influx of Germans in the early 1750s, expressed concern and wanted to limit their further immigration.[24] He asked, "Why should Pennsylvania, founded by the English, become a Colony of Aliens, who will shortly be so numerous as to Germanize us instead of our Anglifying them?"[25] Despite

---

[20] Thomas Jefferson, *The Works of Thomas Jefferson* (G.P. Putnam's sons, 1904), 64.

[21] "Thomas Jefferson to William Duane, 12 August 1810," *Founders Online*, National Archives, https://founders.archives.gov/documents/Jefferson/03-03-02-0001-0002. [Original source: *The Papers of Thomas Jefferson*, Retirement Series, vol. 3, 12 August 1810 to 17 June 1811, ed. J. Jefferson Looney. Princeton: Princeton University Press, 2006, pp. 4–7.]

[22] "Jefferson's Letter to Chastellux," September 2, 1785, https://avalon.law.yale.edu/18th_century/let34.asp; "The Examination Number VII, [7 January 1802]," *Founders Online*, National Archives, https://founders.archives.gov/documents/Hamilton/01-25-02-0280. [Original source: *The Papers of Alexander Hamilton*, vol. 25, July 1800 – April 1802, ed. Harold C. Syrett. New York: Columbia University Press, 1977, pp. 491–495.]

[23] Forrest McDonald and Ellen Shapiro McDonald. "The Ethnic Origins of the American People, 1790." *The William and Mary Quarterly* 37, no. 2 (1980): 20.

[24] Franklin said: "The seventh Proposal of discouraging the sending more Germans to Pennsylvania, is a good one." See: "From Benjamin Franklin to Peter Collinson, 1753," *Founders Online*, National Archives, https://founders.archives.gov/documents/Franklin/01-05-02-0046. [Original source: *The Papers of Benjamin Franklin*, vol. 5, July 1, 1753, through March 31, 1755, ed. Leonard W. Labaree. New Haven: Yale University Press, 1962, pp. 158–160.]

[25] Observations Concerning the Increase of Mankind, 1751," *Founders Online*, National Archives, https://founders.archives.gov/documents/Franklin/01-04-02-0080. [Original source: *The Papers of Benjamin Franklin*, vol. 4, July 1, 1750, through June 30, 1753, ed. Leonard W. Labaree. New Haven: Yale University Press, 1961, pp. 225–234.]

acknowledging the Germans' positive attributes, Franklin worried their large-scale unassimilated presence might erode foundational "English Laws, Manners, Liberties, and Religion."[26]

The commonly held American view on immigration was that it should strengthen and not weaken the character of the United States. This instinct was reflected in the *Constitution*, which exclusively served the needs of "the People of the United States . . . ourselves and our Posterity," as well as the first four naturalization acts which limited immigration to "free white persons" of "good character."[27] James Madison said it was "very desirable" to induce "the worthy part of mankind to come and settle amongst us" only on the condition that they "increase[d] the wealth and strength of the community."[28] George Washington believed immigration policy should ensure they "get assimilated to our customs, measures, and laws" to "become one people."[29]

Over time, immigration standards in the United States changed to the point where now almost anyone can enter the country and reap America's benefits. The importance placed on restricting immigration to culturally similar groups gradually diminished, leading to a variety of social challenges. Now many areas of the country are inhabited and controlled by effectively foreign groups of people with little incentive to assimilate. If America ever truly existed as a cohesive nation where immigration and assimilation could occur on a scale that enriched rather than diluted its national character, that era has long since passed.

Perhaps a more fitting perspective on America today is not

---

26 From "Benjamin Franklin to Peter Collinson, 9 May 1753," *Founders Online*, National Archives, https://founders.archives.gov/documents/Franklin/01-04-02-0173. [Original source: *The Papers of Benjamin Franklin*, vol. 4, July 1, 1750, through June 30, 1753, ed. Leonard W. Labaree. New Haven: Yale University Press, 1961, pp. 477–486.]

27 "The Constitution of the United States," 1787, National Archives, https://www.archives.gov/founding-docs/constitution-transcript.

28 "Naturalization, [3 February] 1790," *Founders Online*, National Archives, https://founders.archives.gov/documents/Madison/01-13-02-0018. [Original source: *The Papers of James Madison*, vol. 13, 20 January 1790 – 31 March 1791, ed. Charles F. Hobson and Robert A. Rutland. Charlottesville: University Press of Virginia, 1981, p. 17.]

29 "From George Washington to John Adams, 15 November 1794," *Founders Online*, National Archives, https://founders.archives.gov/documents/Washington/05-17-02-0112. [Original source: *The Papers of George Washington*, Presidential Series, vol. 17, 1 October 1794–31 March 1795, ed. David R. Hoth and Carol S. Ebel. Charlottesville: University of Virginia Press, 2013, pp. 161–162.]

as a singular nation, but as an empire. While it retains vestiges of its Anglo-Protestant roots, primarily in its rural heartland, these regions now wield minimal influence. Donald Trump's populism resonates with this dwindling core, yet its sway diminishes with each passing year. Increasingly, America seems more a collection of diverse nations, distinct regions, and urban centers, each with its own unique identity, loosely bound under one flag. Under a loose federal arrangement, as envisioned by many of the Founders, these differences are less likely to threaten social stability, as states would enjoy greater freedom to govern themselves, thus preserving strong local identities. However, in an increasingly totalitarian state, where every aspect of life is controlled from the center, these differences clash more sharply.

This became apparent to me in a real way when I was making a documentary on the monument crisis in 2021. I spent the morning in Auburn, Alabama, and the afternoon in Portland, Oregon, filming interviews and chronicling monument destruction. Though both regions nominally share a language, their religions, customs, values, politics, fashion, cuisine, and virtually every other aspect of life starkly contrasted. My cameraman and I had a contest to see who could find an American flag in Portland that was not flying obligatorily over a Federal building. I cannot recall if we ever found one. Yet Auburn was covered in them. I was not even sure our own country's flag united us after that trip.

Like all empires, America seems like it is on a road that will eventually leave it conquered or fallen from within. The Romans eventually outsourced influential positions to foreigners which contributed to the downfall of their empire. Similarly, the Soviet Union encompassed satellite states whose allegiance was, at best, tenuous, ultimately playing a role in its own disintegration. The Great American Empire is following a familiar path as it erodes its own core Anglo-Protestant identity.

This does not mean that, even if contemporary America were to decline, there would not be some continuation of the Anglo-Protestant America that once existed. While it may be geographically diminished and include individuals who honor its ethos without having ancestral ties to Britain, it is important to recognize that, on a manageable scale, members of various non-British groups have historically assimilated into American culture and made meaningful contributions without destroying its core identity. As a result, the influence of American culture will likely persist in some form.

There may even be a restoration of the old America if the influence and moral condition of its 'old stock' is revived. Yet without this foundational core identity, there is no hope for restoration. Without it, America's history could still serve as educational material for future societies, offering lessons and templates. However, applying these lessons without the original cultural carriers would not amount to a restoration of America, any more than America's adoption of Greco-Roman principles amounted to a revival of those ancient empires.

PRESERVING THE CORE

Christians of all people should understand and work against the dynamics that lead to social decay and erasure. Foreign assimilation into a nation is possible under the right conditions, but there are limitations in both its extent and the scale in which it can successfully work. High levels of blending inevitably lead to the formation of new nations. The Samaritans are an example of this phenomenon.

According to 2 Kings 17, God judged the Northern Kingdom of Israel through the king of Assyria who captured Samaria and initiated a population replacement program, deporting Israelites to Assyria and importing foreign peoples to settle Samaria. As a result, the remaining Israelites intermingled with foreign peoples and further syncretized their religions, shattering the Northern Kingdom and giving rise to a new Samaritan people who became a source of friction with the Jews who remained in the surrounding region.[30]

---

30 "Ephraim [The Northern ten tribes] will be shattered, so that it is no longer a people." Is 7:8; Josephus, "Of the War, Book II," in *The Jewish War*, accessed October 10, 2024, https://penelope.uchicago.edu/josephus/war-2.html.

The prophets Ezra and Nehemiah worked to prevent a similar outcome, which threatened to undermine the religion, language, and bloodline of the returning exiles from the Southern Kingdom of Judah, by enforcing prohibitions against marriages with the "peoples of the lands."[31] These prohibitions, which Solomon failed to uphold, significantly contributed to the initial division between the kingdoms of Israel and Judah, as his foreign wives persuaded him to permit worship of their false gods.[32]

Passages like these can make modern Westerners—who often downplay the interconnected importance of religion, language, and bloodline in favor of shared liberal values—feel uncomfortable. They place these ideas in the same category as the biological determinism that gained traction in certain parts of the West during the 19th and 20th centuries. In reality, both perspectives are reductionistic products of modernity. The Bible, in contrast, reflects a more holistic pre-modern view of nationality, manifested clearly in the way God established Israel.

According to Genesis 17-22, God established a covenant with Abraham and his natural descendants, promising them a land, defining a holy purpose for them, and instituting circumcision as a sign. Even at this early stage, the sign of circumcision was extended to foreign men who were part of Abraham's household and thus under his authority. Throughout the rest of the Old Testament it was these core descendants, at times connected to assimilated foreigners on the periphery, who reaped national member benefits.

It is important to understand that the Bible always placed an emphasis on these ancestral connections concerning national

---

31 "For they have taken some of their daughters as wives for themselves and for their sons, so that the holy race has intermingled with the peoples of the lands; indeed, the hands of the princes and the rulers have been foremost in this unfaithfulness." Ezra 9:2; "In those days I also saw that the Jews had married women from Ashdod, Ammon and Moab. As for their children, half spoke in the language of Ashdod, and none of them was able to speak the language of Judah, but the language of his own people." Neh 13:23-24

32 "Furthermore, you shall not intermarry with them; you shall not give your daughters to their sons, nor shall you take their daughters for your sons. For they will turn your sons away from following Me to serve other gods; then the anger of the Lord will be kindled against you and He will quickly destroy you." Deut 7:3-4; "Now King Solomon loved many foreign women along with the daughter of Pharaoh: Moabite, Ammonite, Edomite, Sidonian, and Hittite women, from the nations concerning which the Lord had said to the sons of Israel, 'You shall not associate with them, nor shall they associate with you, for they will surely turn your heart away after their gods.' Solomon held fast to these in love." I Kings 11:1-2.

identity. In Deuteronomy 6, Moses reminded Israel that the land, heritage, and covenant belonged to those whose fathers were "Abraham, Isaac, and Jacob."[33] Ezekiel likewise prophesied that the land of Israel belonged to Ezekiel's "brothers," "relatives," "fellow exiles and the whole house of Israel."[34] Even Jesus and Paul treated "kinsman according to the flesh" with a preference not immediately granted to others in the same regions.[35] Israel as a physical nation was intended for the Israelites, and this extended to social structures.

The tribes of Israel were to perpetually control the land of Canaan. The year of Jubilee even reinforced this by reverting sold lands, every fifty years, back to the original families who held them.[36] Israelites were required to forgive debts to fellow Israelites after seven years and were prohibited from charging interest on loans to them. However, toward foreigners they could do both.[37] Israelite slaves could not be held involuntarily in perpetuity, but foreign slaves could be.[38] Foreigners were also forbidden from becoming kings and priests.[39]

Outsiders who wished to integrate into Israel's theocratic society could do so with certain limitations. The mechanism Scripture reveals for foreigners to gain a generous degree of participation was through submission to the covenant.[40] Even then, some groups were totally barred from religious gatherings, such as Ammonites and Moabites, while others, namely Edomites and Egyptians, could only participate after three generations.[41] Outsiders were also required to abide by Israel's laws.[42] If they did, they could receive a measure of

---

[33] Deut 6:10.
[34] Ezek 11:15.
[35] Matt 10:5-6, 15:24, Luke 19:9, John 4:22, Acts 13:14, 13:46, 17:1-2, 18:1-4, 19:8, Rom 1:16, 9:3.
[36] Josh 13-21, Lev 25.
[37] Deut 15:2-3; 23:19-20.
[38] Ex 21:2-6, Lev 25:44-46, Deut 15:12-18.
[39] "You shall in fact appoint a king over you whom the Lord your God chooses. One from among your countrymen you shall appoint as king over yourselves; you may not put a foreigner over yourselves, anyone who is not your countryman." Deut 17:15; "These searched among their ancestral registration, but it could not be located; therefore they were considered unclean and excluded from the priesthood." Neh 7:64; See also: Ez 2:59.
[40] But if a stranger sojourns with you, and celebrates the Passover to the Lord, let all his males be circumcised, and then let him come near to celebrate it; and he shall be like a native of the land. But no uncircumcised person may eat of it. The same law shall apply to the native as to the stranger who sojourns among you." Ex 12:48-49
[41] Ex 21:2-6, Deut 15:2-3, 12-18, 23:3-8.
[42] Lev 18:26.

legal protection and sustenance.[43] However, a small number of foreigners received much more than this.

Doeg the Edomite became "the chief of Saul's shepherds." His later betrayal of David and murder of 85 priests does not exactly make him a poster child for foreign ascendency, but he did attain a high rank.[44] In contrast, Uriah the Hittite was one of David's mighty men who demonstrated remarkable integrity before David had him murdered in order to take his wife.[45] There are also examples of Israelite men who married foreign women, such as Joseph who married an Egyptian, Moses who possibly married a woman from south of Egypt, Salmon who married Rahab the Canaanite, whom James and the author of Hebrews praised for her faith, as well as Salmon's son Boaz who married Ruth the Moabite. Both Rahab and Ruth stand in the genealogy of Christ through Joseph.[46]

Ruth is an interesting case, not only because she became an exception to the rule that Israelites were not to marry Moabites, but she ideally modelled what assimilation should look like on account of love for her Israelite mother-in-law, Naomi. In complete submission, Ruth told her: "Where you go, I will go, and where you lodge, I will lodge. Your people shall be my people, and your God, my God. Where you die, I will die, and there I will be buried. Thus may the Lord do to me, and worse, if anything but death parts you and me."[47] There is no reason to create a rule from this, like some have done, that dismisses Israel's law against intermarrying with Moab. There are extenuating circumstances that support classifying this situation as a special case, such as Boaz being half Canaanite himself and adhering to the custom of Israel's Levirate Marriage law.[48] Yet, Ruth's love for Naomi, and by extension her religion and people, made Ruth an ideal member of Israel—which is not something that can be

---

[43] The laws that applied to them had to be applied with equity: See: Ex. 22:21, Jer. 7:6; They were allowed to flee to cities of refuge. See: Num. 35:15; They were allowed to glean from vineyards and fields and receive portions of the religious tithe and produce during the Sabbatical year: See Lev. 19:10, 23:22, 25:6, Deut. 14:29.

[44] 1 Sam 21:7, 22:9, 18.

[45] 2 Samuel 23:39.

[46] Genesis 41:45, Numbers 12:1, Hebrews 11:31, James 2:25, Matt 1:5.

[47] Ruth 1:16-17.

[48] Ruth 4.

said for many of today's migrant populations. This is an important point that reflects the ideal nature of national bonds.

In Ernest Renan's famous 1882 essay "What is a Nation?" the French academic sought to look past important but technical features like language and race to find the intrinsic sentimental qualities that bound a nation together. Someone can feel pride during an Independence Day parade, and that pride may be prompted by hearing a particular dialect and seeing particular faces. But those things in themselves are not what cause these feelings of smallness and sacrifice. Rather it is the fact that there is a belonging attached to those things. They are one's own language and one's own nationality. Renan wrote:

> The nation, like the individual, is the culmination of a long past of endeavours, sacrifices, and devotions. Of all cults, that of the ancestors is the most legitimate, for the ancestors have made us what we are. A heroic past, great men, glory (by which I understand genuine glory), this is the social capital upon which one bases a national idea. To have common glories in the past and to have a common will in the present; to have performed great deeds together, to wish to perform still more–these are the essential conditions for being a people.

These qualities are reflected in the Shema prayer of Deuteronomy 6:4-9, which instructs parents to collectively affirm their love for God and teach it to their children, as well as in the command from Leviticus 19:18 to love one's neighbor as oneself. Language and ancestry serve as channels for conveying deep attachments to one's own people across generations, solidifying these bonds in traditions such as national celebrations like Passover and memorials like the pile of stones commemorating the crossing of the Jordan River in Joshua 4:6-7. Just as shared commitment, sacrifice, and love hold a family together, they also serve as the binding agents that unite a nation.

This understanding implies that liberal thinkers who base their views of nationhood on a social contract between individuals and society are wrong. Edmund Burke taught that "society [was] an association of the dead, the living and the unborn." Roger Scruton added that it was a "shared inheritance for the sake of which we learn to circumscribe our demands, to see our own place in things as part of a continuous chain of giving and receiving, and to recognize that the good things we inherit are not ours to spoil."[49] Both the Abrahamic Covenant and the Constitution of the United States inherently prioritize securing blessings for future generations, as do the Magna Carta and the First Charter of Virginia, along with many other nationally significant political documents. It is natural to love one's own, but in modern times our general government often seems to think its own are foreigners.

As I write this chapter, I am reminded of a situation in 2024 when the government imported up to 20,000 Haitian migrants to Springfield, Ohio, a city with only 60,000 residents, thereby straining local infrastructure, increasing property costs, and fostering unsafe conditions. Local residents expressed frustration, noting that the migrants' housing and grocery needs were fully covered by government funds. That same year, FEMA's inadequate response to two hurricanes brought to light its allocation of over $1.4 billion within a two-year period for migrant care. A border security and foreign aid bill also designated $60 billion for military aid to Ukraine, $14 billion to Israel, and just $20 billion for United States' border security. Previous generations of Americans would have a hard time conceiving of this apparent preference for foreign peoples over one's own.

There was always a foreign contingent living among Israel. Moses recounts that even during the Exodus "a mixed multitude" left Egypt with the Israelites.[50] But they were never to threaten the Israelite way of life. Israel could benefit from foreign laborers, but even at the height of Solomon's reign with his foreign workforce, it is only estimated that ten percent of the population was foreign.[51] A core group of Israelites continued to set the cultural tone for their own country. Can the same be said for modern Western nations, which,

[49] Roger Scruton, *How To Be a Conservative* (A&C Black, 2014), 20.
[50] Ex 12:38.
[51] Deut. 24:14–15; Samson Liao Uytanlet and Juliet Lee Uytanlet, *Manual for Sojourners: A Study on Peter's Use of Scripture and Its Relevance Today* (Wipf and Stock Publishers, 2023), 13.

thanks to advancements in transportation, quickly take in large percentages of people—numbers that, had they arrived in pre-modern times, would have been considered an invading force?

In 2004, political scientist Samuel P. Huntington wrote:

> America's core culture has been and, at the moment, is still primarily the culture of seventeenth- and eighteenth-century settlers who founded American society. The central elements of that culture can be defined in a variety of ways but include the Christian religion, Protestant values and moralism, a work ethic, the English language, British traditions of law, justice, and the limits of government power, and a legacy of European art, literature, philosophy, and music.[52]

Today, it is doubtful that Huntington's description from over two decades ago still accurately reflects present-day America. He expressed concern that immigration was eroding this "core culture" and now lives to see this prediction realized.

America has traditionally done a decent job, compared to other countries, of incorporating many kinds of different people. This is due in large part to its vast virgin lands, general Christian openness, and economic opportunity. Throughout most of our history, minority groups did not generally have the ability to politically threaten the core—until the rise of New Left identity politics. As a result of changing circumstances, members of different groups are now balkanizing themselves into states and regions where they share similar values. Whether this reinforces local and regional attachments remains to be seen, but one thing is for sure: the emerging United States will be much different in character than the country it was for its entire previous existence.

To stabilize the country and ensure its survival, we must nurture the iconic American Anglo-Protestant identity. Achieving this will require the implementation of certain limiting principles. While

---

[52] Samuel P. Huntington, *Who Are We?: The Challenges to America's National Identity* (Simon and Schuster, 2004), 40.

this is not an exhaustive list, here are a few practical considerations. First, we should end the practice of allowing dual citizenship, as it implies dual allegiance. Second, English should be established as the official language of the United States. Third, we should impose strict limits on immigration, prioritizing individuals who align culturally, and this should include deporting those in the country illegally. Fourth, we should incentivize domestic births and strengthen family units. Fifth, we should consider ways to promote and educate the public about American heritage, legends, and lore. Sixth, affirmative action-style quota systems that provide advantages to minority groups should be ended, as they have limited efficacy and have been used to diminish Anglo-Protestant influence. Finally, governmental and civic organizations should once again privilege Christianity, especially in regions such as the Bible Belt where the public supports this.

In conclusion, the concept of the "proposition nation" does not exist in reality. It is used to justify the erosion of national identities. Christians should oppose this idea because it disregards God's natural order which establishes relationships that form nations with their own unique characteristics. This aspect of God's creation is worth defending against the forces of globalism, as it organizes humanity, provides identity, and assigns vital responsibilities. Immigration should generally be managed at a scale that allows host nations to absorb newcomers without jeopardizing their core identity or creating divisions that diminish their national cohesion. There will come a day when representatives from every nation will gather around God's throne in praise, united in the Christian faith yet maintaining their unique national identities. Until that day, Christians in the West should strive to "make disciples of all the nations" while preserving their traditional ways of life.[53]

---

53 Matthew 28:19

9

CONSERVATIVE
NAZI HUNTERS

*Organizations of what one might call a patriotic and traditional
type are labelled crypto-Fascist or 'Fascist-minded'*

George Orwell–What is Fascism? (1944)

I t goes without saying that the modern Left views their political
opponents as proto-Nazis. This of course puts them in the envi-
able position of wearing the white hat regardless of the strength
of their arguments. The sheer volume of media attacks on Donald
Trump for somehow gleaning from Adolph Hitler is overwhelming. Before the 2024 election, *Vox* carried the subtitle: "Trump isn't
Hitler. But when it comes to the courts, he's successfully borrowing
the Nazi's playbook." The association this time is that in the same way
Hitler used his arrest for the Munich Beer Hall Putsch to promote
himself, so Trump was also using his arrest for election interference
to promote his candidacy.[1] Of course, modern Leftists fail to see the

---

[1] Nicole Narea, "Why Trump Seems to Grow More Popular the Worse His Legal Troubles Become," *Vox*,
August 25, 2023, https://www.vox.com/trump-investigations/2023/8/25/23845591/donald-trump-
charges-january-6-trial-hitler-putsch-trial.

parallels between their leaders and Nazis on things like race obsession, healthcare, and environmental policies. Only conservatives are guilty of adopting Nazi beliefs.

Ironically, modern conservatives foolishly seem determined to appropriate this lazy smear for themselves as a defense mechanism and a way to convince their voter base that political progressives are the "true Nazis" and thus win the moral high ground. Before adopting this tactic, it is wise to consider where it came from, who benefits from it, and how conservatives traditionally critiqued Nazism.

Although the strategy of connecting one's opponents to Nazis is more aggressive and common today, the Paris Peace Treaties were hardly dry when it started. In 1950, Frankfurt School psychologist Theodor Adorno published *The Authoritarian Personality,* which suggested things like parental authority, traditional gender roles, family pride, preserving heterosexuality, defending American culture, and Christian beliefs signaled "implicit prefascist tendencies."[2] During the 1952 presidential campaign, Democrats weaponized this association game.

President Harry Truman blamed Republicans for things like opposing civil rights, restricting immigration, and promoting the belief that Soviet subversives had infiltrated the State Department. This "big lie," he said, was "deadly to the American tradition of liberty" and the kind of weapon "used by the Nazis, the Fascists, and the Communists." He warned the National Jewish Welfare Board that Americans should be "vigilant" to oppose "the philosophy of racial superiority developed by the Nazis" from reemerging in the United States "under the guise of anticommunism." He even linked Republicans' opposition to government-subsidized jobs programs to an unwillingness to "defend ourselves against the aggression of the Nazis and the Fascists" and to "do business with Hitler" instead. Ironically, all of this was aimed at Dwight Eisenhower, who defeated

---

2 Jon Harris, *Christianity and Social Justice: Religions in Conflict* (Reformation Zion Publishing, LLC, 2021), 12.

actual Nazis, but who was now guilty of accepting "the very practices that identified the so-called 'master race.'"[3]

Today's American Left increasingly destroys more and more cultural artifacts, organizations, and people through this effective strategy. Everything from MAGA Republicans to Moms for Liberty are smeared as Nazis or as part of the growing list of supposedly repackaged Nazi beliefs like white supremacy, Kinism, Christian Nationalism, and Confederate sympathizing. Such has always been the post-WWII Left's undeveloped understanding. They seem to think that anything with a hint of concern for the preservation of European heritage, tradition, or culture will produce another Hitler and Holocaust. Being "anti-Nazi" now requires one to purge Western societies of their very identities.

American political conservatives have long pointed out the Left's hypocrisy on this point. James Burnham expressed concern in 1961 that the United Nations exclusively focused on racialism from "Western whites" such as Nazis and Klansmen, while ignoring "the anti-white outrages of the black Congolese, the anti-Semitic activities of North African Arabs . . . the Mau Mau terror," and other examples.[4] The United States Department of Justice even sued SpaceX for employing American citizens instead of asylum seekers and refugees. It is a modern sin to prefer one's own people if they are white, and this is somehow proven by the fact that Hitler preferred white people and committed genocide.

Of course, Anglo-American conservatives have always opposed Nazism but on different grounds. Early post-war conservatives believed Hitler's problem was not that he loved his country or his people too much, but rather that he twisted natural affinities for blood and soil into loyalty to a totalitarian ideology. They saw little difference between Nazism and Bolshevism on this point. Neither Fascism nor Communism were capable of achieving their ideal world, and thus they produced rulers committed to fantasies

---

3 Harry Truman, *Public Papers of the Presidents of the United States* (National Archives, 1952), 862-863, 1011, 276.
4 "From a Cold War Notebook," *National Review*, January 14, 1961, 18.

that destroyed the lives of the people they claimed to love. Gerhart Niemeyer asked, "Does it make sense when people, in the name of the good life, initiate wholesale purges, liquidate entire classes of the population, insist on prescribing the detailed structure of a faraway society, maintain an army of spies, and spies against those spies?"[5] The obvious answer is "No." Hitler did not love his own people as much as he did a certain abstract construction of a society people's lives were made to fit into.

National Socialists worked to achieve what Erik Von Kuehnelt-Leddihn called an "irrational mixture of biology and collectivism," and conservatives critiqued them on both counts.[6] They objected to the way Nazis "declassed and denied many privileges" to non-Aryans, which forced upon society a new disruptive hierarchy.[7] They disagreed with the novel way Nazis imagined Jews to be less than people.[8] They pointed out how Nazis developed a welfare state which suppressed individual freedom to live, think, and work. This was the opposite of conservatism, which sought to preserve traditional arrangements formed by Providence over time through experience.[9]

This is why many post-war conservatives rejected the Left's attempts to paint them as Nazis. Kuehnelt-Leddihn said the National Socialists "always belonged to the Left," and the idea that they were "of the 'right' [was] one of the most successful hoaxes in history."[10] In *The Conservative Mind,* Russell Kirk echoed this point. Kirk wrote: "The Nazi and Fascist parties were destructive instruments, made possible by the hysteria and loneliness of the masses who enthusiastically supported them; though now and again these ideologies might endeavor to disguise themselves by talk of 'family' and 'tradition,' this was no better than sham: their nature and object

5 Gerhart Niemeyer said "the two systems are more alike than different." See: Gerhart Niemeyer, "Are Communists Rational," *National Review*, January 5, 1957, 15.
6 Erik Von Kuehnelt-Leddihn, "The Vacant Throne," *National Review*, October 25, 1958, 275.
7 Forrest Davis, "The Right to Nullify," *National Review*, April 25, 1956, 11.
8 Russell Kirk, "Mill's 'On Liberty' Reconsidered," *National Review*, January 25, 1956, 24.
9 "No Program for Youth," *National Review*, October 8, 1960, 205.
10 Erik Von Kuehnelt-Leddihn, "Letter from the Continent," *National Review*, July 13, 1957, 60; Erik Von Kuehnelt-Leddihn, "Letter from the Continent," February 15, 1956, 16.

was revolutionary."[11] Conservatism and Nazism were mortal enemies by nature.

One way to show this more clearly is to examine the way National Socialists viewed religion. Nazi leadership believed Christianity competed with their ideology. Hitler mocked Christianity as a Jewish belief. He said: "I will not tolerate it, if a parson meddles in earthly affairs. The organized lie must be broken, so that the state is absolute lord."[12] Heinrich Himmler said "We shall not rest until we have rooted out Christianity."[13] As a result, the state agents seized most church property, routinely accused ministers of financial misconduct or sexual perversion, eliminated parachurch ministries and information outlets, and arrested thousands of clergy. When jurist Helmuth James von Moltke was condemned to death in 1945 for consulting with clergy on "the practical-ethical demands of Christianity," he said, "Christianity and we National Socialists have one thing in common, and one thing only. We claim the whole man."[14]

This aggressive opposition to Christianity resembled what took place during the French Revolution. Russell Kirk applied Edmund Burke's critique of that event to 20th century tyrants who religiously prioritized the will of the modern state over people's natural interests.[15] In both Jacobinism and socialism the state subordinated every social impulse. Unlike Leftists who share their anti-Nazi enthusiasm with communists, Anglo-American conservatives saw their own disagreement represented more in the German State's religious opponents. Frederick Augustus Voigt noted, "The people who did most against the Nazis were not the Communists, not even the Socialists, but the active Christians and the conservatives, the Jesuits, the ministers, the Junkers, the colonels, the aristocrats."[16]

James Donohoe recounted in his book *Hitler's Conservative*

---

11 Russell Kirk, *The Conservative Mind: From Burke to Eliot* (Regnery, 2001), 487.
12 Adolf Hitler, Heinrich Heim, and Werner Jochmann. *Monologe Im Führer-Hauptquartier 1941-1944.* (Hamburg: A. Knaus, 1980). 303, 150;
13 E.F. von Weizsäcker, *Memoirs of Ernst Von Weizsacker: Chief of the German Foreign Office*, 1938-1943. (Gollancz, 1951), 281.
14 H. Gollwitzer, K. Kuhn, R. Schneider, and M. Miles. *Dying We Live: The Final Messages and Records of the German Resistance.* (Wipf & Stock Publishers, 2009), 129.
15 Russell Kirk, *The Conservative Mind, from Burke to Santayana* (Regnery, 1953), 74-75.
16 "Letter from the Continent," *National Review*, September 8, 1956, 13.

Opponents in Bavaria the way many Bavarian Christians believed "the 'new Germany' had departed from values and traditions of which Germans had once been so proud." Donohoe writes that "most of those who were actively opposed to Hitler in the years after 1933 were equally opposed to the old-fashioned nineteenth century liberalism" as well as Bolshevism. They opposed National Socialism the way Edmund Burke opposed the French Revolution, that is, by appealing to Christianity, traditional social hierarchy, and private property. They defended the "liberty of the Church" because they believed the Christian religion was true, not because they prized a mere freedom to worship in a religiously neutral, pluralistic society.[17]

In modern America, these opponents of Hitler would likely be classified by the media as "Christian nationalists." Yet their instincts mirror that of older generations of Anglo-American conservatives who rightly detected in Nazism the innovations of modernity and rejected them. This older conservative tradition in America rejected progressivism and any ideology people sought "to make the yardstick for all political decisions." Gerhart Niemeyer observed that conservatives who "fought militantly both Nazism and Communism and have seen the destruction wrought by these totalitarian ideologies have acquired a certain primordial fear of all ideological thinking.[18] But wisely, they recognized the political reality that National Socialism had collapsed and was, at most, a historical reminiscence.[19] New threats demanded their attention, which is why they spent little time rehashing their critiques to warn about an enemy already defeated.

Leftists fault anyone who falls short of sharing their obsession with smoking out Nazis as somehow harboring pro-Nazi sentiments. It does not matter how often former President Trump denounced neo-Nazis, white supremacists, and Klansmen, the media still constantly subjected him to renewing his disavowal. These ritualistic purity tests are perhaps what led to the modern political Right's seared

---

17 James Donohoe, *Hitler's Conservative Opponents in Bavaria: 1930–1945; a Study of Catholic, Monarchist, and Separatist Anti-Nazi Activities* (Brill Archive, 1961), 3, 13, 22, 11.
18 Gerhart Niemeyer, "Too Early and Too Much," *National Review*, October 13, 1956, 23.
19 F. A. Voigt, "Germany Revisited," May 9, 1956, 17; *National Review*, July 18, 1959, 201.

conscience on this whole issue. There's a good example of this from a few years ago at a large gun-rights rally in Richmond. A conservative blogger noticed that the event did not seem to be about gun rights at all. Instead, the goal was disproving the Leftist narrative that Nazis and Klansmen are the only ones who care about gun rights, thus painting then Governor Ralph Northam as the true Nazi and Klansman. This, of course, is the same Ralph Northam who thought it was acceptable to do things like raze monuments and kill children after birth. Yet, the message the crowd emphasized with their signs and slogans was how racist he supposedly was, as if that was relevant to his attempted gun grab.[20]

Now political activists on the Right are starting to adopt the Left's framing and priorities. Nate Hochmann, an aide working for the Ron Desantis campaign, was immediately fired from his position after retweeting an exaggerated political video that briefly featured an obscure symbol apparently used by Nazis.[21] Yet, Christina Pushaw, the campaign's rapid response director, defended congratulating a homosexual father who had twins through surrogacy that same month.[22] A historian on the Virginia Board of Historic Resources had to resign from Governor Glenn Youngkin's administration for simply supporting monuments to Confederate soldiers.[23] Yet again, this was the same administration that hosted a series of Pride Month events.[24]

The Left's long "cancel-culture" tradition, now adopted by the Right, is starting to extend to groups like traditional Christians.

[20] Dissident Mama, "Stop Gaslighting Yourselves!," *Dissident Mama* (blog), February 1, 2020, https://www.dissidentmama.net/stop-gaslighting-yourselves/.

[21] Martin Pengelly, "DeSantis Aide Fired after Sharing Video Featuring Symbol Used by Nazis," *The Guardian*, July 26, 2023, sec. US news, https://www.theguardian.com/us-news/2023/jul/26/desantis-campaign-video-nazi-symbol-fired-aide.

[22] Christina Pushaw [@ChristinaPushaw], "@mplpodcast305 @RichardGrenell Congratulating a Friend on Becoming a Dad, and Welcoming New Babies into the World, Has Nothing to Do with 'Pride Month.' Rejecting Identity Politics Means Seeing the Person First, Not Their Orientation. Why Not Tag @rubinreport Btw?," Tweet, Twitter, July 1, 2023, https://twitter.com/ChristinaPushaw/status/1675136566120022016.

[23] Gregory Schneider, "Youngkin Appointee Who Defended Confederate Statues Resigns from Board," *Washington Post*, August 3, 2022, https://www.washingtonpost.com/dc-md-va/2022/08/03/youngkin-appointee-resigns-confederate-statues/.

[24] Sarah Rankin, "Virginia Gov. Youngkin Hosts Series of Pride Events to Mixed Sentiment," *NBC4 Washington*, June 11, 2022, https://www.nbcwashington.com/news/local/virginia-gov-youngkin-hosts-series-of-pride-events-to-mixed-sentiment/3074801/.

Lizzie Marbach, the communications director for Ohio Right to Life, was fired for social media activity culminating in the statement, "There's no hope for any of us outside of having faith in Jesus Christ alone." Republican Congressman Max Miller took offense, claiming it was "one of the most bigoted tweets" he had ever seen.[25] The exclusivity of Marbach's rather conventional claim was beyond the pale in our society of pretended tolerance.

These representative examples of the political Right policing themselves are happening during a time when conservative industry leaders seem more concerned with normalizing homosexuality than responding to the Left's constant attacks on white people. They conceive of America in ways only Progressives used to. To them, America is more the abstract ideas of freedom and equality than it is a tangible place filled with tangible people. As egalitarian sentiments increase, Right-Wingers follow in the footprints laid down for them by radicals. As a result, gatekeepers in politically Right circles are conditioned into suspecting Nazi sympathies simply because someone values a sense of people and place. This became more clear to me recently as I watched conservative and evangelical Christian outlets try to eviscerate Stephen Wolfe's book *The Case for Christian Nationalism.*

Although legitimate critiques exist, most reviews took him to task for alleged fascistic tendencies. Stephen said what many Christian thinkers before him, including Augustine and John Calvin, believed: That "blood relations matter for your ethnicity because your kin have belonged to this people on this land." It did not matter that Wolfe clarified he rejected "modern racialist principles" and was not making a "white nationalist" argument.[26] Paul Matzko in *Reason* magazine wrote that "Wolfe has composed a segregationist political theology."[27] Kevin DeYoung claimed in his review for The Gospel

[25] Max Miller [@MaxMillerOH], "This Is One of the Most Bigoted Tweets I Have Ever Seen. Delete It, Lizzie. Religious Freedom in the United States Applies to Every Religion. You Have Gone Too Far.," Tweet, *Twitter*, August 15, 2023, https://twitter.com/MaxMillerOH/status/1691564395342488045.
[26] Stephen Wolfe, *The Case for Christian Nationalism*, (Moscow, Idaho: Canon Press, 2022), 139, 172.
[27] Paul Matzko, "A Segregationist Case for 'Christian Nationalism,'" *Reason*, May 13, 2023, https://reason.com/2023/05/13/beware-the-christian-prince/.

Coalition that Wolfe's arguments bore "resemblance to certain blood-and-soil nationalisms of the 19th and 20th centuries."[28] Virgil Walker wrote for G3 Ministries that "Wolfe's version of nationalism maintains consistency with the kind of German volkism that paved the way for ethnic German nationalism."[29]

But this was never the problem conservatives had with Nazism until very recently. In fact, some of their critiques were that National Socialists did not value people and place enough. The Nazis violated sovereign borders, persecuted their own countrymen, and destroyed sacred traditions. Thus conservatives viewed the "blood and soil" slogan as merely that, a slogan. To whatever extent conservatives possessed an affinity for their own people, it disagreed with the Nazi instinct to replace natural affections with a love for power and ideology.

What gatekeepers on the modern American Right fail to see is how their willingness to cancel others for violating egalitarian principles shares more in common with the ideologues they claim to oppose than it does with their conservative heritage. Authentic conservatives have a much stronger argument against National Socialism, but it is not one they should need to deploy, given how busy they are fighting actual threats. Younger members of the Right are starting to see the failures of late-stage post-war conservatism. The question is whether they will have the opportunity to conserve conservatism by restoring a Christian moral framework that values people and place while rejecting newly adopted ideologies and tactics that were once revolutionary Leftist but are now bipartisan.

---

[28] Kevin DeYoung, "The Rise of Right-Wing Wokeism," *The Gospel Coalition*, November 28, 2022, https://www.thegospelcoalition.org/reviews/christian-nationalism-wolfe/.

[29] Virgil Walker, "The Dangerous Intersection of Christian Nationalism and Ethnocentrism," *G3 Ministries*, April 27, 2023, https://g3min.org/the-dangerous-intersection-of-christian-nationalism-and-ethnocentrism/.

10

THE WOKE
RIGHT MYTH

'And your defect is a propensity to hate everybody.'
'And yours,' he replied with a smile, 'is wilfully to misunderstand them.'

Fitzwilliam Darcy to Elizabeth Bennett–*Pride and Prejudice*

The term "woke" accompanied the Black Lives Matter movement as a way to describe a heightened awareness of social disparities and the revolutionary spirit required to remove and replace the structures supposedly responsible for them. Like other analytical tools inspired by cultural Marxism such as "identity politics" and "critical theory," "wokeness" targeted the cultural foundations of Western civilization, aiming to replace them with a new order that promised a future form of social equality yet to be realized.

Because of its rigid ideology, its negative consequences, and the extent to which it blamed innocuous and fundamental social features for reinforcing oppression, the woke movement became discredited in the minds of many and the term became a pejorative. Calling someone "woke" today conveys the idea that they are radical activists, bent on destruction, and out of touch with reality. Popular podcaster Tim Pool described "woke" as "cult-like adherence to liberal social orthodoxy."[1]

BATTLE FOR THE SOUL OF THE RIGHT

Although the term originated with the revolutionary Left, some today use it to discredit certain elements on the Right that are less liberal and more aligned with older conservative views. While it is unlikely that applying the term to right-wing movements will gain widespread traction, it does highlight two competing political approaches vying for dominance against the hard Left. One seeks to conserve religion, hierarchy, and tradition against the forces of pluralism, egalitarianism, and ideology, while the other sees itself as the champion of individual rights, freedom, and equality against collectivism, totalitarianism, and bigotry. In short, it really is a battle between conservatives and liberals happening on the Right.

Applying the term "woke" to conservatives seems to have gained steam in 2022 when Kevin DeYoung wrote a review of Stephen Wolfe's book *The Case for Christian Nationalism* entitled "The Rise of Right-Wing Wokeism." DeYoung, a council member at The Gospel Coalition and pastor in North Carolina, described Wolfe's views as "woke" because they conveyed the idea that "oppression is everywhere, extreme measures are necessary, and the regime must be overthrown." Ultimately, Wolfe's alleged error seems to be the extent to which he critiqued positive liberal assumptions concerning capitalism, secularism, and pluralism. He thought these controlling and interwoven conditions of modern life made men weak, undermined ethnic bonds, and threatened Christianity.[2]

Since DeYoung raised the alarm about Christian nationalism, others have started insisting that a "woke right" exists within Christian circles. Yet, the parallels they draw to prove their point are

---

1   Tim Pool, *James Lindsay ROASTED For Fake Christian Nationalist Hoax, Former Liberals SLAMMED For Lying*, 2024, https://www.youtube.com/watch?v=Aq_5owTIoH4.
2   Kevin DeYoung, "The Rise of Right-Wing Wokeism," *The Gospel Coalition*, November 28, 2022, https://www.thegospelcoalition.org/reviews/christian-nationalism-wolfe/.

not very substantive. They also overlook major differences between social justice ideology and the more conservative political thought that animates the Christian Right.

JAMES LINDSAY'S FAILED DECOY

James Lindsay, an atheist and libertarian thinker, claimed he demonstrated the existence of the "woke right" when *American Reformer*, a Christian conservative publication, republished a "modified" portion of the *Communist Manifesto*. Lindsay had rearranged the text to critique liberalism and submitted it under a pseudonym. A closer examination of Lindsay's decoy article reveals that it was neither much of a summary nor a rewrite.

Instead, it was a hollowed-out, fragmented section with mostly new language that actually made the opposite point of the original section from Marx. Instead of arguing against conserving religion and hierarchy, as Marx does, Lindsay argued for a conservative return to these things. Lindsay also stripped away Marx's ideological framework, which reduced every human impulse in history to "class struggles," and did not replace it with anything as universal, abstract, or binary. Instead, he wrote about a threatening liberal order that he confined to the period beginning with World War II.[3]

Despite the significant chasm between Marx's framework and purpose and those presented in the article for *American Reformer*, Lindsay argued that what made the former representative of the "woke right" was the belief that they were dominated by a liberal order that needed to be overthrown—similar to Marx's view that the proletariat must gain power to defeat the bourgeoisie.[4] All the other popular critiques of the woke right seem to make a similar case. If

---

3 Jim Hanson [@JimHansonDC], "James Lindsay Is Mocking the 'Woke Right' (@AmReformer) for Publishing 6 Pgs of the Communist Manifesto . . ." *X*, December 3, 2024, https://x.com/JimHansonDC/status/1864071222780145732; James Lindsay, "The Liberal Consensus and the New Christian Right," *American Reformer*, November 18, 2024, https://americanreformer.org/2024/11/the-liberal-consensus-and-the-new-christian-right/.

4 James Lindsay, "A Communist Manifesto for Christian Nationalists: Testing the Woke Right," *New Discourses*, December 3, 2024, https://newdiscourses.com/2024/12/a-communist-manifesto-for-christian-nationalists-testing-the-woke-right/.

someone on the Right thinks in terms of group interest, believes a powerful hegemony threatens their group, and pursues social domination to meet the threat, they risk being categorized as woke.

A False Equivalence

Seth Dillon, the CEO of the comedy website *The Babylon Bee*, called "the woke right . . . a mirror image of the woke left" since "they use the same rhetoric, the same methods, the same grievance and identity framework."[5] Neil Shenvi, a chemist who runs a Christian apologetics blog, made similar points and added that "the woke right is embracing the ideas and methods of critical theory," namely an oversimplification of social dynamics.[6] Comedian Konstatin Kisin accurately identified some of the civilizational threats conservatives are concerned about, such as the World Economic Forum, mass immigration policies, and anti-family rhetoric. Yet, he compared these threats to the Left's discredited obsession with systemic racism and suggested that the Right might turn to an authoritarian figure if their concerns were not addressed through democratic means. Kisin argued that Tucker Carlson was already laying the groundwork for this shift and was "woke" as a result.[7]

In each case, a false equivalence is drawn between Christian Right thinking and social justice ideology. If acknowledging that powerful forces target certain social groups is seen as appealing to shared rhetoric, then this similarity is irrelevant. The real question is whether the rhetoric is true or is driven by a false ideology. Every political approach seeks to protect preferred groups from perceived threats. Even liberals view themselves as collectively opposing groups that

5 Seth Dillon [@SethDillon], "James Was Able to Trick These Guys into Publishing the Communist Manifesto Because the Woke Right Is a Mirror Image of the Woke Left. They Use the Same Rhetoric, the Same Methods, the Same Grievance and Identity Framework. Their Solutions Differ, but Their Wokeness Is Identical.," Tweet, *X*, December 3, 2024, https://x.com/SethDillon/status/1864036600532865215.

6 Neil Shenvi, "What Is the 'Woke Right'?," *Neil Shenvi–Apologetics* (blog), June 8, 2024, https://shenviapologetics.com/what-is-the-woke-right/.

7 Konstantin Kisin, "Tucker Carlson And The Woke Right–Konstantin Kisin," https://www.youtube.com/watch?v=6cN_mB_D96w.

threaten their agenda. Ironically, much of the critique of the "woke right" is written in this very spirit.

If engaging in political analysis that identifies general threats from powerful institutions and seeks to preserve the social order is equated with critical theory, which aims to deconstruct the social order through an ideological framework, then there is a serious conflation at play. Max Horkheimer, the director of the Institute for Social Research responsible for "critical theory," thought "progress toward utopia [was] blocked" by the "technocracy." He stated that critical theory was designed to emancipate man from this. All political approaches must necessarily analyze threats and provide remedies to them, even liberalism. But this is not the same as seeking creative ways to destabilize and remake society along egalitarian lines.

If seeking power to defeat power is "woke," then so is politics itself. It is curious that conservatives are blamed for a strong centralized government they played the least role in creating. While they aim to preserve local and federal arrangements, conservatives must also build institutions strong enough to counter globalist threats or risk losing everything. Ironically, liberalism's focus on individual autonomy at the expense of society has eroded local ties, fostering decadence that weakens democracy and drives centralization. Conservatives, more committed to transcendent principles than to mechanisms like democracy—which only work under certain conditions—understand that other forms of government may be necessary to confront greater threats. However, their prudence does not mean they neglect efforts to preserve the conditions that make democracy possible, as recent concerns over voter ID and compromised elections demonstrate.

WOKE LIBERALISM?

The criticisms liberals make of conservatives for being part of the so-called "woke right" can also be applied to liberal political ideologies. This is because liberals tend to minimize the features that make "wokeness" unique—its ideological rigidity and egalitarian scheme—and focus instead on the architecture of its arguments. Woke activists recognize dominant power structures, including oppressed and oppressor groups, and strive to defeat political opponents. Liberals take this basic framework and compare it to the way traditional conservative groups approach politics. Since these groups also recognize the role of hegemony, oppression, and the importance of wielding power, then they too must be "woke," or so the logic goes.

Conservative Christians often discuss the secularization of society, their own marginalization, and the need to defeat their enemies on the Left. More broadly, conservatives worry about globalist interests undermining their communities and seek to resist them. Unsurprisingly, none of this is particularly newsworthy, as these concerns are intrinsic to all political approaches, including liberal ones. If recognizing dominant power structures, oppressed and oppressor groups, and striving to dismantle oppressive institutions are enough to define someone as "woke," then liberalism itself should be seen as "woke."

This is evident in the political philosophy of John Stuart Mill. Mill believed that "despotism of custom is everywhere the standing hindrance to human advancement." He thought society's mandates represented a "social tyranny more formidable than many kinds of political oppression."[8] For liberals to make the "woke right" theory work, they would need to carve out an exception for their own belief in the existence of oppressive social hegemonies or else turn a blind eye to the schemes of their own theorists.

To take a practical subject, on the question of Woman's Liberation, Mill believed society had unjustly divided "mankind into two classes, a small one of masters and a numerous one of slaves." This "unjust domination ... appear[ed] natural" to those in the superior position. His remedy was for this usurpation to "be replaced by a principle of perfect equality, admitting no power or privilege on the one side, nor disability on the other." Marriage itself would need to be overhauled.[9] This does sound woke, but the reason is not because Mill sought

---

[8] John Stuart Mill, *J. S. Mill: "On Liberty" and Other Writings* (Cambridge University Press, 1989), 70, 8.
[9] Ibid., 129.

the demise of his enemies. Like all modern liberals who champion a kind of autonomous individualism, Mill's penchant for overturning natural order and custom is what makes him seem "woke," not the fact that he believed nefarious forces should be stopped.

My point is that thinkers who are part of the liberal tradition, classical or modern, all found it necessary to identify threats and defeat them. John Locke rightly saw those who would "harm another" as social threats who should be "restrained" by government coercion. In the universal struggle between law and tyranny, Locke viewed absolute monarchy as a threat to civil order. He argued that "the people" collectively had the right to dissolve legislatures that act contrary to the law and to establish new ones in their place. Yet Locke is not considered "woke right." Neither is the American Revolution.

Even the libertarian Ayn Rand, who eschewed collectivism, could not escape smuggling in a necessary place for collective power against tyranny when she praised America's revolutionary achievement in limiting the role of government. Right or wrong, features like the oppressor/oppressed dichotomy, the existence of hegemony, and the importance of pursuing power are part of any political approach. For these concepts to be baptized into wokeness, there must be a commitment to egalitarian social justice ideology from the outset.

For instance, woke activists do not merely acknowledge oppression in general terms—they view it as stemming primarily and universally from specific identity groups. White people, heterosexuals, Christians, and males are often seen as chiefly responsible for society's problems. This perspective defines oppression through an egalitarian lens, where disparities in wealth, privilege, and other metrics are seen as evidence of oppression. However, activists choose these disparities selectively, focusing only on situations where they favor presumed marginalized groups. Ultimately, the game is rigged from the start to produce certain conclusions that ultimately justify social revolution against order, tradition, and hierarchy. If anything, liberals tend to share more similarities with the "woke" neo-Marxists they so despise than traditional conservatives do.

Both liberals and woke activists often operate through ideological frameworks that impose rigid, reductionist, and simplistic principles on complex political decisions. While liberals tend to emphasize "freedom" and woke activists prioritize "equality," both treat these concepts as expansive, universal principles that must override any tradition or custom that stands in their way. For James Lindsay, this perspective extends to supporting legalized pornography, abortion rights, and "LGBT equality," all in the name of individual rights.[10]

Conservatives, on the other hand, have traditionally seen their role as counter revolutionaries in defense of the good, true, and beautiful as mediated through tradition and applied to unique situations. They certainly hold to a good vs. evil binary and conceive of it in spiritual terms, but this battle takes different forms and cannot be generally reduced to social structures or the concerns of one cultural moment, such as battles between democracy and monarchy or labor and business. This gives them latitude to make prudential decisions, since not every issue is bound up in some rigid totalizing principle. It also ensures they value the use of power to stop evil. They are also generally more favorable to gradual approaches to social change over revolutionary ones. Obviously, none of this sounds remotely woke unless the term simply refers to recognizing enemies and using power to defeat them.

Perhaps what traditional conservatives and woke activists have in common in a significant way is not the architecture of their arguments, but instead a shared recognition that they are both interested in obtaining and using power to further their political goals—even if their goals are the opposite of one another. Modern liberals, on the other hand, often appear to believe they can rise above group identities, political conflicts, and the pursuit of power, even as they form groups and exercise power to challenge those who threaten their different visions for individual autonomy.

---

[10] James Lindsay, anti-Communist [@ConceptualJames], "Amateur Porn Is Freedom.," Tweet, *X*, December 7, 2019, https://x.com/ConceptualJames/status/1203442305069387776; James Lindsay, anti-Communist [@ConceptualJames], "@MacCarey1 @DickPatriarchy This Is Undoubtedly True. My Original Tweet Was Not an Endorsement of an Abortion Ban Because It Will Work out Cheerfully in Some Small Percentage of Women (Who Still Should Have Been given the Choice over Their Own Bodies).," Tweet, *X*, May 15, 2019, https://x.com/ConceptualJames/status/1128679906743857155. Helen Pluckrose and James Lindsay, *Cynical Theories: How Activist Scholarship Made Everything about Race, Gender, and Identity—and Why This Harms Everybody* (Pitchstone Publishing (US&CA), 2020), 19;

SOME LIBERAL SELF REFLECTION

The main issue with "Woke Right" rhetoric is the fact that liberals, whether they go by that name or not, are deceiving themselves into thinking they can transcend the political. Liberals view themselves as advocates for human rights, grounded in the ideals of individual autonomy, democracy, and pluralism. They typically position themselves as the antithesis of fascism, communism, and other totalitarian schemes. However, what they frequently fail to grasp is how their political philosophy undermines the traditional societies that provide the stability for many of their own policies to function effectively.

Every society, even Western liberal democracies, naturally form hierarchies where some groups dominate while others are subordinated. In the United States, English is predominantly the language spoken in public spaces. City skylines often highlight Christian symbols more than those of other faiths. Major sports events primarily feature men. Holidays that are nationally recognized focus on events and characters from America's own unique past. Minority groups who reject these default social arrangements must create their own subcultures within the broader society.

There is no escaping hierarchy, group dynamics, political threats, critical analysis, or the pursuit of power—at least if one wants to engage politically in this world. It is only in high-trust societies that free trade is possible, personal liberty can thrive, and heavy-handed central authority is less likely to emerge. America once embodied this ideal more fully. To preserve our cherished rights, America must return to the virtues her citizens once held in greater measure. This means rejecting the ideology of "wokeness" and the egalitarian nonsense designed to undermine the West, replacing it instead with Christianity and an ordered liberty. There is nothing "woke" about that—although perhaps preventing the re-establishment of these traditional characteristics, under the guise of combating oppression, could be.

11

THE INESCAPABILITY OF
IDENTITY POLITICS

*Man is by nature a social animal; an individual who
is unsocial naturally and not accidentally is either
beneath our notice or more than human.*

Aristotle

When most conservatives consider identity politics, they think of it as a creature of the Left—and with good reason. The term "identity politics" was first used by self-proclaimed "Black feminists and Lesbians" in the 1977 *Combahee River Collective Statement*. The primary authors, Demita Frazier, Beverly Smith, and Barbara Smith, believed that "racial, sexual, heterosexual, and class oppression" formed an interlocking system that "Black feminists" were well positioned to oppose.

In their minds, black liberation and feminist movements stood against certain kinds of oppression while reinforcing others. Although the *Statement* authors were socialists, they did not believe socialism itself was capable of destroying "capitalism and imperialism as well as patriarchy." Therefore, their revolutionary task was to work within various identity-based movements on the Left to finally accomplish an ultimate liberation from white Christian males and the system they created to benefit themselves.

Essentially, the Left's identity politics acknowledged the myriad of ways a dominant majority suppressed victim minority groups. It also sought to mobilize these victim groups into an alliance capable of competing against the majority. We can see the effectiveness of this strategy over the past two decades as Left-wing institutions concentrated their resources on different issues from same-sex marriage to firearm restrictions.

Their coordination represents an unofficial political spoils system where resources are routed to various causes in exchange for participation in other progressive efforts. Activists for racial justice are expected to support feminists who are in turn expected to support LGBT+ causes, etc. As momentum begins to fade with one cause, another is brought to the forefront. This works well politically, not just because it maintains constant pressure on the Right, but also because it weaponizes a communal aspect of human nature that modern conservatives, broadly speaking, refuse to acknowledge.

It is inescapably true that people will think of themselves in particular ways based on where they live, what they enjoy, who they associate with, and other factors. Some identity markers are superficial, such as membership in a bowling league. But others are deep enough to cause feuds, wars, and political movements when threatened. The Left knows this and uses such differences as a means to gain political power in their cosmic quest for universal justice. In contrast, the Right's political messaging and goals are reversed.

THE RIGHT'S IDENTITY CRISIS

Political conservatives' messaging focuses on universal ideas and individual self-interest, even though they are invested in the goal of preserving a particular way of life. In reviewing more than 1,000 political ads before the 2022 mid-term elections, *The Washington Post* found that Democrats highlighted concerns specific to particular groups such as abortion, Medicare, and special interests, while Republicans focused on issues that impacted everyone, like taxation, inflation, and crime.[1]

Donald Trump is an exception in that he is the first major Republican in recent memory to overtly court the support of working class whites, Christians, and other groups by appealing to their particular interests. In 2016, when Hillary Clinton identified half of Trump's supporters as "deplorable" and "irredeemable" for being "racist, sexist, homophobic, xenophobic, [and] Islamophobic," Trump took credit for them, defended them, and attacked Clinton. He said, "People who warn about radical Islamic terrorism are not Islamophobes. They're not. They're decent American citizens who want to uphold our tolerant values and keep our country safe."[2] Trump's willingness to defend ordinary Americans attracted the support of disaffected rust belt voters.

Compare this to Presidential candidate Mitt Romney's reaction when Vice-President Joe Biden said Republicans would put people "back in chains" in 2012. Instead of defending the voters in his party, Romney lamented how Biden's "reckless accusations . . . disgrace[d] the office of the presidency."[3] Romney's way of framing the problem in terms acceptable to everyone, including Democrats, is still standard Republican procedure, and it seems to assume we still live in time of relative homogeneity like we did half a century ago.

During the Cold War, Anglo-Protestantism still dominated culture, people expected immigrants to assimilate, and the threat imposed by another superpower united all citizens against a common foe. All Americans stood for freedom against totalitarianism and made it a priority in the voting booth. This broad understanding of what appeals to Americans still permeates much discourse on

---

1 Harry Stevens and Colby Itkowitz, "What More than 1,000 Political Ads Are Arguing Right before the Midterms," *Washington Post*, October 25, 2022, https://www.washingtonpost.com/politics/interactive/2022/political-ads/.

2 "Donald Trump Calls on Hillary Clinton to 'Retract' Her 'Basket of Deplorables' Comment," *ABC News*, September 12, 2016. https://abcnews.go.com/Politics/donald-trump-hits-back-hillary-clinton-basket-deplorables/story?id=42033561.

3 Steve Holland and Jeff Mason, "Biden Draws Romney's Ire with 'Chains' Comment," *Reuters*, August 15, 2012, https://www.reuters.com/article/idUSBRE87E00Z/.

the Right. Republicans commonly campaign to restore what they believe is the country's default setting against the identity politics that threaten this unity.

Conservatives who lived through the Cold War knew that Soviet forces had infiltrated previous movements on the Left, such as the Civil Rights and Antiwar Movements, in order to exploit social weaknesses and turn Americans against themselves. This understandably made conservatives suspicious of social movements that separated groups of people from the mainstream and promoted ingroup preferences among them. John Wayne's 1972 recitation of a poem called "The Hyphen" characterizes this sentiment well.

Wayne stated:

We all came from other places,
Different creeds and different races,
To form a nation. To become as one.
Yet look at the harm a line has done.

Wayne explained that when people call themselves things like "Afro-American" or "Irish-American," they were actually "a divided American." The poem concluded by championing American freedom and equality which "can span all the differences of man." He warned that such divisions, if left unchecked, would ultimately destroy America by turning it into something resembling Nazi Germany or Soviet Russia.

Wayne's concern was shared by much of the Right's intelligentsia, who rooted the source of American homogeneity in a commonly shared commitment to the individual. Frank Meyer said "all value resides in the individual; all social institutions derive their value and, in fact, their very being from individuals and are justified only to the extent that they serve the needs of individuals."[4] Thinkers like William F. Buckley, George Will, and F.A. Hayek made similar statements.[5] In theory, this universal thinking set a low bar that allowed

---

[4] Frank Meyer, *In Defense of Freedom and Related Essays* (Indianapolis: Liberty Fund, 1996), 8.
[5] George Hawley, *Conservatism in a Divided America: The Right and Identity Politics* (University of Notre Dame Pess, 2022), 62-69.

Republicans to attract a more diverse group of people to their movement. Unfortunately, it simultaneously weakened the Right's social vision and diluted the interests of traditional Americans who made up its base of support.

As wealth creation became more important than regional distinctions and foreign intervention a greater concern than domestic cultural rot, some voters suspected that behind the individual freedom message was a commitment to corporatism and globalism. Even when the religious Right campaigned for Christian sexual ethics, they increasingly watered down their Christian character with broad terms like "Judeo-Christian," "family values," and "people of faith." Advocating on behalf of a religious or cultural group was something the Left did, but conservative politicians felt they were not supposed to. One of the things that separated them from the Left was the fact that their message still applied to every American. Some political conservatives took pride in this fact, but others charted a different path.

During the Republican National Convention in 1992, presidential candidate Patrick Buchanan delivered his "Culture War" speech. Although he highlighted general themes such as job creation and foreign policy successes, he also took aim at homosexuality and pornography normalization, abortion policy, "radical feminism," religious discrimination, and environmentalism. In a famous line, he stated: "This election is about more than who gets what. It is about who we are. It is about what we believe, and what we stand for as Americans. There is a religious war going on in this country. It is a cultural war, as critical to the kind of nation we shall be as was the Cold War itself, for this war is for the soul of America."[6] Buchanan spoke the language of particular identity later channeled in part by Donald Trump.

Like Buchanan, Trump also acknowledged the cultural differences between two groups of Americans and championed one vision over the other. He prioritized citizens over asylum seekers, jobs for families over corporations, and American interests over "defending democracy" around the world. Trump supporters called this

---

6 Patrick Buchanan, "Culture War Speech" (Republican National Convention, August 17, 1992), https://voicesofdemocracy.umd.edu/buchanan-culture-war-speech-speech-text/.

philosophy "America First," and Americans who stood in the way of it were enemies, not because they disagreed with abstract notions of freedom, but because they lacked national loyalty. After years of Republicans emphasizing what they believed were American ideals, universal to all peoples, Trump emphasized the American people themselves and sought to protect their identity.

Although his record on the sexual revolution is mixed, Trump's instinctual resistance to its latest innovations is also based on identity. He chastised then President Biden for recognizing Transgender Visibility Day when it fell on Easter because it disrespected Christians. He then declared November 5th, the day he won the Presidency, to be "Christian Visibility Day."[7] Leftists in the institutional media accused Trump of divisiveness. One op-ed implied he was bigoted by allegedly signaling to white Christians and diminishing the plight of people who considered themselves transgender.[8] Ultimately however, it is the fact that Donald Trump considers the United States to be culturally Christian that offends liberal sensibilities.

In the Leftist framework, identity politics are justified because they represent alleged victim groups in a crusade for equality. Yet when people like Patrick Buchanan or Donald Trump signal support for particular groups, the media portrays them as bigots, since their policies benefit the white working class, middle America, and evangelical Christians who are allegedly oppressors by definition. This is how the Left can treat identities on their side as candidates for universal celebration and protection while rejecting similar treatment for identity groups opposed to them.

This is why even standard Republicans who use universal messaging and avoid signaling support for particular groups cannot

7 Benny Johnson [@bennyjohnson], "TRUMP: 'What the Hell Was Biden Thinking When He Declared Easter Sunday to Be "Trans Visibility Day"? Such Total Disrespect to Christians... November 5th Is Going to Be Called "CHRISTIAN Visibility Day", When Christians Turn out in Numbers That Nobody's Ever Seen before'" Https://T.Co/qu3uquKfqc," Tweet, *X*, April 2, 2024, https://twitter.com/bennyjohnson/status/1775287061181767792.
8 Philip Bump, "Analysis | Trump's 'Christian Visibility Day' Bit Overstates His Christian Support," *Washington Post*, April 3, 2024, https://www.washingtonpost.com/politics/2024/04/03/trump-christian-visibility-day/.

escape charges of bigotry from the Left and are hardly competitive among cultural minorities. Democrats offer what appear to be an array of specific benefits preferable to the broad Republican message intended for everyone. Thus, the people who by default support even the most lackluster Republican campaigns are the same ones who stand to lose in the Left's culture siege. They behave as groups even if their groups are not acknowledged. The media then smears Republicans anyway for dog-whistling for the support of alleged majority oppressors like white people, men, and Christians. It turns out that avoiding identity politics is still a decision to attract certain identities.

If there is a lesson to be learned from America First politics, it is that thinking in terms of identity is both unavoidable and perhaps necessary to break the Left's stranglehold on framing who is and who is not a victim. Acknowledging and rewarding vilified or forgotten demographics can motivate them and may even expand one's base of support. Leading up to the 2024 election, institutional media noticed through polling data that Trump expanded his support among black and Hispanic voters. Perhaps this is attributed to his message which both acknowledged them and promised to help their families against crime and joblessness. This is something the Democrats have repeatedly failed to remedy. It is reasonable to think that if Trump could make good on his promise to help working class white people, why not other groups as well? This is something other Republicans could capitalize on, but many are afraid to identify with people the Left considers "deplorable." However, the fact is, in a certain sense identity politics is unavoidable even for Republicans who see America as a universal idea.

Politics by nature includes an "us vs. them" element. I remember in 2016 when Hillary Clinton chastised Donald Trump for dividing America along an "us vs. them" battle line. Yet she herself employed the same binary thinking she accused Trump of harboring. Clinton's actual point was that there are those who do not want division (i.e. us) and there are those who do want division (i.e. them). Both their strategies recognized division.

Political theorist George Hawley, in his book *Conservatism in a Divided America*, observed that "tribalism, in one form or another, seems to be an inescapable element of democratic politics" and "at some point…one must work with human nature as it is."[9] Despite the influence of neutralist classical liberal thinking, mainstream conservatives engage in partisanship. They also appear to defend more traditional gender roles and advocate for natives over foreigners. Some have started to mimic the Left by enacting broad hate speech laws against antisemitism in deep red states. All of these messages advocate for certain exclusive identities: Republicans, women, citizens, and Jewish people. If Republicans were honest with themselves, they have never exclusively advocated for rootless American individuals.

DEFEATING THE LEFT'S IDENTITY POLITICS

It is time for the modern political Right and its evangelical base to reject the fear and ideology that keep it from stating the obvious. The Left's "identity politics" are at war with both the natural order and our traditional American heritage. Conservatives object to this vision because they wish to preserve ways of life unique to their Western Christian cultures. This may vary based on region, but overall the United States, as political theorist Barry Shain put it, is based on "British institutional development and Reformed Protestantism."[10] The Left rejects these features and uses identity politics to expunge and dilute them. They accomplish this in two ways.

First, they socially construct group identities whose sole purpose is to mimic and replace actual institutions like the nation, the church, marriage, and the family. The Left is able to advance the interests of unassimilated peoples at taxpayers' expense, using the proposition nation which erodes the distinction between native and foreigner. They grant the same public access and privileges to Satanism that Christianity enjoys. They allow mothers to abort their children apart from the father's input and children to have gender reassignment

---

9   Hawley, 2, 4
10 *The 1607 Project: Virginia First* (Last Stand Studios, 2024).

surgeries apart from the parents. They treat homosexual couples and sexually deviant living arrangements as if they are marriage and family units. Ultimately, they justify the wicked and condemn the righteous for resisting their evil.[11]

Second, the Left foments and capitalizes on resentment to persuade racial and religious minority groups to think of themselves in political opposition to the majority. In recent years, through campaigns to stop "Islamophobia" and "Asian Hate," as well as the very successful "Black Lives Matter" movement, political progressives have fundamentally changed policy and damaged the reputations of Christians and white people. Whatever their intentions and legitimate historical grievances, the Left ultimately gives a false impression about their enemies and functions as a malicious witness.[12]

To say the Left's identity politics are an exercise in evil and slander may be controversial, but it is necessary to face reality. There is no way to compromise with people bent on using a tool designed to destroy one's way of life. It is an attack on America's civilizational foundation. The New Testament teaches Christians to prioritize family members, other believers, and fellow countryman over other groups. Yet it is precisely this ordering the left seeks to undermine for traditional Americans, and so far it has worked.[13]

Some evangelicals are concerned if they advocate for themselves as Christians—seeking the benefits a political society can afford them and working to identify that political society as Christian—that they are engaging in a right wing version of identity politics, opening the door for white supremacy, or rejecting the "sojourner identity" Christians are supposed to have in the world.[14] However, most of these objections are easily dispelled by making simple distinctions.

It would be inaccurate to say that Christians who advance

---

[11] Prov 17:15.
[12] Ex 23:1.
[13] I Tim 5:8, Gal 6:10, Matt 10:6, 15:26, Rom 9:3.
[14] Alan Atchison, "Christian Nationalism Is a Threat to National Security," *Capstone Report* (blog), May 22, 2023, https://capstonereport.com/2023/05/22/christian-nationalism-is-a-threat-to-national-security/41615/; Carl Trueman, "Identity Politics on the Right," *First Things*, December 8, 2022, https://www.firstthings.com/web-exclusives/2022/12/identity-politics-on-the-right; Jesse Johnson, "Coveting Caesar's Throne: Navigating Christian Nationalism in an Election Year" (Shepherd's Conference, Grace Community Church, March 28, 2024), 47:20, https://www.youtube.com/watch?v=nif61IJiphQ.

interests from a uniquely Christian tradition, instead of universal values, are simply parroting a right wing version of the Left's identity politics where only the names have been changed. As previously discussed, the Left's identity politics is designed to destroy and replace Western Christian hegemony, which is really just traditional American culture. Some versions of it also assume that certain identities produce uniquely valid truth claims based upon their social standpoint. Christians obviously oppose these features, since they believe truth is objective, slander is evil, and natural ordering should be protected. But the idea that social groups exist and possess certain interests, like avoiding persecution for example, is woven into the fabric of reality. At the very least, Christians should work toward propagating the identities God established through creation and custom while rejecting ones that threaten them.

The fear is that if Christians can justify their collective action for a government that favors Christianity, white supremacists will seek to establish an exclusively white ethnostate. This reflects a number of misunderstandings. The major one is probably thinking that liberal democracies somehow prevent the kind of identity-based politics that led to the German Nationalism of the 1930s. We have already discussed how the Left unabashedly uses identity politics and the Right, while believing it does not, also appeals to identity groups. Whether or not Christians seek political power as Christians does nothing to change this dynamic.

Furthermore, the nature of the United States reduces the possibility of an ideologically white ethnostate from forming. The country has always included ethnic minorities, with an Anglo-Protestant core reflected in its major customs, laws, lineage, and religion. Subcultures who do not want to maintain certain Anglo-Protestant traditions, such as Jewish immigrants or Amish communities, have generally gained levels of regional autonomy. Although there have been times Americans favored European immigration over other continents, this never led to exclusively white residents or citizens.

If a white ethnostate ever did begin to form, it would likely be due to the Left's constant attacks on white people, causing them to believe their destinies are bound together in the face of a common enemy. Even then, this shared fate would likely not be enough to overcome the differences between people who think of themselves more by region and place of origin than they do by an abstract "white" identity. If nations are extensions of families as the Bible teaches, the diverse array of Americans classified as white would make up multiple nations.[15] Either way, such a development could not be attributed to Christians simply advocating for themselves.

Those who think that Christians forsake their sojourner identity when they invest in political affairs as believers see a conflict where none should exist. Christians can still believe heaven is their final destination when involving themselves in the temporal world. If they can invest in making their families, churches, and businesses more Christian, there is no reason to believe they cannot do the same with their government.

American Christians and political conservatives should unashamedly use political power to advocate for identities that are part of God's good order and discourage identities that are not. In the United States, it is still taboo for pedophiles, gangsters, and human traffickers to seek political representation, even though they are at a social disadvantage. Many of the Left's innovative grievance groups should be viewed this way. They are simply organizations of people who share a common enthusiasm for perversion.

Instead, people should think of themselves in terms of who God made them, where He placed them, and what social groups they belong to with legitimate political interests. In Scripture we find positive examples of people advocating politically for themselves, their region, their religion, their family, and their nation.[16] Protecting justice, upholding righteousness, and securing peace for one's own is part of loving neighbor. This is why it is good for American public policy to outlaw abortion, restrict pornography, protect the border, privilege Christian civic rituals, allow gun ownership, and punish

---

[15] Gen 12:3, Psalm 22:27, Amos 3:2, Eph 3:14-15.
[16] Acts 16:37, 22:25, Neh 2:5, Exodus 9:1, 1 Tim 2:2, Gen 44:33-34, 1 Sam 25:25, 1 Kings 3:16-27, Jer 29:7, Est 7:3-6.

crime, to name just a few current issues. Objectives and priorities may change based on circumstance, but God's ordering and His moral law do not.

Scripture also teaches that God expects civil magistrates to treat people in their jurisdiction with equality before the law. They are even judged by God based on how they treat or mistreat their most vulnerable subjects.[17] This means that people do possess God-given rights based upon God-given responsibilities. Unlike the Left's identity politics, which have no moral reason to prevent the violation of someone's rights, Right-leaning Christians are not free to reward one social group by taking fundamental God-given rights away from another group. Part of our Anglo-Protestant inheritance is a system of law designed to protect "life and liberty," by which Sir William Blackstone meant the ability to fulfill "natural duties" like worshiping God and raising children.[18]

While the term "identity politics" belongs to the Left with all its baggage, separating identity from politics is ultimately impossible because of human nature. People want groups to belong to. In a healthy society, national, regional, familial, and spiritual identities help fulfill this longing. But during a time of social breakdown, ideologies, frivolous activities, and novel identities fill the void. This is why we have "furries," "bronies," and even "Trekkies." It is one reason why so many social justice warriors and "cat moms" are single women. It is why many young urban men join gangs and why white middle class men without support networks commit suicide. Reversing this trend will not be easy, but it is possible.

Richard Weaver wrote in his 1963 essay "Two Types of American Individualism" that for two millennia the West possessed a certain kind of individualism wholly different than the kind bandied about by modern liberals and libertarians. He called this notion "social bond individualism" because it "battle[d] unremittingly for individual rights, while recognizing that these have to be secured within the social context." We are all born into a world not of our making,

---

17 Prov 29:14, Dan 4:27.
18 Sir William Blackstone, *Commentaries on the Laws of England: In Four Books* (Callaghan, 1872), 31.

we receive an inheritance from those who went before us, and we are expected to maintain it for "ourselves and our posterity."

Both Christians and political conservatives must reject the temptation to battle identity politics by adopting the revolutionary anarchic individualism of today which subverts society by showing indifference "for all that civilization . . . has painfully created."[19] Instead, they should get involved in their local communities once again. We can do things like join civic organizations, participate in government, produce local art, shop at farm-markets, and get to know our neighbors. Activities like these will help establish a place of belonging, form a local identity, and secure a natural hierarchy. This is infinitely more important and more fulfilling than sitting on the sofa perusing social media or watching television for hours. It is hard to love one's neighbor if one does not participate in life with them. This is how we defeat identity politics by replacing it with the truth.

---

[19] Richard Weaver, "Two Types of American Individualism," Modern Age, 1963, 122, 134.

12

THE WAR ON
DEFINITIONS

Recovery (which includes return and renewal of health) is
a re-gaining—regaining of a clear view. I do not say "seeing
things as they are" and involve myself with the philosophers,
though I might venture to say "seeing things as we are (or
were) meant to see them"—as things apart from ourselves.

J.R.R. Tolkien

It is important to understand the mental shift developing as the West slides from a world oriented around higher purposes to one centered on temporal desires. A new way to define and categorize reality, consider problems, and approach solutions now captivates the minds of a population largely oblivious to the change. Christians are no exception. People yearn for an older more rooted way of living yet fail to see how their social views prevent that world from reemerging. This feeling of nostalgia and incompleteness increasingly shows up in various places, from the movement to consume locally-sourced food to the trad wife phenomenon.

People still long for the benefits that accompany traditional living with its hierarchy, loyalty, and belonging, yet rarely embrace the costs associated with it. A trailer for a recent Western-themed Hallmark film features a cowboy exclaiming, "I'm part of this community. Rodeo is about family. We support each other. We forgive past wrongs."[1] Somewhere in the back of our minds we wish to belong to such a place, but it only seems to exist in the fantastical worlds of royal families and rural life. In the real world, we are told by most authorities that community and family can mean almost anything and obligations to them are more chosen than expected.

People take DNA tests to know their ancestry yet believe race is only a social construct. They attend gender-reveal parties before a child enters the world, yet think of gender in the same way. Some even believe ending the life of the child they celebrate is morally permissible. Feminists tend to want men who look and behave in masculine ways, yet regurgitate the mantra that masculinity is toxic.[2] A self-proclaimed feminist admitted in the *Washington Post* that though she dates all kinds of men, she "end[s] up being attracted to the men who come off as 'traditionally masculine.'"[3] What explains these contradictions?

REIMAGINING THROUGH REDEFINITION

The Apostle Paul taught in Romans 1 that apart from sinful desire, people both understand the reality of God's design and operate according to it. He wrote that it was natural for women to be sexually attracted to men. In Proverbs 30, Agur son of Jakeh observed similar behavior. Like animals, people exhibit instinctual patterns.

---

1   *Trailer–Ride–Coming to Hallmark Channel Sunday March 26, 2023*, https://www.youtube.com/watch?v=DupufyqZty4.

2   Eric Dolan, "Interactions between Height and Shoulder to hip Ratio Influence Women's Perceptions of Men's Attractiveness and Masculinity," *PsyPost*, January 14, 2023, https://www.psypost.org/interactions-between-height-and-shoulder   to   hip-ratio-influence-womens-perceptions-of-mens-attractiveness-and-masculinity/; Kim Elsesser, "Who Should Pay For Dates? How Chivalry Contributes To The Gender Pay Gap," *Forbes*, February 12, 2020, https://www.forbes.com/sites/kimelsesser/2020/02/12/who-should-pay-for-dates-how-chivalry-contributes-to-the-gender-pay-gap/; Chris Riches, "That's Rich... Women Decline to Date Men Who Earn Less–However Good," *Express*, February 3, 2016, https://www.express.co.uk/lifestyle/life/640467/Rich-decline-date-men-earn-less-good-looking-dating;

3   Shannon Lell, "I'm a Feminist Who's Attracted to 'Manly Men,'" *Washington Post*, September 13, 2016, https://www.washingtonpost.com/news/soloish/wp/2016/09/13/im-a-feminist-whos-attracted-to-manly-men/.

He compared "a king when his army is with him" to a strutting rooster and mighty lion. Some behaviors were too deep for him to understand, including "the way of a man with a maid." Jesus also referenced the instinctual obligation that even evil fathers have toward their sons when they ask for a loaf of bread or a fish.[4]

Although humans possess a sin nature through the Fall, God still designed them originally to act in certain ways and to yearn for good, true, and beautiful things such as marrying members of the opposite sex and caring for children. Sinful inclinations suppress, twist, and replace these natural desires while mixing them with selfish motivations and goals. But they are not completely destroyed.

This is why people today may redefine marriage, yet still fail to abandon the ideal of binding oneself romantically to a life-long companion. The most hardened progressives continue to use terms like nation, family, and gender as if they mean something fundamental about the world, while claiming they are in fact open to definition. This schizophrenic behavior is not a delayed effect where archaic vestiges of the past still linger through language. Rather, it reflects the impossibility of trying to emancipate the world from the way it was designed.

Although global managers may claim to reshape the world, all they can really do is pretend they don't live in the world God has already made. They may label any group they choose a "family"—whether it's coworkers or open relationships—but in doing so, they merely mimic an actual family unit. Much like the idolaters of the Old Testament who gave divine qualities to idols made of wood and stone, today's idol makers believe they can remake reality simply by renaming it. The more people accept and honor these misapplied labels, the more confidence they gain in their delusions. But in the end, they will come to realize that reality has remained unchanged all along, despite their efforts to redefine it.

The primary way elites bent on remaking reality reinforce their fantasies is through the abuse of language. George Orwell, in his

---

4 Rom 1:18-27, Prov 30:30-31, 18, Matt 7:9-10.

famous 1946 essay "Politics and the English Language," described how "political language . . . [was] designed to make lies sound truthful and murder respectable, and to give an appearance of solidity to pure wind." In Orwell's time, bombing villages became "pacification," driving people from their homes was a "transfer of population," and forced labor camps were "eliminat[ing] unreliable elements."[5] Today, political discourse is much worse.

Our ruling class uses terms like "democracy" to subvert popular elections, "justice" to protect criminals, and "inclusion" to exclude decent Americans from influential positions. Some pundits mockingly refer to our present situation as "clown world" because of how often the terms we use mean the exact opposite of their actual meaning. Fortunately, there is an ancient remedy for our crisis of meaning.

The prophet Isaiah condemned "those who call[ed] evil good, and good evil; who substitute[d] darkness for light and light for darkness; who substitute[d] bitter for sweet and sweet for bitter!"[6] There is no reason for Christians to accept a new dictionary produced by alchemists bent on casting civilization over the cliff of absurdity. Believers have always functioned to preserve cultural integrity as "salt" while pointing to God's truth as "light."[7] In order to do this, Christians should first understand the trick being played on them.

The "Woke" Left, as they are often called, know enough about the things they hate to corrupt the way people think about them. History, for them, is a progression toward a utopian world of peace and equality. After successfully ending customs of the past designed for oppression—things like arranged marriages, monarchies, and feudal labor relationships—they now must target the patriarchal, nationalistic, and ecclesiastic institutions that continue this oppression. Their twisted definitions, like their revisionist history, are solely meant to propel this revolution.

For example, in a CNN interview with Victoria Nuland, the

5 George Orwell, "Politics and the English Language," *The Orwell Foundation*, April 1946, https://www.orwellfoundation.com/the-orwell-foundation/orwell/essays-and-other-works/politics-and-the-english-language/.
6 Is 5:20
7 Matt 5:13-16

former Under Secretary of State, she claimed that Congress would continue to give money to Ukraine in order to "defend democracy & freedom" against "tyrants like Putin." Yet, since 2022, Ukraine has suspended its elections, shut down eleven political parties, and banned the Ukrainian Orthodox Church. Ukraine seems to be no more a bastion of "democracy & freedom" than Russia.[8]

However, "democracy" is no longer just about citizen participation in government. It is now about using civil institutions to promote social equality. According to the mainstream narrative, democracy is threatened when the Russians subvert social media platforms, Donald Trump questions the election process, and Christian nationalists use government to promote their particular values.[9] Yet Left-wing groups such as Black Lives Matter, trade unions, and migrants in Western countries are said to promote democracy because they represent oppressed groups and appeal to universal rights.[10]

Ukraine is part of what Victoria Nuland described as a "free and open international order" because it embraced the influence of the West, which facilitated "cooperation on climate action, migration, food security, and shared prosperity."[11] As a result, the Biden administration felt an obligation to support Ukraine financially, just as they believed it was their role to combat disinformation, challenge voter ID laws, and root out so-called patriotic extremists within the military—all in the name of defending democracy. What was once a commitment to actual democracy has now evolved into a

---

8 Tom Elliott [@tomselliott], "Victoria Nuland on More Ukraine Spending: 'We Will Do What We Have Always Done, Which Is Defend Democracy & Freedom around the World ... And by the Way, We Have to Remember That the Bulk of This Money Is Going Right Back into the U.S., to Make Those Weapons' Https://T.Co/6P98dCLKqN," Tweet, *X*, February 24, 2024, https://twitter.com/tomselliott/status/1761451250954989687

9 Katherine Stewart, *The Power Worshippers: Inside the Dangerous Rise of Religious Nationalism* (Bloomsbury Publishing USA, 2020). 2, 6, 275.

10 Barbara Ransby, "Opinion | Black Lives Matter Is Democracy in Action," *The New York Times*, October 21, 2017, sec. Opinion, https://www.nytimes.com/2017/10/21/opinion/sunday/black-lives-matter-leadership.html; Charles Dunst, "Immigrants Are Key to Fighting Off Authoritarianism," *Time*, May 15, 2023, https://time.com/6279622/immigrants-authoritarianism/; Hamilton Nolan, *"Unions Are Laboratories of Democracy": Hamilton Nolan on Joe Biden, Gawker, and the Power of Labor*, interview by Jack McCordick, February 12, 2024, https://www.vanityfair.com/news/unions-democracy-hamilton-nolan-joe-biden-gawker-labor.

11 Elliot; "Democracy," Center for American Progress (blog), July 8, 2021, https://www.americanprogress.org/topic/democracy/.

commitment to a broader, global utopian vision. The term "diversity" operates in a similar way.

Not long ago, I attended a college graduation ceremony where every speaker felt compelled to emphasize their commitment to diversity, as if it were a deity demanding universal devotion. They told the audience that diversity had enriched the campus and helped graduates reach their full potential. It was credited with enhancing leadership skills and even hailed as the reason the day was possible. What struck me, however, was that the ceremony itself was almost entirely lacking in diversity—except for the overabundance of times the term was mentioned.

Today, diversity is not about including different kinds of people and their customs so much as it is an ideological commitment to multiculturalism. An advocate for diversity does not need to befriend anyone of a different religion or participate in a foreign activity. All they must do is advertise their commitment to diversity, perhaps disparage their own culture if their family traces back to Europe, and maybe hire someone with a foreign background. There is no need to get one's hands dirty by actually spending time with people who are different. Something similar can be said for justice.

The term "justice" is no longer about universally applying the law to different cases so much as it is a commitment to equal social outcomes. Racial justice, for example, brings attention to "the ways that discrimination, policing, prosecutions, and incarceration practices impact Black communities."[12] Climate justice focuses on the "the disproportionate impacts of climate change on low-income and BIPOC communities."[13] In each situation, whether it's justice for migrants, people who identify as LGBTQ+, or women, justice refers to calibrating rewards and punishments so they are evenly represented in different groups irrespective of merit and guilt. Ironically, using "just" to describe a person who treats others fairly has all been eliminated from our vocabulary. Someone who cares about justice

12 "Race & Justice | NAACP," accessed February 27, 2024, https://naacp.org/issues/race-justice.
13 "What Is Climate Justice?," UC Center for Climate Justice (blog), accessed February 27, 2024, https://centerclimatejustice.universityofcalifornia.edu/what-is-climate-justice/.

now is more likely to be identified as an activist who agitates for their cause. Virtue is no longer fundamental to democracy, and personal commitment is no longer required to be inclusive or just.

FROM VIRTUE TO IDEOLOGY AND BACK

This deemphasis on virtue highlights a key distinction between traditional Western civilization and the one emerging today. Without internal virtues like honor and duty, society cannot function. Instead, people will turn on one another, driven by selfish interests. For society to endure, it requires a group of people who are willing to uphold social stability with reverence and devotion. This is where legends, ceremonies, and heroes play a crucial role. They pass on a cultural inheritance that inspires people to emulate noble examples, which in turn helps to preserve civilization.

Until recently, the civilizational importance of promoting virtue was widely recognized. Plato wrote, "The State which we have founded must possess the four cardinal virtues of wisdom, courage, discipline and justice."[14] John Adams echoed this sentiment in 1776 when he stated, "Public Virtue cannot exist in a Nation without private, and public Virtue is the only Foundation of Republics."[15] People assumed civilization was fragile and would slip into anarchy or despotism if virtue was not maintained.

The redefinition of words today reflects how character qualities are being replaced by social formulas. Apparently, virtuous leaders are no longer necessary for civilization to continue. Neither does it matter if the people who share a civic life together are similar, virtuous, or capable. What matters is that their governing principles center on things like diversity, equity, and inclusion. This is a reorientation away from internal virtue and toward a theoretical arrangement.

Western democracies are not as different as they would like to think from Marxist nations in places like Communist China and

---

[14] Plato, *The Republic* (Penguin UK, 2007), 7.
[15] John Adams, "From John Adams to Mercy Otis Warren, 16 April 1776" (University of Virginia Press, April 16, 1776), http://founders.archives.gov/documents/Adams/06-04-02-0044.

how they functioned in this regard. In these totalitarian systems, leaders often relied on corruption and deception to gain power and recognition. Their version of virtue was measured not by personal character, but by their allegiance to a particular economic system. For example, it did not matter how morally upright a person was if they owned a business that violated the Communist system. Loyalty to the party and its principles was the highest virtue, often promoted through any means necessary. Even though the West's systems are more rooted in a liberal conception of individual freedom, one wonders if they are overall less corrupt.

Terms like democracy, diversity, and justice have become casualties of a social revolution that exploits their positive reputations to promote a new totalitarian vision—one that seeks to erase difference and enforce equality. In this brave new world, Christians stand as holdouts, loyal to the old definitions, but not out of resistance to change. Rather, they remain committed to representing the world as it truly is, and because of this, they can stand firm with confidence. They must recognize the tricks being played on them and see the urgent need to take the reins of cultural leadership, since they uniquely understand human nature and need.

Christians know God designed people to belong to families and nations and gave them unique languages to speak. He designed men and women differently, telling them to get married, have children, and spread out. He gave families regions to belong to and property to work. He administered penalties for violating the rights of others. He also made a way for individuals to be forgiven for their sins and restored to a relationship with Him. It is easy for Christians to forget about the world God made when they are bombarded with messaging designed to sell fantasies that appeal to sinful desires. Nevertheless, the true world does not cease to exist because of new inaccurate definitions.

Christians can use their knowledge of human nature and God's design to their advantage when fighting back against the lies of our age. They can open up their homes to those from broken ones. They can uphold positive examples of marriage, family, and gender roles to people who never experienced them. They can eat healthy and adorn their bodies with dignified clothing. They can infuse custom and ritual into their own unique areas to develop a sense of neighborliness and civic pride. They can make positions of authority worthy of respect by serving constituents, congregations, and employees. Christians may be persecuted along the way, but they should know that these actions work to foster healthy and happy communities specifically because they correspond to human nature and God's design. This kind of cultural leadership will require courage. This starts with a willingness to correct the record.

It is not Christians, but the pagan Left who are in fact the ones misgendering when they use "preferred pronouns." It is not Christians who hate sexual deviants, but those who condemn them to the prison of their own sinful desires. It is not Christians who advocate misogyny, but activists who erase the very definition of a woman. It is not Christians who believe that white people are inherently superior, but rather progressives who assume that white people must interact with or support minorities for them to achieve meaningful significance.

Christians today far too quickly accept their position as a lower caste incapable of influence. It is hard to square this with the belief that God is in fact the creator. It may feel like Christians are forced to live in an increasingly pagan world. However, since God is the creator, it is pagans who are inescapably forced to live in a Christian one. Presbyterian pastor Maltbie Davenport Babcock understood this when he penned the lines to the famous hymn: "This is my Father's world. O let me ne'er forget; That though the wrong seems oft so strong, God is the ruler yet." Christians should be confident in the truth of their convictions and not shy away from defending them with "gentleness and reverence."[16]

There was a time when the rebels of society rejected rules they knew reflected priorities higher than the ones they had for themselves. But they were anomalies benefitting from the stability a

---

[16] 1 Pet 3:15

traditional society afforded them. Church bells chimed and neighbors helped each other. Rebels knew they could fall back on this organic safety net if they were in trouble. Today, this safety net is fading not only from existence but from memory. It is now up to Christians to rebel against the low trust society they have inherited and restore it to a place that reflects the design of its Creator.

In an age dominated by technology and artificial intelligence, one thing seems certain: people will increasingly value authenticity. Those who are willing to risk themselves to speak the truth and love others will be recognized and respected, standing in contrast to those who simply toe the party line and reap rewards from elite institutions. Christians are uniquely positioned to lead this shift away from the artificial world of human theories and back to the reality of God's design.

13

OUR LEADERSHIP CRISIS

A steady rise to a position of preeminence most often comes with hard work, constant effort at self-improvement and devotion to principle.

Dwight D. Eisenhower

Today, models for assessing leadership ability largely focus on personality traits or loyalty to the managerial class, a trend that extends even into Christian circles. I remember a few years ago attending a weekend church-planting assessment hosted by the North American Mission Board in which the initial phase concentrated on categorizing each participant according to a Myers-Brigg's assessment. The curriculum assumed that personality determined leadership quality. Many evangelical organizations embrace the Enneagram for the same reason.[1] Unfortunately, this approach

---

[1] The Texas Annual Conference for the United Methodist Church supplies a roster of Enneagram specialists for their own leadership formation. See: "Enneagram–Texas Annual Conference of the United Methodist Church," December 27, 2022, https://www.txcumc.org/leadership-formation/ministry-specialist/enneagram/; Brian Lowe, the Acts 29 Southeast Director endorses an Enneagram assessment intended to help Christians "get trained to lead others spiritually." See: "Gospel Enneagram | Home | United States," gospelenneagram, accessed July 9, 2023, https://www.gospelenneagram.com; Evangelical influencers like Russell Moore and Lisa Vischer recently participated in an Enneagram summit that included sessions on things like "leadership styles," "handling conflict," and "relating to your co-workers." See: "Get the All Access Pass!," accessed July 9, 2023, https://www.tylerzach.com/aap.

reflects an erroneous modern shortcut to manufacture leaders by tapping into some kind of scientific formula rather than doing the hard the work of discipleship.

Leadership cannot be created like a car on an assembly line. Leadership is less about personality and more about character proven through experience. During my church planting assessment we formed teams who worked toward various tasks as observers watched to see who would emerge as leaders. There is a certain wisdom to this, but it neglects the bigger picture. One snapshot moment during a social experiment should have mattered much less than the character references and professional experience I was never required to provide.

For years, many Christian youth groups followed a similar path by unofficially selecting ministry candidates based upon their popularity during high school.[2] Some of today's most famous preachers, such as Steven Furtick and J.D. Greear, act and dress in ministry settings as though they never graduated.[3] Many attend their churches and follow their teachings, but it seems less to do with their leadership than it does their likability. There is a conflation today between stewardship and style.

OUTWARD APPEARANCE

It would be foolish to think appearance does not factor in determining a leader, but it is certainly not the most important factor. King Saul was tall and handsome, people praised Absalom for his looks, and King Nebuchadnezzar chose to educate young Jewish men who were not only intelligent, but also good-looking. There is a natural human tendency to gravitate toward people who appear

---

2 Thomas Bergler explained how Youth For Christ sought teen leaders who were "'attention getter[s]' or 'extrovert[s]' that 'consonantly has other kids following [them].'" They "subtly redefined spiritual leadership by making it look a lot more like business leadership." See: Thomas Bergler, *The Juvenilization of American Christianity* (Wm. B. Eerdmans Publishing, 2012), 202-203.

3 Both are known for their casual approach to preaching and, at times, silly antics. See: J.D. Greear Dancing in Church (Whitney Houston Karaoke) LGBT Staff Member, 2019, https://www.youtube.com/watch?v=bptLlYx9t-s; Steven Furtick Elevation Jr Church For Grownups (Pastor John MacArthur Rebukes), 2019, https://www.youtube.com/watch?v=Fs-Nceerq5g.

healthy, strong, and beautiful. Yet, appearances can be deceiving. Although the Lord chose David who was "ruddy, with beautiful eyes and a handsome appearance" to succeed Saul as king, He also told the prophet Samuel not to consider appearance or height, because "God sees not as man sees, for man looks at the outward appearance, but the LORD looks at the heart."[4] For the institutions Christians depend on to produce leaders, this is a difficult problem.

It is much cheaper to manufacture people who match fashionable optics than it is to cultivate and evaluate internal virtues. Technology makes this process even easier now that anyone can use camera angles, filters, and home studios to look and sound a certain way. No one needs to know the real person behind the curtain. The only important thing is what people see. This is obviously a broken paradigm, and by God's providence this approach to leadership selection is faltering.

Business executive Phillip Barlag makes an interesting point in his book *The Leadership Genius of Julius Caesar*. He states:

> People want to know that their leader has skin in the game. They want to see that the leader is right there with them in the trenches, fighting the same battle. Being insulated from an organization erodes a leader's moral credibility. On the other hand, leading from the front builds moral credibility. It gives you the opportunity to create a common will and to demonstrate good faith to your organization. If a leader is willing to put their life—or in modern terms, their career—on the line during a critical moment, then the team is much more likely to want to join in the fight.

Traditionalists, including evangelicals in the West, are targeted increasingly by other more influential institutions. Simultaneously, they sense that their own leaders would rather negotiate terms of surrender rather than defend them. Couple this with the fact that leadership formulas are cheaply made and easy to reproduce, and it

---

4 1 Sam 9:2, 10:23, 2 Sam 14:25, Dan 1:4, 1 Sam 16:7.

is not hard to understand how Christian organizations like Together for the Gospel failed for the last decade of its existence to successfully propel younger names into broader popularity. At the same time, uncompromising established voices like John MacArthur have a staying power in conservative evangelicalism that other established voices, such as Alistair Begg who compromised on a crucial issue, does not.[5] This dynamic helps explain how David Platt is running his church into the ground, why churches are leaving the Acts 29 church planting network, how the once disgraced pastor Mark Driscoll made a comeback because of his anti-regime sentiments, and why Russell Moore complains about Southern Baptists preferring Donald Trump to himself.[6] Having skin in the game is not the only metric to determine good leadership, but it is superior to the polished media image that still dominates the face of evangelical institutions.

Under normal circumstances, one would think that these factors create an opportunity for bolder voices to ascend the ranks of leadership. In one sense they do. Through social media, some independent voices are breaking into conferences and publishing, building new institutions, and sometimes challenging status quo compromise. The internet creates a place where talented young men overlooked by legacy organizations can build support and gain influence. Yet the fact that so many potential leaders are overlooked while unimpressive men fill high positions reveals a second kind of flaw in our current leadership mode

---

5 John MacArthur, despite being out-of-step with evangelical fashions, has a reputation for not compromising on issues like Covid lockdowns, social justice, and LGBTQ normalization, while Alistair Begg was recently dropped from one of the largest Christian radio networks for comments normalizing same-sex wedding ceremonies. See: Billy Davis and Steve Jordahl, "Radio Ministry Drops Pastor over Same-Sex Wedding Comments," *American Family News*, January 24, 2024, https://afn.net/culture/2024/01/24/radio-ministry-drops-pastor-over-same-sex-wedding-comments/
6 "The Real David Platt – Sunlight Is the Best Disinfectant," accessed June 14, 2024, https://therealdavidplatt.com/; J. Chase Davis [@jchasedavis], "Recently @Acts29 Completed Their Annual Process Where Member Churches Renew Their Partnership with the Network. Just 220 Churches in the United States Renewed. That Is down from 509 Just over a Year Ago. @Acts29 Lost 57% of Their American Churches.," Tweet, X, April 18, 2024, https://x.com/jchasedavis/status/1781047668447310066; Russell Moore, *Losing Our Religion: An Altar Call for Evangelical America* (Penguin, 2023), 6; Russell Moore, despite leading the Southern Baptist ERLC and serving as a professor at one of the largest evangelical seminaries, has a reputation for compromise. He now leads Christianity Today, which is largely considered a progressive evangelical outlet by conservatives.

Managerial Elites

In 1941, political theorist James Burnham was the first major thinker to identify what he referred to as the "the managerial revolution." He argued that as private corporations and government bureaucracies grew, they became less accountable to owners and oversight. This elevated managers into important roles of unaccountable control where they could pursue their own class interests while disregarding the people whom their organizations were expected to serve. According to Burnham, the New Deal was a descent into managerialism more than it was socialism.

In this new order, property owners and managers traded places. Gone were the days of the philanthropic captains of industry. Gone still more were the days of a duty-bound landed gentry. Now the dominant social power belonged to "administrators, experts, technicians, [and] bureaucrats who [found] places throughout the state apparatus."[7] In a time when human resource departments seem to run the world, Burnham's analysis is prescient.

In order to climb the ranks, employees and staffers must prove their loyalty by seeking the interest of management. This often eliminates, at early stages, those who want to represent the people their organizations supposedly serve. It also suppresses the principled and courageous, trading them instead for scheming company men. Although technology helps to reinforce this arrangement as weak men exert more control and authority than they otherwise could, it is not an entirely new phenomenon.

In the classic work *The Prince*, Renaissance philosopher Machiavelli wrote about two different skill sets he believed should characterize political leaders. He called one set the lion and the other the fox. Lions used overt shows of force to control their kingdoms, while foxes resorted to deception and manipulation. According to Machiavelli, the effective prince possessed both of these traits. That

---

7 James Burnham, *The Managerial Revolution: What Is Happening in the World* (Lume Books, 2021), 238.

way he could defend himself against both an enemy's snares (strategic maneuvers) and wolves (force).[8]

Sociologist Vilfredo Pareto later theorized that either foxes or lions dominate the government depending on cyclical social conditions.[9] Lions achieved control in times of crisis when tough decisions were needed to restore order. Foxes infiltrated these administrations over time, eventually leading to their inevitable weakness and collapse. This theory cannot account for all scenarios, but patterns do emerge. Throughout Scripture, God raised up patriarchs, priests, judges, prophets, kings, and apostles who accomplished great feats for the Lord and their people, only to be followed by lesser men who did not adequately preserve those accomplishments.

It is safe to say that the current managerial class is mainly composed of foxes who feel threatened by lions. One consequence is their attempt to assert authority across as many areas as possible. Foxes will bypass lions to prevent them from gaining control, vilify them through isolation if they do gain control, and neutralize them by placing them in a supervised environment. Additionally, if recent studies are indicative, we do not simply have foxes at the helm, but unstable foxes. The National Education Association recently declared a mental health crisis among the faculty and college staff responsible for training modern elites.[10] This means that if Pareto's pattern holds, we are likely nearing the natural end of rule by foxes.

Regimevangelicals

This also means we are nearing the end of neo-evangelicalism. Neo-evangelicals today—as represented by institutions like *Christianity Today*, The Gospel Coalition, The Evangelical Theological Society, and the most-attended Christian seminaries and conferences in the country—tend to mimic secular social elites and prioritize their acceptance. Carl Henry, who is considered by some to be the founder

---

8 Niccolo Machiavelli, *The Prince*, trans. Tim Parks (Penguin, 2009), 69-70.
9 Geraint Parry, *Political Elites* (ECPR Press, 2005), 52-53.
10 Mary Ellen Flannery, "The Mental Health Crisis Among Faculty and College Staff," *neaToday*, March 7, 2024, https://www.nea.org/nea-today/all-news-articles/mental-health-crisis-among-faculty-and-college-staff.

of neo-evangelicalism, noticed in 1947 that contemporary thinkers dismissed Fundamentalists. To solve this problem and regain a hearing in "contemporary thought," he called on evangelicals to develop a "world program" on social issues, adding that a "single voice that speaks for Jesus" on the world stage "can be a determinative voice" since "nations are keyed to powerful leaders."[11]

This seemed good in principle, but in practice neo-evangelicals shifted from modeling a classic and biblical understanding of leadership to emulating modern leadership methods. Fuller Theological Seminary, Henry's flagship neo-evangelical seminary, opened the Institute for Christian Organizational Development in the early 1980s, led by professor of Christian leadership and management Dr. Walter Wright. Wright supervised "management professionals" who brought principles from the finance, communications, and academic world "into dialog with the Christian faith." The Institute treated management and leadership as if they were synonymous, and management simply meant, "the art of getting things done with and through people."[12] Virtue, in this arrangement, was external in the sense that it served to maintain standards of institutional civility. It was a formula that inevitably produced foxes oriented to the techniques of other foxes.

Neo-evangelicals also pioneered the popular "servant-leadership" models for home and church leadership. These tend toward weakness because they reconcile Christian leadership with modern pacified approaches to masculinity. Male leadership transforms into a docile prioritization of meeting the needs of wives, children, and others over male objectives. Evangelical author Aaron Renn critiques these models promoted by big names like Tim Keller, John Piper, and Russell Moore because they fail to match Christ's example. Jesus exerted authority, overruled the desires of those He served, and sacrificed for a higher mission. He served others, but His habit was not

11 Carl F. H. Henry, *The Uneasy Conscience of Modern Fundamentalism* (Wm. B. Eerdmans Publishing, 2003), 169, 528.
12 Walter Wright, "Editorial," *The Management of Ministry: The Ministry of Management*, December 1983, 2; Gary Demarest, "A Word to Pastors," 3. Max DePree, "What Is Leadership?" 5.

to let them choose how He served them or to domesticate His goals by defining them based upon the desires of women and children.[13]

In my experience, both managerial techniques and soft approaches to male leadership are woven into the fabric of modern evangelicals at very deep levels, even in places associated with conservative theology. I remember submitting my required "servant-leadership" essay with my undergraduate application for The Master's College. At Liberty Baptist Theological Seminary, I took a Marital Counseling class that was partially based upon a servant-leader model. In my Pastoral Ministry class at Southeastern Baptist Theological Seminary, we were taught managerial techniques to diversify and modernize churches along with vision casting and delegation.

Not all of this was bad. In fact, much of what we learned was true and potentially helpful. Yet each situation represented an effort to cultivate a kind of male leader characterized by qualities more common among women, such as sensitivity, gentleness, indirectness, tolerance, approachability, and subservience. These are not inherently bad qualities and can be useful in certain contexts. However, they are not the primary traits traditionally associated with strong male leadership, whether in Scripture or in the context of antiquity.

My major point is that modern elites, including Christians, conceive of leadership in terms of external management techniques, not internal virtues. Even when internal virtues are emphasized or exemplified, they are not primarily leadership qualities, and they do not resemble the courage, strength, and honor that characterized great leaders of the past. These conditions produced a situation where evangelicalism's managerial elites cultivate and oversee a stable of shallow personality-driven and slightly effeminate spokesmen. This hegemony is popularly referred to as "Big Eva," the "evangelical industrial complex," or "regimevangelicals." This industry is currently fracturing, along with secular institutions, as leaders of legacy organizations discredit themselves and public confidence diminishes.

Western Christians should be prepared for this impending

---

[13] Aaron M. Renn, "The Problem With Servant Leadership," August 30, 2022, https://www.aaronrenn.com/p/servant-leadership.

collapse, including in their own organizations. A very real leadership vacuum is growing, and no amount of managerial elites, servant-leaders, or empty personalities can fill it. The implications of this are serious. Proverbs 11:4 warns, "Where there is no guidance the people fall, but in abundance of counselors there is victory." The future of our civilization depends on the vision, strength, bravery, confidence, and wisdom of real world leaders. These qualities are nowhere better taught, exemplified, and cultivated than throughout the pages of Scripture.

RETURN OF THE KINGS

There are many books on leadership, but most simply offer managerial formulas, team-building ideas, and manipulative techniques. However, the Bible contains resources to understand how to be the kind of person who is as "shrewd as [a] serpent" and "bold as [a] lion."[14] It goes beyond Machiavelli's fox and lion combination to inspire a morally upright prince, not just a successful one. It does not artificially produce leaders with heads full of systems and methods. Rather, it builds the kind of person who is able to prudentially wield power when circumstances call for it. It may not teach the latest tricks to achieve organizational efficiency, but it does shape a virtue that works to form true greatness.

Modern Christian leaders have lately attacked the concept of the "Christian Prince" because they seem to believe it conflicts with democracy.[15] There is much that can be said about the extent to which Western countries are actual democracies, whether democ-

---

[14] Matt 10:16, Prov 21:1; I support the use of "fox" as a pejorative the way Jesus did in Luke 13:32 of Herod.

[15] Owen Strachan: "We don't need a Christian Prince—King Jesus already has that role filled." Paul Miller: "[Stephen] Wolfe's Christian prince has a far more expansive mandate than our liberal democracies do." Andrew Walker: "This imagined omnicompetent talisman might as well be Vladimir Putin, which may be okay if Christian authoritarianism is in the offing." See: Owen Strachan [@ostrachan], "We Don't Need a Christian Prince—King Jesus Already Has That Role Filled. We Do Need an Army of Godly Fathers Who Step up, Take Responsibility for Themselves and Their Families, Act Righteously in Public, Disciple Others, Stand down Evil, and Live in Joy by the Grace of God.," Tweet, *X*, May 24, 2024, https://x.com/ostrachan/status/1794054639786029215; Paul D. Miller, "A Tale of Two Books, One Podcast, and the Contest over Christian Nationalism," *Christianity Today*, December 20, 2022, https://www.christianitytoday.com/ct/2022/december-web-only/stephen-wolfe-case-christian-nationalism-paul-miller.html; Andrew Walker, "Book Review: The Case for Christian Nationalism, by Stephen Wolfe," 9Marks, December 9, 2024, https://www.9marks.org/article/a-baptist-engagement-with-the-case-for-christian-nationalism/.

racy is an ideal arrangement, or whether a Christian prince must be tyrannical, dictatorial, and statist. But it is more important to first understand that the Christian prince is an old concept symbolizing the ideal Christian ruler, and therefore it is in keeping with Scripture and Christian tradition.

From Tertullian to Shakespeare, the concept of the Christian Prince was an important feature of Christendom, making its way into lessons, lore, and legal documents.[16] Christianity's emphasis on inner virtue defined and limited the qualities of strength and cunning championed by Machiavelli. The goal of a Christian Prince was not simply operational success but honorable service. The Anglican *Book of Common Prayer* charged Christian princes to defend the Faith and to promote both spiritual welfare and the temporal interests of their people.[17]

In 1516, Erasmus defined this figure in *The Education of a Christian Prince*, which he dedicated to Prince Charles V of the Habsburg Empire. Erasmus's teachings were widely circulated and influenced both Protestant and Roman Catholic rulers.[18] In *Education* he emphasized a sovereign's inner virtues, stating: "The prince should watch his morals and actions, careful always to be cautious and dignified; value the truth; worship God; act in a manner appropriate to the circumstances at hand. . . He should surpass all in virtue."[19]

In 1523, Martin Luther advised potential magistrates who converted to Protestantism. Many of his principles are both biblically rooted and applicable to many leadership settings. Chiefly, Luther taught that a Christian Prince should not use his office for "selfish

---

16 Tertullian, "To Scapula," in *The Ante-Nicene Fathers: The Writings of the Fathers Down to A. D. 325 Volume III Latin Christianity*, ed. Reverend Alexander Roberts, James Donaldson, and Arthur Cleveland Coxe (Cosimo, Inc., 2007), 106-107; Augustine, *The City of God*, Volumes I & II, ed. Anthony Uyl and Marcus Dods (Ontario, CA: Devoted Publishing, 2017), 101; *Henry the V* was Shakespeare's ideal Christian Prince. See: Kenneth Muir, *Shakespeare Survey* (Cambridge University Press, 2002), 61-65; The term "Christian Prince" is seen in both the 1584 "Charter to Sir Walter Raleigh, and the 1606 "First Charter of Virginia."

17 *The Book of Common Prayer* (Cambridge, 1662), 329. https://www.churchofengland.org/sites/default/files/2019-10/the-book-of-common-prayer-1662.pdf; It should be noted that there were ecclesiastical limitations on the magistrate. For example, Princes were not permitted to minister God's Word or the Sacraments. See: 338.

18 Nancy Spannaus et al., *The Political Economy of the American Revolution* (Executive Intelligence Review, 2015), 82-83.

19 Desiderius Erasmus, *The Education of a Christian Prince*, trans. Lester Born (New York : W.W. Norton, 1936), 48.

profit" but "toward the profit, honor and salvation of others."[20] The Prince must punish evildoers but consider the cost to his own people of going to war.[21] When at war, he must use violence including "kill[ing], rob[bing], and pillag[ing] the enemy."[22] Luther said the Christian Prince should be "wise enough to master both the law and his advisers."[23] This meant learning his subject's condition and not overly relying on others to tell him.[24] It also meant cultivating a healthy suspicion, since all men are capable of betrayal, and those who seek power for themselves should not be given it.[25] Ultimately, Luther taught that the Christian Prince should be humble by depending on God for strength and wisdom.[26]

This archetype for leadership does not stand out to us because it represents a clever strategy or an innovative system. One cannot use it to curate someone's image in a deceptive way. Neither can it be reconciled with feminism. What stands out about the Christian Prince is the fact that he is a great man. What he does flows from who he is. The authors of Scripture repeatedly emphasized this connection between virtue and ability.

In Exodus 18, Moses delegated political power to "able men who fear God, men of truth, those who hate dishonest gain."[27] In Deuteronomy 17, God forbade kings from multiplying horses, wives, and personal wealth. Instead, they were to write for themselves a copy of God's law, read it every day, and in so doing learn to fear God, keep His commandments, and remain humble.[28] Paul's qualifications for elders and deacons focus on internal virtue, including faithfulness, wisdom, kindness, responsibility, and strength.[29] In each case, the respect that qualified someone for leadership did not come automatically. It had to be earned.

---

[20] Luke 22:25.
[21] 2 Sam 3:27, 20:10; 1 Kings 2:5.
[22] Genesis 14:14.
[23] Proverbs 26:16, Ecclesiastes 10:16, 1 Kings 3:9.
[24] 2 Chron 19:4.
[25] 2 Sam 16:28, 17:1, John 3:20-21.
[26] 1 Kings 3:9; Martin Luther, "Secular Authority: To What Extent it Should be Obeyed," in *Works of Martin Luther with Introductions and Notes*, vol. III (Philadelphia: A. J. Homan Company, 1930), 263-271
[27] Ex 18:21.
[28] Deut 17:16-20.
[29] Titus 1:6-9, 1 Tim 3:1-13.

Leadership ability is not identified by certificates or through completing formulaic programs. Instead, it is observed over time as potential leaders face situations that expose their character. This is what Jesus was getting at in Matthew 20 when He contrasted the way "the Gentiles lord it over" their subjects with the way His disciples were to sacrifice for others. Sacrifice cultivates greater trust than does simply occupying an authoritative position. Numerous Proverbs reinforce the truth that titles do not make leaders, but virtue does.[30]

This was reinforced to me at an early age in the Christian family I grew up in. My grandfather was a carpenter by trade. He told stories about all the "educated fools" he came across in the military and on the job. They possessed the authority to supervise, but often lacked the common sense or work experience that could have made them good at their job. As a result, they often caused problems, hurt people, and were thus ignored. They felt threatened by the resulting lack of respect they received, which made them more tyrannical as they attempted to assert their authority rather than earn it.

I learned this firsthand when I entered the workforce as a furniture repairman for a large corporation. There always seemed to be a distance between the warehouse managers and those who actually handled customers and repaired furniture. The best managers were the ones who gave us the tools we asked for and listened to our requests. Unfortunately, many managers thought the motivational tricks, inspirational speeches, and negative incentives they learned in business school were enough to achieve success. The result was discouraged employees and contempt for out-of-touch managers. The *de facto* leaders became technicians and coordinators who learned how to help their coworkers by overcoming these obstacles and "working the system." Unfortunately, this same dynamic can manifest itself in Christian institutions.

My dad, who served as a pastor for the majority of his life, used to tell me that a leader is the one who leads, not necessarily the one

---

[30] Prov 16:12, 28:16, 29:2, 4, 14.

with a title. I have seen this simple truth prove itself regularly in seminaries, churches, and ministries. People may assent to the dictates of a person with position because they fear the consequences of doing otherwise. But further down the chain of command, employees with virtue and skin in the game become the true respected leaders. This situation explains why people think the leadership class is fake. It also reinforces the necessity for elevating truly virtuous leaders into positions of authority.

We live in a time similar in some ways to what Erasmus described in 1515. He said:

> The guardians of a prince aim never to permit him to become a man. The nobility, feeding on public corruption, endeavor to make him as effeminate as possible through pleasures, lest he learn what a prince ought to know. Villages are burnt, fields are devastated, temples pillaged, innocent citizens slaughtered, all things spiritual and temporal destroyed while the king plays at dice or dances, or amuses himself with fools, or in hunting and carousing.[31]

Like self-serving princes, many members of today's detached leadership class seem to have little to qualify them for their positions beyond loyalty to their own class and titles that sound impressive. As conditions continue to worsen, people who anticipate the return of "King Richards" will start to depose their "Prince Johns." Traditional Christians are uniquely positioned to provide these leaders of the future, as they are the last major group in the West to hold to a sense of order and virtue.

---

[31] *The Political Economy of the American Revolution*, 82.

14

WHAT MAKES A LEADER?

I cannot trust a man to govern others who cannot govern himself.

Robert E. Lee

During the height of the Covid panic in 2020, I entered a barbecue restaurant and quickly realized that the owners had not taken any of the precautions required by the state to remain open. I asked an older man cutting up some meat behind the counter if he had any rules about social distancing. He paused. His jaw firmed up as he raised his head to look me in the eye. He said, "I swear, this country is run by queers and women." Of course, a simple "no" would have sufficed. But this man was angry, and he wanted to make a point to someone he did not know about the country's problems as a whole. In his mind, the United States lacked male leadership, and the Covid crisis exposed this weakness.

AGAINST THE GYNOCRACY

One of the first assumptions in Scripture concerning leadership roles is that they generally belong to men. This is not because men are more valuable than women. Neither is it because God arbitrarily decided to grant men certain roles and women others. It is rather because of the way men and women are designed. The Apostle Paul prohibited women from "exercis[ing] authority over a man" in church. Women were also to be "subject to their own husbands" in the home.[1] The Patriarchs, the twelve Apostles, and the authors of Scripture were all male. It was also assumed throughout Scripture that military and political leadership belonged to men, except in special cases associated with shame or God's judgement.[2] Laws concerning rulers and warriors always assumed they were male.[3]

Paul grounded the reason for male headship in creation. In 1 Corinthians 11:8 he stated that "man does not originate from woman, but woman from man." The Apostle Peter reinforced this when he described a wife as "someone weaker, since she is a woman."[4] Jesus had every opportunity to overturn the social dynamics that placed men in positions of authority. Instead, He continued to maintain them in His own circle. Before the advent of 19th century feminism, Christians had always maintained that social and political leadership naturally belonged to men.[5]

This does not mean women cannot engage in business as the wife of Proverbs 31 did, or teach children as Lois and Eunice did, or influence kings like Esther did, or casually share God's truth publicly as Anna did, or even go into battle when men refuse to like Deborah did.[6] But it does mean that God designed women primarily to nurture and not to dominate. From the beginning of creation, Eve was to be a "helper suitable for [Adam]."[7] Some egalitarians teach that the Hebrew term for helper [*ezer*] does not have to refer to a subordinate, but as Craig Blomberg points out:

[1] 1 Tim 2:12, Titus 2:5.
[2] Judges 4:9, Is 3:12.
[3] For example: God instructs kings in Deut 17:17 to not "multiply wives." There is no exception clause for queens multiplying husbands. In the context of laws of warfare, Deut 20:7 says: "And who is the man that is engaged to a woman and has not married her? Let him depart and return to his house, otherwise he might die in the battle and another man would marry her." There is no exception clause for women engaged to a husband.
[4] 1 Peter 3:7.
[5] Zachary Garris traces some of this. See: Zachary Garris, *Honor Thy Fathers: Recovering the Anti-Feminist Theology of the Reformers* (New Christendom Press, 2024).
[6] Prov 31:24,2 Tim 1:5, Esther 8:5, Luke 2:38, Judges 4:9.
[7] Gen 2:18.

"What makes an *ezer* a 'helper' in each context is that he or she comes to the aid of someone else who bears the primary responsibility for the activity in question." Man was already tasked with ruling creation, and his naming the animals and then naming Eve signified this rule.[8]

Unfortunately, females often wind up in leadership positions they are not suited for because powerful institutions seem to prefer females in lead roles. Even in the military, leadership vetting and training are no longer tailored for men. This incentivizes many males to either pursue independent leadership in small operations with less influence or to accept subordinate roles in larger institutions. Recent statistics show an increasing gap between the number of females graduating college as opposed to males.[9] The result of this is a more effeminate society, where expectations for males are low and it is acceptable for them to lack initiative and fortitude. Sometimes this is called a gynocracy.

Social justice activists see gynocracy as a needed corrective to centuries of patriarchy. What they fail to understand is that this inevitably leads to weakness and decadence. We have become a society where virtue is destroyed, frivolity is exalted, and evil is no longer subdued. Political leaders with God-given maternal instincts apply their nurture to migrants, sexual degenerates, and other alleged victim groups, regardless of the consequence to their own countries.[10] Soft men use their office for personal ambition and prevent strong men from competing with them. Yet if strong men do not ascend the ranks of leadership, the West will not survive long.

---

[8] Gen 1:26, Craig Blomberg, "Women in Ministry: A Complementarian Perspective," in *Two Views on Women in Ministry* (Zondervan Academic, 2010), Kindle location: 2426.

[9] Kim Parker, "What's behind the Growing Gap between Men and Women in College Completion?," *Pew Research Center*, November 8, 2021, https://www.pewresearch.org/short-reads/2021/11/08/whats-behind-the-growing-gap-between-men-and-women-in-college-completion/.

[10] Critics on the right, broadly speaking, are quick to point out that men can also compromise and conservative women tend to do better on social issues than liberal men. While generally true, women are much more likely to support liberal causes than men, especially unmarried women who have a greater freedom to apply their maternal instincts toward alleged victim groups. See: Lydia Saad, "U.S. Women Have Become More Liberal; Men Mostly Stable," *Gallup*, February 7, 2024, https://news.gallup.com/poll/609914/women-become-liberal-men-mostly-stable.aspx.

INTERNAL VIRTUE

Promoting males to leadership positions is obviously not enough to save our way of life. We also need virtuous men. Both the Classical and Christian tradition acknowledge "cardinal virtues" that other important qualities rest upon. In Plato's *Republic*, these are wisdom, bravery, sobriety, and justice.[11] Contrary to pagan philosophers, Augustine argued that these virtues "cannot exist save in those who have true piety."[12] He thought virtues were rooted in the spiritual realm and directed toward eternal ends. He believed the purpose of following a virtuous path was to prepare people for heaven more than it was to avoid misery and guarantee happiness on earth. Impious people can use virtues for temporal gain but compromise them if their goals are unmet. This proved such people are not virtuous in the first place. This is why I distinguish between external and internal virtue.

Today, there is a helpful move toward assisting males rediscover virtue as manifested by popular thinkers like Jordan Peterson, Brett McKay, and others. Sometimes this movement is called the "manosphere." While manosphere thinkers rightly critique many of the problems of modern life, their greatest motive seems to be self-improvement. The drugs, pornography, and video games that waste so much male energy are gateways to anxiety and depression. Manosphere influencers teach men to pursue exercise, relationships, and excellence instead. This does generally lead to happier lives, as it should. Yet, as Augustine argues, true virtue transcends even earthly rewards.

This is one reason the Anglo-American tradition required public servants to take an oath of office, generally made upon a Bible. This arrangement naturally favored Christianity and certainly disfavored atheism. John Locke, who argued for liberty of conscience, believed atheism should not be tolerated because it undermined the "bonds

---

11 James Adam, ed., *The Republic of Plato*, Book 4 (Cambridge, 1900), 427e https://www.perseus.tufts.edu/hopper/text?doc=Perseus%3Atext%3A1999.01.0168%3Abook%3D4#note-link95

12 Augustine, *The City of God*, Volumes I & II, ed. Anthony Uyl and Marcus Dods (Ontario, CA: Devoted Publishing, 2017), 307.

of human society."[13] In a world where people believed in divine rewards and punishments, oaths like this made sense, although they seem vestigial in modern urban contexts. After a statesman demonstrated virtue to his peers, he confirmed it before God. It was the final step to ensure his integrity.

Internal virtue is not something those without it can use for organizational efficiency or some other external objective. Virtue does, to be sure, arrange laws and mores according to divine standards, but that is its fruit and not its essence. Instead, virtue resides internally within the spirit of a person such that God and others know them as righteous or wicked. Scripture identifies figures like Noah, Job, Joseph the wife of Mary, John the Baptist, and Lot as righteous men.[14] They were not perfect, but a love for God and others characterized them. It is ultimately this love that internal virtue rests upon.

The first cardinal virtue is wisdom or prudence. To be wise is to possess the ability to apply God's designs and teachings to concrete situations. God naturally designed wisdom to come with age and experience.[15] Even Jesus increased in wisdom as he grew older.[16] Yet, in Ecclesiastes, King Solomon contrasts "a poor yet wise lad" with "an old and foolish king who no longer knows how to receive instruction."[17] It is not enough to simply let time pass in order to gain wisdom. Humility must also be present.[18]

The New Testament teaches those who lack wisdom to ask God for it.[19] Solomon did this and received a "wisdom [that] surpassed the wisdom of all the sons of the east and all the wisdom of Egypt."[20] This produced in him an uncanny ability to understand human nature, draw moral lessons from creation, and navigate difficult ethical dilemmas. Throughout the book of Proverbs, Solomon

---

[13] John Locke, "A Letter Concerning Toleration," 1689, https://press-pubs.uchicago.edu/founders/documents/amendI_assemblys7.html.
[14] Gen 6:9, Job 1:1, Matt 1:19, 6:20, 2 Peter 2:7.
[15] Job 12:12.
[16] Luke 2:52.
[17] Eccl 4:13.
[18] Prov 13:10.
[19] James 1:5.
[20] 1 Kings 4:30.

contrasts the "fool" who is "wise in his own eyes" with the wise man.[21] The main difference between the two is not intelligence but "the fear of the Lord."[22] There can be no wisdom without a love and preference for God's ways.

Someone shows they do not fear the Lord when they close themselves off to His input or the input of other wise people. Defective leaders reject wisdom because they only trust themselves or receive advice from flatterers. A good example is King Rehoboam, who "forsook the counsel of the elders which they had given him, and consulted with the young men who grew up with him and served him."[23] The results were disastrous, and the Kingdom of Israel was divided. Unlike Rehoboam, a wise leader listens, learns, and applies.

A wise leader also enjoys a mature confidence in his decisions because they are grounded in higher principles, vetted by wise people, and reflect reality. Solomon instructed his sons to "keep sound wisdom and discretion" for the security and confidence they brought.[24] Someone who makes decisions based on "selfishness or empty conceit" can project misplaced confidence in themselves.[25] But people motivated by vanity fail to successfully meet their obligations as leaders. Scripture is full of examples including Pharaoh, Nebuchadnezzar, Belshazzar, Saul, and Herod. Our current leadership class lacks the healthy confidence wisdom provides—and it shows.

The lack of resistance to Covid lockdowns, BLM riots, election interference, and other unpopular regime-approved actions expose a lack of bravery or courage. This second cardinal virtue is deeply embedded in biblical examples and strongly associated with faith. Stories like Joshua and Caleb spying out Canaan, David and Goliath, Jesus at Gethsemane, and Peter and John before Annas all reinforce the importance of facing fear for a higher purpose. In Hebrews 11, the author recounts many others who "from weakness were made strong" and accomplished valiant acts.

---

[21] Prov 26:11-12, 24:3-7.
[22] Prov 9:10, Psalm 111:10.
[23] 1 Kings 12:8.
[24] Prov 3:21-26.
[25] Phil 2:3.

American history is also filled with courageous examples. This used to be the major narrative that characterized most popular retellings of the country's past. Explorers, colonists, soldiers, and settlers all sacrificed to form our homeland. Today this has given way to an emancipation narrative where improvements in social equality are what make America great. This shift in how we understand ourselves appears to coincide with a decline in men's courage. A growing number of men have a hard time facing the sacrifices attendant to marriage and family, let alone defending our country from enemies. This severely hampers the quality of our leadership.

A motto attributed to Davy Crockett, "Be always sure you're right, then go ahead!" encapsulates the relationship between wisdom and courage. Leaders should carefully and confidently forge a path forward while meeting unavoidable challenges with bold action. Stonewall Jackson demonstrated this in his life when he told an acquaintance during the War Between the States that he did not concern himself with his own death during battle. He predicted that all men would be equally brave if they too believed God fixed the time of their death.[26] He consumed his life with a divine mission that drove him into the depths of danger. This does not mean he lacked fear, but he knew how to face it. In the words of John Wayne, "Courage is being scared to death but saddling up anyway."[27] Without an ability to face one's own fears there is no hope in leading others to face theirs.

Spiritual leadership is no different. The Bible expects pastors to fulfill the image of a shepherd facing wolves and lions.[28] The author of Hebrews says they are to keep watch over the souls of their sheep.[29] This is no small task when Peter describes "the devil" as a "roaring lion, seeking someone to devour."[30] This is why timid people are not suited for leadership, let alone pastoral ministry. They care too much

---

[26] George Francis Robert Henderson, *Stonewall Jackson and the American Civil War* (Longmans, Green and Company, 1898), 200.

[27] *The Hollywood Reporter*, vol. 310 (Wilkerson Daily Corporation, 1989), 16.

[28] Acts 20:28: "Be on guard for yourselves and for all the flock, among which the Holy Spirit has made you overseers, to shepherd the church of God which He purchased with His own blood."

[29] Heb 13:17.

[30] 1 Peter 5:8.

for their own comfort and reputation to risk upsetting the status quo. Sadly, this characterizes all too many in pastoral roles. Yet at the heart of leadership lies not a love for oneself, but a love for others. In order to love them well, a leader must also protect them from his own sinful impulses. This is where the cardinal virtue of sobriety or temperance comes in.

Solomon compared "a city that is broken into and without walls" to "a man who has no control over his spirit."[31] Though Samson was a judge of Israel who demonstrated bravery on behalf of his people, his special weakness for women became his demise. The headlines today are regularly filled with similar stories of politicians and pastors who lacked the discipline to say "no" to their desires. It is significant that Paul disqualified men who were weak when it came to women, wine, anger, and money from seeking pastoral office.

Because the heart of man produces sin, Scripture instructs believers to be more cautious about themselves than any other person.[32] Throughout the New Testament there is a constant emphasis on the need to mortify the desires of the flesh.[33] A man characterized by indulging his vices, even secret ones, includes others in the consequences of his own actions. This is why it is important for leaders to demonstrate their responsibility and care for others before ascending to power. Potential elders are to manage their households well and show consistency with outsiders before holding office. This principle of faithfulness in little leading to faithfulness in much applies to leadership more generally. Without personal sobriety it is difficult to work toward public justice.

As a virtue, justice describes someone who gives to each person their due. This includes rewards and punishments. A just parent knows when to discipline their child. They also know when to give them candy. Justice also encompasses what is fitting according to the transcendentals of the good, true, and beautiful. A just man upholds righteous standards in every arena. He shuns vulgarity, protects

---

[31] Prov 25:28.
[32] Matt 15:19.
[33] Col 3:5.

innocence, and exercises good taste. A just artist understands how to portray violence or romantic passion without resorting to grotesque or explicit imagery. A just man sees how his actions affect others, knows when to show mercy, and does not fail to do right when it is in his power to do so. Justice informs wisdom, bravery, and sobriety. Justice is also a fundamental attribute of God.

It says in Psalm 89:14 that "righteousness and justice are the foundation of Your throne." Jesus exemplified this during His earthly ministry as He confronted the Pharisees for distorting justice, ministered to those whom they overlooked, and ultimately died to appease the justice of God and save His people.[34] We find in Christ a man who both punishes evil people and dies to save them.[35] No one has ever personified justice more profoundly.

Christ also resisted Satan's temptations. Although they were personally attractive, their purpose was to derail Him from His mission.[36] If Christ were to bow to Satan, it would demonstrate injustice, as He would be giving worship rightfully due to God to Satan instead. But God cannot be bought and neither should His representatives. God told Moses to appoint judges who would only pursue justice and not distort it through partiality or bribes.[37] This is key to understanding whether someone is actually just.

A just man understands his obligations and supports the most suitable arrangements for the people he serves. His judgements are calibrated to the North Star of divine law, and natural priorities inform their application. Solomon prayed that he would be a just king who would vindicate the afflicted, save the needy, and crush the oppressor as he inherited his father's kingdom.[38] He assumed his good work would most directly apply to Israel, his providentially selected people. Part of being a just ruler is applying justice to whom it is due. Much of what plagues modern leadership positions is a failure to meet this basic threshold.

---

[34] Matt 23, Luke 5:30-31, Rom 3:25-26.
[35] Phil 2:8, 2 Cor 5:10.
[36] Luke 4:1-13.
[37] Deut 16:18-20.
[38] Psalm 72:4.

Good leaders reach for a purpose higher than themselves, rooted in justice, and translate this purpose into an achievable vision for their people. They shun laziness, embrace sacrifice, and take their role seriously. James warns that teachers in the church will incur a "stricter judgement." They are not free to do whatever they want, because they steward a church that ultimately belongs to Christ.[39] Ultimately, all leaders are stewards who will answer to God for the way they led people under their influence.

What are needed today are men of virtue who are willing to lead. This does not mean perfect men. The Bible is filled with men like Moses, Gideon, and Peter who were all afraid before taking the responsibility God gave them. They faced their fear because they knew there were things more important than their own self-preservation. The sons of Issachar were "men who understood the times, with knowledge of what Israel should do." Not only did they possess wisdom, bravery, sobriety and justice, but also a willingness.[40] In order to develop men of caliber who are willing to lead, we must first provide more opportunities for them to learn, grow, and even fail at times.

DEVELOPING LEADERS

Organizations like the Boy Scouts used to assist young men by providing them with good examples, teaching them useful skills, and giving them an occasion to prove themselves in leadership hierarchies. Unfortunately, like other fraternal male groups, they eventually included homosexuals and women, thus threatening group cohesion, lowering standards, and increasing the threat of sexual abuse. Today, there are almost no mainstream exclusively male organizations.

This means that more than ever, fathers, pastors, and other community leaders must take young men under their wing and administer the kind of uniquely male rites of passage that have been universal in all societies. Virtuous male leaders hardly ever spring out

---

39 James 3:1, Acts 20:28.
40 1 Chron 12:23, 32, 38.

of vacuums. They are cultivated in the community of men and patterned after noble examples. In a real sense, the existence of orderly society depends on a web of limiting forces that incentivize men toward their obligations to family, community, and country.

In more agrarian contexts, this kind of natural aristocracy arises organically. A young man learns early that survival depends on honoring father, working hard, and maintaining a good name. Life's temporal rewards are simple and patterned after traditional living. A man becomes a man when he has proven his competence and physical ability to govern a farm and family. He becomes a good man when he does this well in the sight of God and neighbor. This system is still propagating itself, as evidenced by the themes present even in modern Country songs, but it cannot sustain the leadership class in an industrial society.[41]

When Jesus worked to replace arguably one of the most corrupt religious establishments in antiquity, He did so by discipling twelve ordinary men over a three year period. They learned firsthand what it meant to sacrifice, trust God, and love others. Jesus led by example, and then gave His disciples tasks to achieve under His guidance, such as healing, feeding crowds, praying, and spreading His message.[42] Today's challenges demand a similar model.

We cannot depend on our governing, business, medical, or church arrangements in their current state to produce qualified leaders. We must instead do what we can to identify willing followers, as Jesus did, and cultivate their character through example and experience. My church regularly hosts a "young men's challenge" to assist fathers in taking their responsibility seriously, while welcoming young men into the community of men. We also facilitate male discipleship, host monthly men's lunches, and hold annual men's retreats as a way to provide exclusive male spaces. This may not seem like much, but it goes a long way toward helping young men who increasingly come from dysfunctional backgrounds without positive examples.

This may seem obvious, but a natural way for men to become

---

[41] See: "Buy Dirt" by Jordan Davis and "This is my Dirt" by Justin Moore.
[42] Mark 6:7-13, Matthew 10:1-8, Matthew 14:13-21, Matthew 6:5-15.

involved in each other's lives is simply to show hospitality. The strongest relationships are often built around shared interests or proximity. These organically form as people take the necessary steps to show hospitality. Informal gatherings to discuss the topics of the day, enjoy fellowship, or work on projects are the stuff life is made of. These gatherings naturally build mutual bonds and hierarchical arrangements. I have seen this work first hand to encourage character formation.

One of the greatest opportunities Christians have to impact the next generation of leaders is to host high school and college ministries in stable homes. A surprising number of young people are unacquainted with basic stability. The visual depiction of a husband and wife who love each other and work together for the common interest of their home is enough to inspire many to pursue this arrangement themselves. It also builds the trust necessary to gain a hearing with those who otherwise might not be open.

At the end of the day, there is no formula or program that can manufacture a virtuous leader. It takes time, involvement, experience, and labor to determine where someone is, where they need to go, and how they can get there. The ultimate answers will not be found in education programs that focus on little more than knowledge and political alignment. They are found where they always have been found: in the ordinary day-to-day rhythms of life, as exemplary figures pass down their leadership qualities to admirers.

The Bible has inspired the greatest leaders of the past, even though it is primarily a book of stories. It contains both examples of what and what not to do.[43] Repeatedly, it instructs believers to imitate the pattern laid down by godly figures.[44] In a society starved for good leadership examples we must look to the Scriptures, history, and lower-level leaders today who personify admirable traits. Building a new leadership class must include shared experience with virtuous men, in addition to practically applying leadership qualities in challenging scenarios.

---

[43] 1 Cor 10:11, Rom 15:4.
[44] 1 Cor 11:1, Phil 3:17, Heb 13:7.

Because God calls every man to lead in some capacity, whether in the home or at work, there are always opportunities to train for greater responsibility. Hiring managers should look past certifications and familiarize themselves with the lives of aspiring leaders where they can. Companies should consider it a liability to overlook the competency and character of job applicants who have already demonstrated their capabilities. Perhaps competitive managers should require that pastors and community leaders vouch for someone's character before they take an important job. This may seem invasive, but consider that before WWII, banks in even some progressive areas essentially required church membership to obtain a mortgage.[45]

If we are to see virtuous leaders return, it is essential to sort for actual leadership qualities, including loyalty to God and local region over the managerial class. Increasingly, top companies are ditching college degree requirements and replacing them with apprenticeships.[46] The more this happens and the more success these companies enjoy, the better chances are for challenging the current managerial class.

True leaders are not empty personalities, effeminate servant-leaders, or managerial elites. They are virtuous men whose character is built over time and revealed when placed in challenging circumstances. Their loyalty is given to those whom they love and serve in God's providence. When they make mistakes, like a wise man they learn from them. They bravely suffer depravation for their people and discipline themselves to carry out their mission. They cast a just vision and work hard to achieve it. Jesus was the pinnacle of this kind of leader, and just as He will return one day, so will they.

[45] Bob Buford, *Halftime: Moving from Success to Significance* (Zondervan, 2011), 21-22.

[46] Ethan Dodd, "You No Longer Need a College Degree to Work at These 7 Companies," *Business Insider*, March 25, 2023, https://www.businessinsider.com/google-ibm-accenture-dell-companies-no-longer-require-college-degrees-2023-3.

15

ACT LIKE MEN

*The wonderful liquor of youth had evaporated rapidly, and
his character had crystallized as rapidly into the hardness of
manhood. The warfare, the blood, the evil pleasures which he
had seen had been a fiery, crucible test to his soul, and I love
my hero that he should have come forth from it so well.*

Howard Pyle
(on Myles Falworth's coming of age in *Men of Iron*)

I
f there is one common denominator behind the various social
maladies impacting the world today, the dearth of genuine masculinity would certainly be a contender. Issues like sexual confusion, family breakdown, crime, and political corruption would all
be solved if men acted like men. Yet increasing numbers of men are
leaving the workforce, retreating into digital fantasy, and failing to
take responsibility. Christian senator Josh Hawley said in a speech
that "many men in this country are in crisis . . . And that's not just a
crisis for men. That's a crisis for the American republic."[1] It is also a

---

1 "The Future of the American Man" (National Conservatism Conference II, 2021), 3:30 https://www.
youtube.com/watch?v=mRzvinE4IaE.

crisis for the church. Without shepherds the sheep scatter. This makes them more vulnerable to wolves willing to fill the leadership vacuum. We need strong virtuous men more today than perhaps we ever have.

A frequently quoted proverb states: "The only thing necessary for the triumph of evil is for good men to do nothing." Some may ask whether men who do nothing are actually good. They may be, according to modern standards that reinforce male passivity. But it was not this way throughout most of human history, and it should not be this way today. Even pagan societies recognized that in order to survive, they needed a form of masculine strength, even though it was incomplete and marred by sin.

We see this during Israel's war with the Philistines. First Samuel 4 records the way Israelite soldiers paraded the ark of the covenant in battle with the hope that God would reverse their defeat. It states in verse five that "as the ark of the covenant of the LORD came into the camp, all Israel shouted with a great shout, so that the earth resounded." Some translations say "the earth shook," and some commentators conclude a literal earthquake took place.[2] This struck fear in the minds of the Philistines. Israel they could defeat, but they had little confidence they would be successful against the God who "smote the Egyptians." In order to persuade themselves to fight, they said: "Take courage and be men, O Philistines, or you will become slaves to the Hebrews, as they have been slaves to you; therefore, be men and fight."[3]

We see this same kind of language in the inspirational addresses that precede great battles, such as in the "St Crispin's Day Speech" in William Shakespeare's *Henry V* or Winston Churchill's "Finest Hour" speech before the Battle of Britain.[4] In a small way, some of the pep talks during sporting events resemble this spirit. In all

2   New King James Version says "earth shook," Christian Standard Bible says "ground shook"; James E. Smith, 1 & 2 Samuel (College Press, 2000), 187; Ralph Klein, *1 Samuel*, 2nd ed., vol. 10 (Zondervan, 2000), 137.
3   1 Sam 4:8-9.
4   "And gentlemen in England now a-bed shall think themselves accurs'd they were not here, and hold their manhoods cheap whiles any speaks that fought with us upon Saint Crispin's day." See: William Shakespeare, *The Plays and Poems of William Shakespeare* (E. Fleischer, 1833), 430; "Every morn brought forth a noble chance and every chance brought forth a noble knight, deserve our gratitude, as do all the brave men who, in so many ways and on so many occasions, are ready, and continue ready to give life and all for their native land." See: Winston Churchill, "We Shall Fight on the Beaches" (London, June 4, 1940), https://winstonchurchill.org/resources/speeches/1940-the-finest-hour/we-shall-fight-on-the-beaches/.

these cases men recognize that in order to defeat a threat they must remember who they are.

The word translated "men" in 1 Samuel 4 is directly linked to "courage" and "fight." People naturally recognize that one of the important features a man possesses involves strength, both physically and emotionally, when properly channeled men use this strength to protect themselves and the ones they love. This means that in addition to their spiritual worth, God designed men with a temporal purpose as part of their nature. Throughout Scripture we find God often responds to threats facing His people by commanding men to be men.

Paul's final exhortation in his first letter to the Corinthian church includes this language: "Be on the alert, stand firm in the faith, act like men, be strong."[5] The phrase translated "act like men" in the NASB appears in other translations as "quit you like men," "be men," "do manfully," "play the man," "be brave," "be valiant," and "be courageous."[6] The root word implies "sexual differentiation."[7] It occurs in a group of commands associated with military action during a time of great confusion. The specific situation Corinthian Christians found themselves in demanded male fortitude more than feminine nurturing.

Christians in the modern West might relate to some of the problems associated with the Corinthian church. They faced a spiritual crisis and a leadership vacuum. They fractured over allegiance to various teachers, tolerated sexual sin, harbored dysfunctional marriages, dishonored the Lord's Supper, and competed with each other for recognition in the church. Paul warned them against participating in things as basic as temple prostitution, suing each other in secular courts, and confusing gender roles. In order to climb out of their spiritual slump and restore order, Paul instructed them to cultivate traits associated with masculinity.

In verse thirteen he extolls different facets of vigilance. He tells

---

5 1 Cor 16:13
6 King James Bible, Youngs Literal Translation, Douay-Rheims Bible, The Moffatt Bible, New King James Version, Aramaic Bible in Plain English, New International Version.
7 Geoffrey William Bromiley, *Theological Dictionary of the New Testament, Volume I* (Wm. B. Eerdmans Publishing, 1964), 362.

them to continuously guard against threats, make their defensive position on the high ground of faith, draw upon manly instincts, and exercise strength. He then reminds them in the next verse of why they fight: "Let all that you do be done in love." The chief problem afflicting the Corinthian church was an overall failure to prefer each other over themselves. Paul devoted all of chapter thirteen to this root issue. Instead, they were to sacrifice their personal desires in battle for the sake of their fellow brothers and sisters. Finally in verses fifteen through eighteen, Paul instructs them to form ranks behind men committed to ministry.[8] The Corinthian church needed more vigilance, love, and leadership to avoid destruction.[9]

The early church recognized this same language from Old Testament passages found in the Greek Septuagint translation. The phrase translated in 1 Corinthians thirteen as "act like men, be strong" appears in a similar form during the conquest of Caanan, when both Joshua and the people of Israel were instructed multiple times to "be strong and courageous." Likewise, King David told his son Solomon to "Be strong, therefore, and show yourself a man."[10] These commands reveal a shared understanding of what being a man meant to their original audiences.

Defending Masculinity

Today, as our world challenges gender norms, some self-proclaimed Christians join the confusion by suggesting that modern evangelicals are a "cult of masculinity." Kristin Du Mez, a history and gender studies professor at Calvin University, wrote in her *New York Times* best-selling book *Jesus and John Wayne* that Christian men who think "patriarchal power," "masculine aggression," and "sexual desire" are biblically justified contribute to sexual abuse.[11]

---

[8] "Subjection" (hupotassō) is a military term for aligning oneself within a chain of command. See: Bob Utley, *Paul's Letters to a Troubled Church: 1 & 2 Corinthians* (Bible Lessons International, 2013), http://www.freebiblecommentary.org/new_testament_studies/VOL06/VOL06A_16.html.
[9] 1 Cor 10:9-10.
[10] Deut 31:7, 23, Josh 1:6, 10:25, 1 Kings 2:2.
[11] Kristin Kobes Du Mez, *Jesus and John Wayne: How White Evangelicals Corrupted a Faith and Fractured a Nation* (National Geographic Books, 2020), 277.

What she and others fail to realize is that these features are inescapably part of God's design, whether they are explicitly endorsed in Scripture or not. All men possess certain attributes, but not all use them for good. If good men suppress their strength while evil men encourage theirs, this will leave the victims of so-called "toxic masculinity" undefended. The biblical authors understood this. They did not sense the need to justify fundamental male traits. Instead, they simply recognized God's design from creation and encouraged men to use their more aggressive natures for good. This is why the Apostle Peter instructed husbands to live with their wives "in an understanding way, as with someone weaker, since she is a woman."[12] Up until recently, people universally recognized this fact, which is part of the reason only men filled roles that involved the use of force, like soldiers and police.

Even though women have the same intrinsic worth as men, they do not possess the same nature or fulfill the same role. The biblical authors assumed this. From the beginning, God designed woman to be man's helper in the task of subduing and ruling the earth according to Genesis.[13] The model woman and wife has children, manages her household, beautifies herself and her surroundings, cares for her family in ways which may include engaging in business enterprises, shows hospitality, teaches wisdom, helps the needy, and serves the church.[14]

On the other hand, God equipped men for leadership roles in society. Jesus chose twelve men to be apostles, God limited the office and function of pastor to men, the biblical authors were men, as were the Levitical priests who also decided legal cases.[15] The biblical authors did not forbid women to perform political duties, but they did assume the responsibility to lead in the home, church, and government belonged to men. When women fulfilled political roles, it was either out of necessity or a sign of judgement.

---

12 1 Pet 3:7.
13 Gen 2:18, 1:27.
14 Prov 31:10-31, 1 Tim 5:14, Acts 16:14, Rom 16:1, Phil 4:3.
15 1 Pet 3:1, Titus 1:6, 1 Tim 2:12, Deut 17:8-20; Heretical groups like the Montanists gave "great [priestly] positions of leadership to women," but this was not the accepted practice within orthodoxy. See: Augustine, *The Works of Saint Augustine*, ed. John Rotelle, trans. Roland Teske, vol. 18 (New City Press, 1995), 38.

In Judges 4, the prophetess Deborah told Barak that God had commanded him to lead an army against the Canaanite king Sisera, with the guarantee that Israel would achieve victory. However, Barak would only do so if Deborah went with him. Because of this weakness, Deborah replied: "I will surely go with you; nevertheless, the honor shall not be yours on the journey that you are about to take, for the LORD will sell Sisera into the hands of a woman."[16] After the Canaanite's defeat in battle, Sisera escaped and sought refuge in an Israelite tent, where Jael the wife of Heber killed him by driving a tent peg through his head. Deborah and Barak praised Jael for defeating Sisera, but this did not erase the fact that it was Barak who should have defeated him. Likewise, the prophet Isaiah lamented during his time that Judah's oppressors were children and their rulers were women.[17] This was a clear sign of judgement.

At one time in the not-so-distant past people thought even the idea of women voting in political elections was unbecoming. Consider that in 1895 less than 4% of women in Massachusetts voted in a non-binding referendum to support women's suffrage. The *Atlantic* ran a piece in 1903 that claimed the reason for this lack of popular support was that women understood they were suited to nurture, not coerce. Participating in government directly meant entering a political war where policy decisions forced people into compliance. Therefore, it belonged in the same category as police and soldiers carrying out the government's will. The author of the piece, a theologian named Lyman Abbott, insinuated that voting was beneath the "higher work" given to women. This higher work included nurturing through things like caring, education, keeping home, and charity. Women carried out the ministry of life that men, using the machinery of government, were charged to protect.[18]

This does not mean that women should not vote when given the opportunity or fill some positions that men normally hold in the absence of virtuous men. In a way, that is what Moms for Liberty

---

16 Judges 4:9
17 Is 3:12
18 Lyman Abbott, "Why Women Do Not Wish the Suffrage," *The Atlantic*, September 1, 1903, https://www.theatlantic.com/magazine/archive/1903/09/why-women-do-not-wish-the-suffrage/306616/.

is currently doing. Because Scripture places the responsibility to educate and discipline children chiefly with fathers, it would seem that public schools who violated their trust should receive push-back from them before their wives.[19] Yet most of the public outrage over grooming children comes from concerned moms instead. The moms who step into this role without their husbands leading the way should be commended, but it does beg the question: "Where are the dads?"

The answer of course is that men are increasingly conditioned to relegate their masculinity to common boyhood activities like sports and games, but they do not have the confidence to live up to their potential and take hold of the mature responsibilities that accompany manhood. Paul condemns this penchant for taking the path of least resistance in 1 Corinthians 6:9. He states: "Do not be deceived; neither fornicators, nor idolaters, nor adulterers, nor effeminate, nor homosexuals, nor thieves, nor the covetous, nor drunkards, nor revilers, nor swindlers, will inherit the kingdom of God."

Some translations, like the ESV, combine the Greek word μαλακός, translated "effeminate," with ἀρσενοκοίτης, translated "homosexuals" into "men who practice homosexuality" to designate both the passive and active partners in a homosexual relationship. While the full expression of μαλακός includes this kind of passive sexual behavior, Jesus used it in Matthew 11:8 to describe "a man dressed in soft clothing." Outside of Scripture, contemporary historians applied the term to men with an easy life and cowards who refused to fight.[20] It is reasonable to conclude that Paul was actually condemning male passivity in the strongest terms. This also contrasts with his later command to "act like men." Paul believed manhood was intrinsically tied to a certain kind of forcefulness.

Being a man means doing "away with childish things" and embracing the duties of manhood.[21] God equips men with the capacity for physical labor and the mental fortitude needed to protect, provide,

---

[19] Prov 13:24, Ex 6:4, Col 3:21.
[20] Zachary Garris, *Masculine Christianity* (Crosslink Pub, 2021), 37.
[21] 1 Cor 13:11

and prosper. Real men harmonize their lives with a prewritten template God wired into creation, the highest expression of which is found in Jesus, who perfectly executed His purposes, masculine and otherwise. Right now a war is being waged regarding whether this standard even exists in reality or if it is simply a social construct.

Claiming men should be manly is heresy in a modern world saturated with egalitarianism and androgyny. In 2019, *GQ* magazine concluded, in a survey on changing gender norms, that men increasingly thought of themselves in gender neutral ways.[22] An article in *Psychology Today* asked whether millennial men rejected manhood, based on studies suggesting they placed lower priorities on things like physical and financial strength.[23] According to recent surveys, over half of Zoomers believe "there are more than two genders," while less than half of the fighting age men are willing to defend the United States if invaded.[24]

Recovering Manhood

The United States, including her churches, are in trouble, but fewer people seem to notice and more seem to oppose a return to masculinity. This is where the words of the early church father Athanasius ring out truly. When someone informed him during the Arian controversy that the world was against him, he replied: "Then I am against the world." This is the moment for true men to face their fears and take charge.

Men like Athanasius, who make their stand with God alone if necessary are indeed an endangered species yet Scripture is filled with their examples. An old Sunday-school children's song encouraged young people to: "Dare to be a Daniel, Dare to stand alone! Dare to

22 Condé Nast, "The State of Masculinity Now: A GQ Survey," *GQ*, October 15, 2019, https://www.gq.com/story/state-of-masculinity-survey.
23 Douglas LaBier, "Are Millennial Men Rejecting 'Manhood'?," *Psychology Today*, June 9, 2018, https://www.psychologytoday.com/us/blog/the-new-resilience/201806/are-millennial-men-rejecting-manhood.
24 Jean Twenge, "How Gen Z Changed Its Views On Gender," *Time*, May 1, 2023, https://time.com/6275663/generation-z-gender-identity/; Lora Korpar, "Majority of Americans Would Stay and Fight If Russia Invaded U.S.: Poll," *Newsweek*, March 8, 2022, https://www.newsweek.com/majority-americans-would-stay-fight-if-russia-invaded-us-poll-1686050.

have a purpose firm! Dare to make it known." Men like Noah, Moses, Joshua, David, Elijah, Peter, Stephen, Paul, and Jesus all possessed this daringness. They were not lazy, timid, weak or cowardly. Even those who struggled in these areas were told to reject these tendencies.

For example, during the tail-beginning of Emperor Nero's persecution against Christians, Paul sent a final letter to his disciple Timothy who pastored the church at Ephesus. In this letter, Paul warned the young man about internal dissension in the church, false teachers who would likely challenge his authority, and the kind of opposition that led to Paul's own imprisonment and eventual death. He told Timothy to "be strong in the grace that is in Christ Jesus" and to fulfill his ministry. He encouraged him saying, "God has not given us a spirit of timidity, but of power and love and discipline." Therefore, it was up to Timothy to use the gifts God gave him, to "endure hardship" and to focus on achieving his goals.[25]

Paul used masculine examples like the determined soldier, the honorable athlete, and the hard-working farmer to illustrate what he expected from him.[26] None of this contradicted the patience and gentleness that Paul believed should mark Timothy even when correcting others.[27] This blend of strength and kindness characterized the kind of hero who once universally captivated the minds of young men in Christian societies.

Even without this biblical template, American men who grew up before the 1970s enjoyed imperfect yet masculine role models, whether in space, sports, film, or their World War II veteran fathers. In the American context, most of this culminated in the image of a rugged self-sufficient cowboy who honored a moral code and used his skills to protect the community from danger. He inherited his reputation from cavaliers and medieval knights. These legendary figures set a standard for men encapsulated in the term "chivalry."

Chivalry referred to a force that bound men together in the common pursuit of a higher divine purpose. This purpose guided

[25] 2 Tim 2:1, 4:5.
[26] 2 Tim 2:3-6.
[27] 2 Tim 2:24-25; 4:2, 5.

social relationships and infused them with significance. People did not exist for their own pleasure but to serve the needs of their neighbors before God. Harvard literature professor William Henry Schofield described "the true knight" as someone who "gave up all thought of himself." He pursued nobility instead of wealth. He was generous, courteous, just, and honest. Most importantly, he protected women and the helpless.

In contrast to the heroes of the Greco-Roman civilization who inflicted pain without mercy, Christians developed a code of ethics that "in addition to loyalty, faithfulness, and truth" also prized "mercy, meekness, and pity."[28]

C.S. Lewis believed producing chivalrous men was necessary to maintain lasting happiness and dignity in society. He said it offered "the only possible escape from a world divided between wolves who do not understand, and sheep who cannot defend, the things which make life desirable." Christianity thus resisted the kind of brutish men who in pagan civilizations seized power, oppressed their populations, and quelled dissent. They could only do this because enough of their sons grew up to be both fierce and meek simultaneously. Social institutions demanded aggressive men be humble, and gentle men be valiant. These two impulses, which Lewis observed "have no natural tendency to gravitate towards one another," combined to form the chivalrous knight.[29] They are the same virtues Paul refers to in 1 Corinthians 16:13-14. The command to "act like men" is coupled with the duty to "let all that you do be done in love."

Though there are many exemplary men throughout history, Jesus stands above them all as the perfect man. From a young age He disciplined himself by "increasing in wisdom" and working a strenuous job as a carpenter. He lived a Spartan lifestyle, often going without food, walking everywhere, and rarely having a place to sleep. He taught with authority, stood up for His friends, defended the weak, called out spiritual bullies, overcame Satan's temptations, and drove

---

[28] Schofield, William *Henry. Chivalry in English Literature: Chaucer, Malory, Spenser and Shakespeare*, (Harvard University, 1912), 4-5.
[29] C.S. Lewis, *Present Concerns* (Houghton Mifflin Harcourt, 2002), 14-16.

the moneychangers out of the temple with a whip. He willingly suffered more physical and emotional pain than any man. He said himself: "Do not think that I came to bring peace on the earth; I did not come to bring peace, but a sword."[30]

Yet He also described Himself as "gentle and humble in heart." He respected women and loved children. He was patient, forgiving, and compassionate. He wept over the death of His friend Lazarus and the destruction of Jerusalem. He obeyed His Father and provided for His mother. He healed the sick. He sought the comfort of His friends. He took the form of a slave and washed His disciples' feet. And in the most loving act ever recorded, He laid down His life for His friends.[31] If there is any kind of person this world needs more of, it is men like Jesus.

Families, churches, and society as a whole are in need of real men. While many potential candidates exist, too few today have received the guidance and encouragement from fathers and mentors to inspire them to fulfill their calling. Yet God's Word assures them that being a man is not only possible but expected. The command to "act like men" implies that it is within their ability to do so. In fact, this is how God originally designed men to function. He has also graciously provided His Word, filled with examples of true masculinity, as well as contemporary models of what it means to be a man in His Church. Men have all the tools they need to be true men. Now is the time to put aside distractions, cut out vices, pursue higher virtues, and strive for physical, mental, and spiritual strength. Now is the time for men to step up and be who God has called them to be.

---

[30] Luke 2:52, Mark 6:3, John 4:34, Mark 6:31, Luke 9:58, Matt 7:29, Matt 12:3-8, Mark 5:1-20, Mark 7:6-13, Luke 4:1-13, John 2:15, Matt 10:34.
[31] Matt 11:29, Mark 10:13-16, Mark 14:8-9, John 3:1-21, Matt 18:22, Matthew 15:32, John 11:22, John 6:38, John 19:26, Matthew 10:8, Luke 19:41, Phil 2:7, John 15:13.

16

POWER IS NOT
A DIRTY WORD

Order is Heaven's first law; and, this confess'd,
Some are, and must be, greater than the rest.

Alexander Pope

Perhaps the greatest challenge facing post-civil rights conservatives and their evangelical base is their own reluctance to assert power in support of their agenda. Instead, they focus on preserving a "neutral" liberal-dominated, shifting status quo while opposing so-called "radicals." No matter the issue—be it the national debt or combating public immorality—even when the Right achieves political victories, they do little more than slow the momentum of the leftward direction already in motion. To make matters worse, institutions that serve as gateways to social power frequently gatekeep conservatives. In addition, evangelicals tend to avoid breaking into elite circles and instead prioritize less controversial careers that enable them to start families earlier. It is in this context that I wish to argue for a new priority. Given current challenges, Christians should pursue power for the purpose of loving their neighbor.

The most recent political enemy for the Right, the social justice movement, aggressively started attacking things like marriage and monuments around 2015. This was not only a political move, it was also a religious crusade designed to deconstruct the Anglo-Protestant identity that once ruled the United States. The movement gained steam by appealing to language cultural Christians recognized.

Every Sunday-school-attending kid thought terms like tolerance, acceptance, and love were good qualities to have—and in the right context they were. But the architects of our present world applied them to degenerate behavior. They believed people should be forced to tolerate sexual deviants, then accept their identities as legitimate, and finally to love depravity by celebrating it for an entire month.

At the same time, the premium placed on inner virtue—along with qualities like bravery, fortitude, and sacrifice—gave way to a focus on support for outcomes that aligned with diversity, equity, and inclusion. As vice was normalized, virtue shifted from being a reflection of personal character to being defined by how one thinks society should be shaped. The changes over the past ten years are truly revolutionary. The question many whiplashed Christians are still asking is: "How did this happen so quickly?" The answer is obvious but seldom articulated.

Christians must recognize that these anti-Christian gains were not made through cultural subversion alone, but also through political exertion. Every winning issue social justice activists pushed—from impeding police work to compromising women's sports—was accompanied by policy changes. What was a fringe group of radicals only a few decades ago now sits in positions of influence throughout the country. The only recourse on a social level is to seize power from them. Unfortunately, Christianity's own elite class tends to neutralize their own followers by vilifying power and ambition. Most major Christian influencers invest their energy, not in opposing the enemies of God, but in pacifying God's people to not oppose them at all. For them, the only acceptable Christian behavior seems to be winsomely attempting to impress their enemies to think well of them.[1]

WIELDING POWER

Contrastingly, Scripture outlines multiple positive examples of godly heroes opposing evil through the use of power: Moses challenged Pharaoh's political authority, God expected Israel to enforce civil penalties to purge evil (Deut 19:19, 22:21), the exploits of David and his mighty men demonstrate the importance of military strength, Elisha and Jehu seized the throne of Israel and used their power to punish evildoers (2 Kings 9-10), Esther leveraged her influence with King Ahasuerus to ensure Haman's punishment (Esther 7), Jesus frequently asserted His authority to oppose evil, even using a whip at one point (Matt 21:12-17), Paul referred to magistrates as God's servants to carry out wrath on wrongdoers (Rom 13:4), and Paul also planned to overpower arrogant men with truth (1 Cor 4:18-21). There are many more examples, some directly applicable to our current social situation and some not. Clearly, power in itself is not a bad thing if wielded properly.

Most objections to Christians pursuing power concerns the improper use of it. Christians should not take revenge, become arrogant, or use power as a means to vanity. However, in order to honor God and deliver the weak and needy from the hand of the wicked, power is sometimes required.[2] Most Christians recognize that pastors should exercise authority, as should parents and husbands. Still, in the political realm, many are hesitant. They view it as impolite, too aggressive, or in conflict with their image of Jesus as a servant. Nevertheless, the same principles that govern the proper use of power for pastors, parents, and husbands should apply to public servants as well. It is an act of love toward one's neighbor—even if they are not Christian—to confront the public evil that tempts and oppresses them.

---

1 See "Losing His Religion" in the Appendix.
2 Ps 82:3-4

Historically, Americans have favored self-proclaimed Christian politicians, and while this tendency is changing, even now a majority of Democrat congressman identify as either Protestant or Catholic. Their commitment to these faith traditions is certainly questionable, but there is still an appearance of religiosity present at our highest public levels. Yet surprisingly, evangelicals—who make up about 28% of the U.S. population—are significantly underrepresented in other influential sectors. They account for only about 4% of the scientific community, 7% of the legal elite (by one estimate), likely less than 8% of journalists, and fewer than 19% of college professors.[3]

From my experience, evangelicals often encourage their young men to channel their leadership skills into ministry, which is commendable. Christians need more strong, principled pastors. However, other fields also need virtuous leadership. If the compromises of 2015 did not teach us, the compromises of 2020 should. If we want to take back the dictionary, reinstate virtuous standards, and realize change, more Christians should pursue power in business, law, media, medicine, academics, and government. They should do so to promote good and oppose evil. To accomplish this on a broad scale will require Christians to mobilize and sacrifice.

First, they will need to start matching the Left's enthusiasm to sacrifice for their political causes. It is common knowledge on the Right that conservative political organizations are usually hurting for money. Progressive foundations possess over ten times the total assets and over seven times the average assets of their conservative competition.[4] In 2020, Bloomberg published a shocking chart which compared Biden donations to Trump donations among the top one hundred employers with the most employees. The United States

---

3 Joseph Liu, "Scientists and Belief," *Pew Research Center*, November 5, 2009, https://www.pewresearch.org/religion/2009/11/05/scientists-and-belief/; Dan Crane, "Are Evangelicals Underrepresented Among the Legal Elite?," *Law and Religion Forum*, April 29, 2013, https://lawandreligionforum.org/2013/04/29/are-evangelicals-underrepresented-among-the-legal-elite/; Andrew Beaujon, "There's No Good Data on How Many Christians Are in Newsrooms," *Poynter* (blog), April 12, 2013, https://www.poynter.org/reporting-editing/2013/theres-no-good-data-on-how-many-christians-are-in-newsrooms/; "Are American College Professors Religious?," *HuffPost*, October 7, 2010, https://www.huffpost.com/entry/how-religious-are-america_b_749630.

4 David Horowitz and Jacob Laksin, *The New Leviathan: How the Left-Wing Money Machine Shapes American Politics and Threatens America's Future* (Crown Forum, 2012), 185.

military, Marines, and the NYPD were the only employers whose employees swung solidly toward Trump. Conservatives shared the chart extensively on social media as evidence of their lack of institutional influence.[5] To counter this will require political conservatives and their evangelical constituency to open up their pockets. It will also require fiscal reform to ensure nonprofit organizations are not able to use public resources or tax exemptions to advance partisan agendas, particularly by accumulating large endowments without fulfilling their charitable missions.

A new generation of religious Right leaders will also need to think outside the box about how they fortify their institutions to withstand Leftist influence. Historian Robert Conquest is credited with first articulating the oft repeated principle: "Any organization not explicitly right-wing sooner or later becomes left-wing."[6] Unfortunately, numerous examples—from the Boy Scouts to major Christian denominations—have demonstrated the truth of this claim. In a climate where revolutionaries relentlessly push to reshape every institution according to their egalitarian ideals, it is crucial for conservatives to strengthen legacy institutions that remain uncorrupted, identify those that have been corrupted so they can be allowed to die, and build a cancel-proof parallel economy. Innovators like Nate Fischer at New Founding are already working on solutions to some of these challenges. In short, conservatives should not shy away from having a clear in-group preference for those who share their priorities.

Finally, Christians have something necessary to offer political conservatives, and that is a real alternative to the revolutionary utopian vision offered by progressives. Too often Christians who lean left think they are advancing their own moral vision by conflating the Left's purposes with their own. In reality, the Left operates on an aped version of Christian eschatology, where human effort will inevitably lead to a glorious state of equality. They see themselves as being on the right side of history when future generations look

---

5 Jackie Gu, "Who's Giving to Trump and Biden? Top Donors by Company," *Bloomberg*, November 2, 2020, https://www.bloomberg.com/graphics/2020-election-trump-biden-donors/.
6 John Derbyshire, "Conquest's Laws," *National Review*, June 25, 2003, https://www.nationalreview.com/corner/conquests-laws-john-derbyshire/.

back to judge their predecessors. This conviction is why they are willing to risk so much—imprisonment, poverty, and even death—for their cause.

Modern Christians in the West should take inspiration from their forebears, who also endured great sacrifices—from the early Church to the victims of 20th-century communist regimes. Protecting family and country, upholding creation's natural order, and fostering true worship are sacred missions that God will honor. As long as Christians remain fearful of the media's power to cancel them and allow that fear to shape their actions, there can be no ultimate victory for conservative Christians, even in the temporal realm. This fearful compromised spirit that seeks to cede power to revolutionaries bent on destroying them is a major part of the problem modern Christian leaders have.

RECONCILING CHRISTIANS TO TRASH WORLD

Not long ago, *Christianity Today* ran a piece by former Fuller Theological Seminary president Richard Mouw entitled, "Theocracy Is Not the Enemy of Pluralism." In it, one of Tim Keller's major influencers laid out his case for Christian involvement in cultural matters. According to Mouw, evangelicals have vacillated between two erroneous approaches for far too long. In one approach, which Mouw admits he grew up in, evangelicals were largely patriotic and passive. They accepted things as they were, accomplished their civic duties, but failed to push for social change. Another approach, represented by Jerry Falwell and the Religious Right of the 1980s, was aggressive in its imposition of Christianity in the public square through legislation and political campaigns. Neither approach, according to Mouw, reflects a good example of Christian duty to the world around them.

Of course, what Mouw leaves out are the cultural changes that provoked a concerted evangelical engagement where there had not been any before—with the exception of Mouw and his group of progressive evangelicals like Jim Wallis and Ron Sider, who formed

"Evangelicals for McGovern" in 1972 and drafted the left-leaning "The Chicago Declaration" in 1973. Meanwhile, right-leaning evangelicals enjoyed what Aaron Renn calls the "positive world" and did not see the need for overtly Christian political action. However, throughout the 1960s and '70s, seismic shifts from Warren Court decisions to loosening sexual morals inspired backlash, as evangelicals began to realize they were losing their country's Christian character.[7]

It is this character Mouw seeks to undermine with his third cultural engagement option. In the beginning of the article, Mouw makes it clear he not only wants a religiously neutral society, but one bereft of many Christian values. Forcing what he calls a "theocratic understanding of reality on others" violates their ability to choose obedience to God. This translates concretely into his opposition to censoring foul language on television. Though he does not directly address pornography, drag queen story hours, or self-described transgender athletes, it would be interesting to find out if his logic is consistent. Why not discourage Christians from opposing these examples of public indecency as well?

Mouw describes his approach as "desperately needed today in our increasingly polarized society." Evangelicals, he said, need to "labor patiently alongside others—persons of other faiths and of no faiths at all—in seeking workable solutions to the complex challenges we face as a nation." Of course, this is vague enough to conjure up images of hippies singing kumbaya with no practical policy plan. Is it not enough to be united together in peace? As one "crunchy" woman I met recently said: "That gives me the feels." Feels or not, Mouw certainly does have a plan. He just does not spell it out for the readers of his *Christianity Today* article.

In 2007, Mouw signed a statement on Christianity and Islam called "A Common Word," which highlighted similarities between the Quran and the New Testament regarding love for God and

---

7 Aaron Renn coined the "positive world," "neutral world," and "negative world" categories for understanding shifts in how American cultural elites view Christianity. Before 1994, people viewed Christianity as a net positive socially. Around 2014, Christianity received a negative connotation. See: Aaron Renn, "The Three Worlds of Evangelicalism," *First Things*, February 1, 2022, https://www.firstthings.com/article/2022/02/the-three-worlds-of-evangelicalism.

neighbor. In 2012, he signed on to the Evangelical Immigration Table, which many have pointed out is tied to the Soros-backed National Immigration Forum. In 2017, he signed a statement in the *Washington Post* that urged "President Trump to Reconsider Reduction in Refugee Resettlement." In 2020, Mouw signed the AND Campaign's "2020 Presidential Election Statement" to "promote social justice and moral order." He also signed the Asian American Christian Collaborative's "Statement on Anti-Asian Racism in the Time of COVID-19." Finally, later that year Mouw also signed a statement urging pro-life evangelicals to vote for Joe Biden.

Mouw ends his article stating: "We live in times when our fellow human beings desperately need to encounter evangelicals for whom being theocratic means actively serving the cause of a loving Savior." Apparently, loving Christ means backing ecumenicism and supporting Democrat Party priorities. Mouw is right to say he supports a "pluralistic society" but wrong to frame it as if this is somehow part of his Christian duty and the only faithful option for Christians who wish to be involved. Christians who are disgusted by the trash world their children are inheriting increasingly think it is time once again to ditch pluralism and affirm publicly that Christ is King—not the neutralist pluralism that centers man's autonomy.

SHAPING THE GOP: THE EVOLUTION OF EVANGELICAL INFLUENCE

The Republican Party has been the political home for evangelical Christians for the past fifty years. The 'solid South,' once a stronghold of the Democrats, is where most evangelicals with traditional Christian values live. Over time, this region shifted its allegiance to the Republican Party, a change largely driven by the Democrats' adoption of policies hostile to Christian beliefs. While the modern mainstream retelling of this shift focuses on the civil rights era and racial issues, the real turning point came in the 1980s.

During this decade, evangelical support for the GOP grew as Democrats increasingly embraced positions on issues like abortion, the Equal Rights Amendment, and soft policies toward the Soviet Union that many religious conservatives viewed as morally unacceptable. Although topics like affirmative action and gun rights also played a role, the central concern for evangelical leaders was that the Democratic Party had become aggressively anti-Christian. Jerry Falwell, in a 1985 interview with *TIME* magazine, expressed this fear succinctly: 'If the Democrats win, I don't know what will happen to us.'[8]

Understandably, this symbiotic relationship between the Republican Party and evangelical Christians continued into the Trump-era as Democrats increasingly demonstrated their opposition to traditional Christian beliefs. This has caused some Christians who disapprove of Donald Trump's own immoral past, including his softness on abortion and same-sex wedding ceremonies, to question this arrangement. However, today's arrangement with America First Republicans is different than the previous one with establishment Republicans and may offer greater opportunities for traditional Christians to make actual gains. To understand this, it is first important to know how evangelicals and their social concerns fit into the Republican establishment over the past half century.

The relationship we are used to between the religious Right and the Republican party did not always exist. In fact, in the early 1970s, Wes Granberg-Michaelson reported that "in seminaries and social action bureaucracies of the church in the United States, it [was] becoming acceptable and almost chic to confide to others that you are a Marxist."[9] Mainstream evangelicals like Carl Henry, the founding father of neo-evangelicalism, Paul Rees of World Vision, and Foy Valentine of the SBC all signed the Leftist "Chicago Declaration." Valentine even helped the SBC pass a resolution that maintained abortion was permissible in some cases. In 1976, Jim Wallis predicted that "more Christians" would "come to view the world through Marxist eyes" due to "young evangelicals" and their "zeal

---

8   Robert Ajemian, "Religion: Jerry Falwell Spreads the Word," *TIME*, September 2, 1985, https://time.com/archive/6704527/religion-jerry-falwell-spreads-the-word/.
9   Wes Granberg-Michaelson, "Liberating the Church," *Sojourners*, September 1, 1976, https://sojo.net/magazine/september-1976/liberating-church.

for social change."[10] Neither abortion nor homosexuality were that much of a concern. Contemporary observer Richard Quebedeaux believed young evangelicals were trending Left.

It is important to understand that these progressive evangelicals were primarily made up of aspiring elites and a different group from the non-elites who mobilized politically in the 1980s. David Swartz reported that "well over two-thirds of the evangelical left held education, social service, and religious jobs."[11] Yet the ideological narrowness of this movement made it hard for the evangelical Left to appeal to the working class demographic which eventually composed the populist religious Right. Identity politics tore apart the group that drafted the "Chicago Declaration." This, coupled with Jimmy Carter's failed presidency and the replacement of "positive world" with "neutral world" realities, gave rise to the religious Right.

In reaction to the Equal Rights Amendment and issues that began filtering into local communities—such as ending school prayer, abortion, homosexual adoption, equal protection, and religious tax exemption—rank and file evangelicals started organizing groups to represent their concerns. Then throughout the 1990s, religious Right populism was institutionalized and integrated into the GOP machine, where their concerns were acknowledged, even while they were kept out of elite ranks where Roman Catholics mainly dominated. The unofficial arrangement between these two groups represented a deal that must be understood if one is to make sense of current conditions. The Christian Coalition, led by Ralph Reed, became the quintessential organization to represent this fusion.

Reed offered Republican campaigns evangelical resources, mailing lists, and volunteers in a cooperative effort to elect candidates. The Christian Coalition backed establishment George Bush in 1990 instead of the populist Pat Buchanan. This strategic error set the religious Right on a course away from its initial populist instincts and toward the pursuit of recognition by powerful elites. In return, Bush

---

10 Jim Wallis, "Liberation and Conformity," *Sojourners*, September 1, 1976, https://sojo.net/magazine/september-1976/liberation-and-conformity.
11 David Swartz, *Moral Minority: The Evangelical Left in an Age of Conservatism* (University of Pennsylvania Press, 2012), 149.

and Quayle signaled to the National Association of Evangelicals and the Southern Baptist Convention that they would include social issues in their platform. Ralph Reed called it "the most conservative and the most pro-family platform in the history of this party."

Abortion was never a top concern for voters nationwide, but it did come to characterize and motivate the religious Right. One of George Bush's advisors told the *New York Times* in 1990 that "the President would ultimately profit from sitting out the [abortion] fight, because even if *Roe v. Wade* was overturned, most states would move to restore abortion rights on their own, thereby distancing Mr. Bush from the fallout from such a Supreme Court decision."[12] This has been the general Republican disposition since then.

When Republicans pushed the 1994 "Contract with America," which hardly mentioned homosexuality and only called to end partial birth abortion, the Christian Coalition supported it. Ralph Reed said: "Our movement is now in many ways thoroughly integrated and enmeshed into the machinery of the Republican Party." The next year he stated, "We have gained what we always sought—a place at the table, a sense of legitimacy and a voice in the conversation." Pat Buchanan rightly observed, "The Coalition has given away any boldness in a search for popularity and consensus."[13]

As the '90s wore on, the Christian Coalition broadened its net by including Jews and Catholics and by endorsing religious pluralism. A generally watered down anti-abortion stance, coupled with a vague notion of "family values," became the religious Right's unique trait, as their leadership pursued an ever diminishing feeling of importance and influence. Most Christians remember the history past this point.

Evangelical organizations, regardless of how principled, tended to focus exclusively on certain social issues, while gaining commitments from presidential candidates who did little to move the needle in their direction. GOP conventions featured prayers from

---

12 Robin Toner, "G.O.P. Group Formed to Support Abortion Rights," *The New York Times*, April 24, 1990, sec. U.S., https://www.nytimes.com/1990/04/24/us/gop-group-formed-to-support-abortion-rights.html.

13 Frances FitzGerald, *The Evangelicals: The Struggle to Shape America* (Simon & Schuster, 2017), 422.

Christians along with Muslims, Sikhs, Jews, and Mormons long before 2024. Christian leaders had their place, but not a monopoly. Meanwhile, the country slid socially left, eventually leading to the election of populist Donald Trump.

Evangelical leaders were weak on the social issues that ignited Trump's campaign, including immigration, outsourcing and corruption. Throughout the 2000s they had largely either continued to ignore or steadily softened on issues such as gun rights, globalism, immigration, the surveillance state, and welfare. Trump was never "their" guy, but he moved the needle for them in ways previous establishment Republicans failed to do on abortion.

Simultaneous with the waning influence of the religious Right was also the ascendence of the once defeated evangelical Left. Figures like Russell Moore, David Platt, and Tim Keller joined other institutional elites to oppose Trump, even watering down their pro-life commitments by incorporating other "life" issues prioritized by the Left. They set themselves up against populism by condemning it in strong terms.

Seeing few alternatives, the vast majority of evangelical voters supported Trump in 2016 and 2020, but their leadership started giving up the influence they previously enjoyed on the political Right. After politically defeating the establishment at the 2024 convention with the selection of vice-presidential candidate J.D. Vance, Trump altered the character of the Republican Party. One of the changes he brought was watering down the party platform on marriage and abortion—a reversal of the deal cut in 1990.

The evangelical political industry could no longer expect the largely vacuous rhetoric establishment Republicans offered them or the feeling of importance that came with it. What they could still expect was a seat at the table. It was a smaller seat in some ways, but it was a seat—not a symbolic overture. This is the key thing to understand. What remains to be seen is how traditional Christians will handle the social changes over the next few years.

Things like the outcry online against a Sikh prayer at the 2024 Republican convention and the overtly moral and Christian language used by America First leaders to describe the Left's agenda for corrupting children and liquidating America's future are the breeding grounds for another authentic religious Right—one that is actually serious, populist, and realistic. Americans have not seen this in full bloom since the 1980s. It is time for it to return stronger than it was even then.

Traditional Christians currently have a limited window of four years to build, grow, and secure as much real influence as possible, trusting that God will reward their efforts, whether in this life or the next. Some critics argue for an ecclesiocentric approach where Christians focus solely on evangelism and church-related activities. However, this perspective does not reflect the daily realities that Christians face, nor does it encompass all the areas where Jesus calls them to be "salt" and "light." While church activities remain essential, it is equally crucial for Christians to secure the influence needed to protect these efforts. Ultimately, God will prevail and determine the "right side of history." In the meantime, let us love God and neighbor by pursuing power in this temporal realm. In the words of Charles Spurgeon: "I long for the day when the precepts of the Christian religion shall be the rule among all classes of men, in all transactions. I often hear it said, 'do not bring religion into politics.' This is precisely where it ought to be brought and set there in the face of all men as on a candlestick."[14]

---

[14] Lewis Drummond, *Spurgeon: Prince of Preachers* (Kregel Publications, 1992), 517.

17

LESSONS FROM
THE WOKE CHURCH
CONTROVERSY

*Give me one hundred preachers who fear nothing but sin
and desire nothing but God, and I care not whether they
be clergymen or laymen, they alone will shake the gates of
Hell and set up the kingdom of Heaven upon Earth.*

John Wesley

Although no major studies exist on the increase in church splits over the past few years, there is little doubt that socio-political disagreements are changing the face of American Christianity. Major Christian outlets like *Christianity Today*, *The Gospel Coalition*, and *Charisma* simply assume this is happening.[1]

---

1 Russell Moore, "What Church Splits Can Teach Us About a Dividing America," *Christianity Today*, September 8, 2022, https://www.christianitytoday.com/ct/2022/september-web-only/russell-moore-sbc-baptist-church-splits-dividing-america.html; Trevin Wax, "Why Are U.S. Churches More Politically Polarized Than U.K. Churches?," *The Gospel Coalition*, January 26, 2021, https://www.thegospelcoalition.org/blogs/trevin-wax/why-are-u-s-churches-more-politically-polarized-than-u-k-churches/; Samantha Carpenter, "Should the Church Be Involved in Politics?," *Charisma*, May 23, 2021, https://charismamag.com/culture/politics/should-the-church-be-involved-in-politics/.

This upheaval likely contributes to trends pollsters detect such as church closings, church shopping, and pastors exiting the ministry.[2] All this is happening at a time when Christians must navigate pressures never faced before in America. If we ignore our fractured condition, we do so at our own peril. It is imperative that we diagnose the problem before us and find a remedy.

My starting assumption is that much of the recent friction surrounding Christians relates to social justice issues and the responses to them, whether from sympathetic, liberal, or conservative directions. Most of my public efforts over the last few years have been concerned with defining, identifying and refuting social justice-related errors within Christianity. I saw firsthand the damage it caused in Wake Forest, North Carolina, both at my seminary and at local churches. One white family at a local Southern Baptist church was told by leadership that they were guilty of racism because a black family in the church shared the same last name with them. This supposedly meant the white family's ancestors enslaved the black family's ancestors. I remember in one class the teacher agreeing that Christians should apologize for the Holocaust. The first challenge I faced was Christians who did not believe this was happening in their circles. I churned out as much content as I could in 2019, exposing evangelical compromise at events like T4G and MLK50. Reactions were initially mixed. The majority of Christians either ignored or denied what was happening, but a growing minority started to notice.

After 2020, proving my contentions became easier. As classrooms met remotely in response to alarms surrounding Covid, parents became aware of the sexual degeneracy and anti-white narratives

---

2 In 2019, Lifeway Research published that "approximately 3,000 Protestant churches were started in the U.S., but 4,500 Protestant churches closed." During Covid lockdowns the next year, Pew Research reported that a third of church attendees chose to "exclusively [watch] services offered by congregations or religious organizations other than the one they typically attend[ed]." In November 2021, Barna found that "38 percent [of pastors] . . . considered quitting full-time ministry within the past year." See: Aaron Earls, "Protestant Church Closures Outpace Openings in U.S." (Lifeway Research, May 25, 2021), https://lifewayresearch.com/2021/05/25/protestant-church-closures-outpace-openings-in-u-s/; "Americans Oppose Religious Exemptions From Coronavirus-Related Restrictions" (Pew Research, August 7, 2020), https://www.pewresearch.org/religion/2020/08/07/attending-and-watching-religious-services-in-the-age-of-the-coronavirus/; "38% of U.S. Pastors Have Thought About Quitting Full-Time Ministry in the Past Year" (Barna Research, November 16, 2021), https://www.barna.com/research/pastors-well-being/.

teachers imposed on their children. Yet many tone-deaf pastors ignored this and continued preaching against alleged racist and homophobic behavior. They also complied with Covid mandates. Some even marched against racial disparities while their churches remained closed. The #metoo movement sacrificed itself backing dubious claims, yet major denominations used the movement's rationale in attempting to eradicate sexual abuse.[3] While secular social justice advocates discredited themselves, Christian leaders decided to follow them off the cliff.

CHRISTIAN LEADERS REACT

In observing the innumerable conflicts related to social justice infiltration, I noticed four basic reactions Christians today may find instructive in navigating the waters ahead. They are practicing, participating, permitting, and preventing social justice. I will briefly illustrate the pitfalls of the first three approaches and then chart a path forward by means of the fourth. Along the way we will expose present weakness and reinforce the authority of Scripture.

First of all, Christians who practice social justice see it as synonymous with foundational orthodox belief. Their pastors claim that social justice is the gospel, part of the gospel, or necessary for the gospel. It would be better to think of them as community organizers or activists rather than as pastors. Their churches function as left-wing political fronts with Christian veneers. Although this description is often associated with those outside the evangelical fold, like Al Sharpton or Jim Wallis, evangelical circles are gradually including this approach. People like Eric Mason, Russell Moore, and Jarvis

---

3 For example, the most influential figure advising evangelicals on abuse-related issues supported Amber Heard and Christine Ford directly. See: Rachael Denhollander [@R_Denhollander], "These Are Incredibly Important Dynamics to Understand with Abuse, Especially the Way Abusers Wield the Trauma They Have Caused, and the Victim's Self-Defense to Flip the Narrative.," Tweet, *Twitter*, July 2, 2022, https://web.archive. org/web/20220702131357/https://twitter.com/R_Denhollander/status/1543220904662106113; Rachael Denhollander, "I'm a Sexual Assault Survivor. And a Conservative. The Kavanaugh Hearings Were Excruciating.," *Vox*, October 15, 2018, https://www.vox.com/first-person/2018/10/15/17968534/ kavanaugh-vote-supreme-court-sexual-assault-christine-blasey-ford.

Williams are good examples of prominent leaders in evangelical organizations who fulfill an activist role.

The drawback to social justice activism is obvious. Liberation theology, critical theory, and Christian feminism are hybrids. Their intention is to make Christianity compatible with egalitarian activism. In doing this they must necessarily overhaul the gospel, since it offers grace to oppressors yet fails to automatically ascribe righteousness to the marginalized. They must also reject the natural order because it produces disparity-inducing hierarchies. What is left is not Christianity at all, but something entirely different.[4] This is why Eric Mason teaches that Christians can learn how to work "for gospel change" from secular social justice initiatives.[5] Christian belief is not even necessary for the kind of change he is working toward. This makes the church obsolete, because its most important function can be accomplished by secular organizations. Even if activist Christians manage to successfully draw large numbers to their ranks, they are not adding to the kingdom of God.

The second approach is led by industry managers. David Wells believed the success of "evangelical institutions during the 1970s and 1980s" caused them to become bureaucratic. This inevitably produced leaders driven more by tactics than theology.[6] Most pastors probably fall into this category based on standard reactions to challenges that emerged in 2020. They tried to compromise with social justice through limited participation. Whatever they believed could be endorsed while still maintaining orthodoxy was. This is where churches became loud on issues like racism, Covid, and abuse but were noticeably quieter on LGBTQ+ and abortion. For example, J.D. Greear, a former president of the Southern Baptist Convention, notoriously said the Bible whispers about sexual sin but Black Lives

---

4 J. Gresham Machen came to similar conclusions about liberal Christianity during the Modernist controversy. See: John Gresham Machen, *Christianity and Liberalism* (Macmillan, 1923), 6.

5 Jon Harris, *Christianity and Social Justice: Religions in Conflict* (Reformation Zion Publishing, 2021), 45.

6 David Wells, *No Place for Truth: Or Whatever Happened to Evangelical Theology?* (Wm. B. Eerdmans Publishing, 1994), 133.

Matter was a gospel issue.[7] This was a formula based on risk-calcula-tion more than anything else.

Pastors knew their congregations were split politically. Even if left-leaning members were a small minority, they did not want to provoke them. This may be due to the fact that progressives are generally less tolerant than conservatives. Pastors knew they could rely on most right-leaning members to accept their decisions.[8] Furthermore, pressure from government, media, and corporate interests often outweighed internal pressure from right-leaning con-gregants. Managerial-minded pastors believed they were capable of navigating this minefield by appeasing woke activists without alien-ating conservatives. But they were wrong.

This came out when evangelical elites painted conservative critics as extreme and repeatedly lashed out against Christians who trusted conservative news outlets over them.[9] Things did not go as planned, trust was broken, and churches split. Pastors who participated in social justice campaigns tried to regain credibility with their con-gregations by shifting slightly to the right, but their credibility was already diminished in minds of many. Compromise with social justice did not work. Neither did cowardice in the face of it.

Perhaps the most lamentable of all four approaches involves leaders who permit what they disagree within areas where they

---

7   Leonardo Blair, "JD Greear Endorses Black Lives Matter as Gospel Issue, Denounces Organization," *The Christian Post*, June 10, 2020, https://www.christianpost.com/news/jd-greear-endorses-black-lives-matter-as-gospel-issue-denounces-blm-organization.html; Kelly Williams, "The SBC and Whether God's Word 'whispers' about Sexual Sin," *The Christian Post*, March 27, 2022, https://www.christianpost.com/voices/the-sbc-and-whether-gods-word-whispers-about-sexual-sin.html.

8   Carrie Sheffield, "Liberals Should Resolve to Be More Tolerant in 2022," December 26, 2021, https://nypost.com/2021/12/26/liberals-should-resolve-to-be-more-tolerant-in-2022/.

9   "Rick Warren said . . . he sees evangelicals shifting into two groups. Some of those that are going to be more nationalist, more maybe anti-immigrant, more tied into what they see on cable news every week and I think that is a very fair reality." See: Ed Stetzer, *Southern Baptists Resist the Pirates & Religious Liberty Goes to Court w/ Ed Stetzer & David French*, interview by Phil Vischer and Kaitlyn Schiess, June 23, 2021, 21:30, https://www.youtube.com/watch?v=yJDRpPRtOcA; "I recognize that some of you have seen on cable news . . . or the deep dark web . . . I know that you're seeing that, but you're going to have to elevate your ecclesiology." See: Ed Stetzer, *Where Are We Going Next?*, interview by Dhati Lewis, June 18, 2021, https://www.youtube.com/watch?v=WwDGDA4YmIE; "You are leaving because you disagree that we said too much, too many things about George Floyd . . . Pastors get to disciple our people about one hour a week and Tucker Carlson, Sean Hannity and Rachel Maddow get them for three hours a night." See: J.D. Greear, "Chapel at Southeastern" (Southeastern Baptist Theological Seminary, January 25, 2022), https://youtu.be/7FCIK8YXqJo; J.D. Greear compared conservative critics to Pharisees and terrorists. See: Plenary Session #1, 2021, https://www.sbc.net/ec-meetings/ec-feb-2021/.

enjoy influence. People assumed Carl Trueman, Kevin DeYoung, Jon Payne and others who critiqued aspects of social justice in the abstract would do more in the concrete. Yet they gave credibility to false teachers when it mattered most. This approach is also a manifestation of the managerialism previously discussed. It tends to preference institutional stability over principle and intellectualizes problems to avoid conflict. This is the most tempting pitfall for theologically conservative pastors who know the right thing to do but fail to do it.

Carl Trueman publicly spoke against critical race theory, yet defended Grove City College when parents and students exposed it for promoting teachings consistent with the theory.[10] Kevin DeYoung also criticized critical race theory, yet signaled agreement when Bobby Scott suggested Christians at the Together for the Gospel conference failed to fully accomplish the "the ministry of reconciliation" because they lacked diversity.[11] Jon Payne condemned Revoice theology, yet referred to key PCA leaders who promoted it and corrupted the gospel as "friends from different perspectives" and "brothers in Christ."

Significantly, these conservative leaders had little trouble condemning certain Christians to their political right in strong and specific terms but failed at key moments to condemn actual false teachers to their left.[12] The popular term for this behavior is "punch right, nuance left." Effectively, this approach permits social justice to gain a foothold by relegating critiques to the academic arena. Christians are hampered by cowardly leaders who fail to protect them from

---

[10] Carl Trueman, "Do I Teach at a Woke School?," *The Institute for Faith and Freedom*, December 6, 2021, https://www.faithandfreedom.com/do-i-teach-at-a-woke-school/.

[11] *Panel: Why We Should Be Critical of Critical Race Theory (CRT)* (Together for the Gospel, 2022), https://www.youtube.com/watch?v=8ITnjO581fU, 8:30, 14:30.

[12] Kevin DeYoung argued strongly against Stephen Wolfe, calling many of his claims "unsubstantiated" and "troubling." See: Kevin DeYoung, "The Rise of Right-Wing Wokeism," *The Gospel Coalition*, November 28, 2022, https://www.thegospelcoalition.org/reviews/christian-nationalism-wolfe/; Carl Trueman critiqued Christian Nationalism by tying it to an alleged "white supremacist." See: Carl Trueman, "Identity Politics on the Right," *First Things*, December 8, 2022, https://www.firstthings.com/web-exclusives/2022/12/identity-politics-on-the-right. Jon Payne chided politically conservative Christians if their excitement for Elon Musk's takeover of Twitter did not match their excitement for sharing the gospel. See: Rod Martin, "Liberal Pietism 101: Make Christians Feel Guilty...," *Facebook*, May 1, 2022, https://www.facebook.com/RodDMartin/posts/pfbid0qjCE3296BXMecjTCYnRcrXRFTKsVCTDVUZUnmoZxASzS4jbBD4xVFB5zLsmJDyRXl.

wolves but often gate-keep out those who will. The impact of this is more weakness and compromise.

The first three approaches can easily be reconciled with social justice. Any involvement in social justice crusades is a good way to introduce false teaching and destroy the unique testimony of the church. Throughout the 20th century, mainline denominations realized what evangelicals are experiencing now: dwindling numbers, diminishing influence, and divided congregations. Stories abound of activist-minded congregants leaving churches when they realize Christianity cannot embrace the full expression of their egalitarian principles. After all, left-wing organizations are better at implementing social justice, and they do not face the hurdles associated with Christianity—such as beliefs in hierarchy, tradition, and loving enemies.

CNN senior political analyst Kirsten Powers illustrated this well. She rejected her cold Episcopalian upbringing in favor of atheism, yet felt unfulfilled spiritually. She temporarily satisfied this longing by adopting Tim Keller's brand of evangelicalism. Keller attracted her with "intellectual sources," "psychological insights," and Biblical application. But there was something wrong. Powers notes that she never heard Keller include "teaching about homosexuality or abortion being a sin or men being the head of the family." When she realized these were "core teachings" of Christianity, she started to see how "harmful" and "disempowering" this thinking was. She totally rejected evangelicalism, but retained a personalized evolving spirituality "[un]distorted and destroyed by the need to dominate and control" and influenced by unorthodox figures like Martin Luther King Jr. and Malcolm X.[13]

Powers is not the only person to receive an inoculation against the gospel from compromised leaders. There is currently an entire movement of former church members using egalitarian standards to allegedly deconstruct their faith. With time people realize that

---

13 Kirsten Powers, "My Complicated Feelings About Tim Keller," Substack, *Kirsten Powers* (blog), May 24, 2023, https://kirstenpowers.substack.com/p/my-complicated-feelings-about-tim; Kirsten Powers, *Saving Grace: Speak Your Truth, Stay Centered, and Learn to Coexist with People Who Drive You Nuts* (Crown Publishing Group, 2023), xi.

Christianity and social justice are religions in conflict. They cannot be reconciled. People will hate one and love the other. This is how acquiescing to social justice ideology serves as an off-ramp from orthodoxy. The question remains, who and what is impervious to this pressure? Who will, like the prophets of old, command Israel to choose whom they will serve in no uncertain terms?

THE LOCAL PASTOR

If we look for the answer to this question in the upper ranks of Christian institutions where the pressure to compromise is greatest, we will be discouraged. Leaders like John MacArthur and Voddie Baucham are rare. They also enjoy a unique freedom to say unpopular things because they control their own independent institutions. Brave Christians like professors Russell Fuller and Gregory Schulz risked their careers to say similar things in institutions they do not control. Attempts to reform organizations like the Southern Baptist Convention or Cru rarely succeed. Trying to change large institutions is not wrong, but it can be expensive.

At times, God allows error as a manifestation of His judgment. Some examples include hardening Pharaoh's heart, using parables to keep the proud from understanding, and giving those who suppress the truth over to a depraved mind.[14] Christians serving in organizations they believe are under judgement should ask whether it is better to redirect limited resources toward more fruitful ends. Weighing this decision means asking whether organizations have already effectively neutralized reform attempts. The Apostle Paul abandoned synagogues that did not receive his teaching. Martin Luther followed this example.[15] We cannot hold on to false hope. Ministry resources should go first and foremost to actual ministry. This is often best accomplished on a smaller scale.

Many local congregations withstood social justice ideology in ways larger organizations did not. My own church exists within the

---

[14] Ex 9:12, Matt 13:10-15, Rom 1:18, 28.
[15] Acts 19:9

suburbs of a large metropolitan area surrounded by "wokeness." Yet it never found common cause with any social justice movement. I have noticed traveling around the country while speaking on this issue that smaller independent churches led by non-professional pastors tend to mount the same resistance. There are several reasons for this.

First, working class pastors are similar to people in the congregations they serve. White evangelical Protestants who regularly attended services voted overwhelmingly for Donald Trump.[16] Yet if someone only concentrated on what major evangelical leaders and outlets said, they might assume the opposite was true. This is because elites generally share more in common with each other than with those whom they serve. Their specialized training translates into professional guild membership. Their career advancement depends more on approval from peers than from organizational members.[17] This makes it difficult for laymen to hold them accountable. These realities all contribute to the massive chasm between elites and common people that exists in large organizations.

However, pastors who are not part of this professional guild rely more on the favor of church members for career stability. More importantly, they generally arise from within congregations and therefore carry with them the identity of their church. They do not think of the church primarily as a tool to increase social harmony or as an engine for administrating popular activities. Nor are they simply expository sermon factories. Instead, they tend to be the way Jesus described shepherds in John 10. They know their sheep and their sheep know them. They sacrifice themselves to defend their flock from predators.

Another reason working-class pastors were able to resist social justice is because their congregations stood with them. When churches split over social justice in 2020, courageous pastors prevented it from taking hold of their congregations. Some of them

---

[16] Justin Nortey, "Most White Americans Who Regularly Attend Worship Services Voted for Trump in 2020," Pew Research Center (blog), accessed June 7, 2023, https://www.pewresearch.org/short-reads/2021/08/30/most-white-americans-who-regularly-attend-worship-services-voted-for-trump-in-2020/.

[17] The revolving door theory.

gained members from compromised churches. Others rose to the occasion and started their own assemblies. There was a demand for authentic leadership, but the supply did not exist through conventional channels. Seminary graduates were more likely to exhibit professional docility than their working class counterparts. Christians were less interested in these activists, managers, and academics, regardless of what certifications they had or doctrinal statements they could sign. Now seminary enrollment is plummeting, even though demand for pastors is high.[18] What passed for peacetime leadership is no longer suitable in a wartime setting. This tendency to trust figures who willingly risk their reputations with elites is emerging on many issues common people care about.

Donald Trump, Jordan Peterson, Elon Musk and others gained credibility with common people by taking stands that cost them credibility with professional peers. All it takes is someone refusing to go along with one facet of the social justice agenda, even if they are on board with the rest of it. When someone says "no" to a force capable of hurting them in order to stand for what is right, it projects strength. A good litmus test for Christian leaders is whether they are willing to simply call false teachers what Scripture calls them.

Throughout the New Testament, Christ and the Apostles warn against the subversive strategy of false teachers. They "come to you in sheep's clothing" (Matt 7:15), they "mislead, if possible, even the elect" (Matt 24:24), they "cause dissensions" (Rom 16:17), they "disguise themselves as servants of righteousness" (2 Cor 11:15), they advocate "a different doctrine" (1 Tim 6:3), they "secretly introduce destructive heresies" (2 Pet 2:2), and they "[creep] in unnoticed" (Jude 1:4). That is why we must "beware of [them]," "keep [our] eye on [them]," "cut off [their] opportunity," "test the spirits," and "contend earnestly for the faith."[19] It does not take much effort to say "no" to false teachers, but it does mean reaping the consequences of their opposition. Perhaps this willingness to risk reputation to

---

[18] Steve Rabey, "Enrollment Declines and Shifts Continue at Evangelical Seminaries," *Ministry Watch*, November 26, 2022, https://ministrywatch.com/enrollment-declines-and-shifts-continue-at-evangelical-seminaries/.

[19] Matt 7:15, 24:24, Rom 16:17, 2 Cor 11:15, 1 Tim 6:3, 2 Pet 2:2, Jude 1:4, 2 Cor 11:12, 1 John 4:1, Jude 1:3.

seek God's approval over man's is the most important reason many working class pastors could resist what elites could not.

Thomas Jefferson thought leadership was best handled by a natural aristocracy who gained ascendence through virtue and ability, as opposed to wealth and nobility. If Jefferson were alive today he might very well replace "wealth and nobility" with "certificates and style." It is this natural aristocracy that effectively resisted what every elite institution forced upon them. This has always been the Protestant way to conserve orthodoxy. As one Catholic blogger put it, the strength of Protestantism was that it "produce[d] thousands of George Baileys, who in various fields and in their own small way were able to transform the world."[20]

In the years ahead it will be the George Baileys who conserve orthodoxy to pass it down to future generations. One contractor outside of Portland planted a successful church after he decided to host outdoor services during the Covid shutdown. Another congregation in Indiana grew from twenty people to two hundred in one year when an elder and retired pastor left a congregation compromised by social justice to start a Bible church. Stories like these are happening in more places than most people realize. One of the great needs now is to encourage this organic leadership development.

Practically speaking this means raising up more pastors from within congregations. This increases accountability and reduces corrupting influences. If seminary training is pursued, it should not be done without heavily weighing the costs and benefits. Some institutions provide online tools that help interns and ministers gain training while serving at their local church. This can reduce the possibility of institutional group-think. Another practical application is investing in smaller ministries.

If global elites achieve their goals, evangelical Christians could be forced into a decision to either completely apostatize or suffer the consequences. Governments do not have the resources to monitor

---

[20] The Social Pathologist, "The Social Pathologist: Some Thoughts on George Bailey and the Incarnation," *The Social Pathologist* (blog), December 24, 2021, https://socialpathology.blogspot.com/2021/12/some-thoughts-on-george-bailey-and.html.

every church, but they can influence large groups of believers by applying pressure on their leaders. This is why large organizations are not viable refuges for orthodoxy during times of persecution. Realizing this may be on the horizon, Christians should look at ways to increase their ministry influence by decentralizing what they can. This does not mean they should not form organizations as prudence dictates, but their main work should always involve the communities in which they are embedded.

In conclusion, there is no perfect formula for resisting social justice or liberal incursions. Like any set of false teachings they must be exposed and refuted. It will require hard and risky work, but good resources are available. The reason false teachings advance in many areas within evangelical Christianity is not because the arguments against them are weak. Rather, it is because leaders refuse to oppose false teaching. This weakness in leadership is a greater problem than social justice or liberalism themselves. It is incumbent on every Christian to identify those whom the Holy Spirit equips, who are qualified to lead, and to encourage them. We need pastors willing to "admonish the unruly" and not just to "encourage the fainthearted."[21] If we do not reward bravery and competence we will reap their opposites. This is the only way to satisfy our current deficit in leadership.

---

[21] 1 Thess 5:14

18

THE WAY FORWARD

If you are on the wrong road, progress means doing an about turn and walking back to the right road; and in that case the man who turns back soonest is the most progressive man.

C.S. Lewis

There are many practical things we can do to reinvigorate our lives with a healthy respect for God's design in the natural order. Although we will always live with the ever-present threat of sin, which works through people to twist our conception of God's order into one fashioned after our own innovations, humans still reflect the imprint of their Creator and thrive the most in societies that recognize this.

There was never a golden civilizational age in the West where people did this perfectly. Yet I am reminded of a line in the 2007 song "Roots," by the English folk band Show of Hands. When referencing the legends, symbols, and other cultural touchstones that once characterized England, they sing:

Haul away boys, let them go
Out in the wind and the rain and snow

We've lost more than we'll ever know
'Round the rocky shores of England

That is the position Western Christians are in. There really was a time we collectively recognized a created order that was good, true, and beautiful. We tried to govern our own lives by it while reflecting this order in our institutions. Such days are gone with the wind. We really have lost more than we'll ever know. Yet, at the same time, we are not starting from a completely blank slate. There is a rich heritage waiting to be discovered and adopted once again.

Many Christians recognize the obvious departures from Christian-infused societies, represented by social celebration of sexual perversions, the erosion of national distinctions, and the separation of current generations from their past. Restoring order on a mass scale while institutions are controlled by corrupt elites is a daunting task. However, there are many ways for us to build and cultivate counter-institutions that reflect the wisdom of the ages and the timeless truths in creation and Scripture. Perhaps, like a person recuperating from amnesia, we will begin to remember what we have lost as we start to familiarize ourselves with what we do know. While not exhaustive, this chapter will provide practical examples of ways we can begin the work of recovery.

THE CHURCH

The best thing for the church to do right now is to be the church once again. I do not mean in the modern sense, which ironically sometimes conveys the idea of being something other than the church by knocking down archaic barriers to alleged authentic togetherness and acceptance. I mean actually quite the opposite. Churches should consider whether it is in their means to bring back things like steeples, graveyards, and traditional music.

In my experience, one of the reasons many evangelicals convert to Roman Catholicism and Eastern Orthodoxy, despite important differences in theology, is the fact that their forms frequently resemble actual churches. Their buildings more often convey a sense of transcendence, their liturgy reminds man of his own mortality, and their music demands a compliance missing in most contemporary Christian music. Of course, both traditions are also infected with modernity in different ways and places, but the contrast between them and popular forms of evangelicalism, which reinvent themselves every decade it seems, reveals serious weakness in the most influential American churches.

This is not to say that aesthetics are more important than theology. People should choose a church primarily based upon things like biblical fidelity, qualified leadership, and opportunities to serve. Yet more recent casual approaches to worship reflect an unspoken drift from a focus centered on divinity to one centered on humanity, and this is, at a certain level, a theological problem. The kind of god whose satisfaction is tethered to mankind's cheap and temporal fancies is not the kind of God depicted in creation or Scripture.

Unfortunately, many modern evangelical churches replace a natural longing for God with cheap thrills and entertaining distractions. This shallow emphasis characterizes everything from liturgy to musical selections to leadership qualities. I remember visiting numerous Southern Baptist churches in the Raleigh area when I attended seminary, and most seemed to follow a similar formula.

A casually-dressed greeter cracks jokes, makes announcements, and affirms how special everyone in attendance is to the church. This is either preceded or followed by a rock band performing a difficult-to-follow praise song. This concert atmosphere continues until a middle-aged man dressed like a teenager appears on stage to give what feels more like a TED Talk than a sermon. Generally, there is a call to receive Christ and then to get involved in church programs. This is either preceded or followed once again by a rock band performing a difficult-to-follow praise song. Of course, if Sunday falls on Christmas, regular attendees are not burdened by the obligation to actually attend church, since church is closed so families have more time together.

In contrast, traditional Protestant liturgies increasingly move hearts toward a confrontation with the holy character of God throughout the course of a service. They often start with lofty music, followed by Scripture reading and corporate singing. God's presence is acknowledged in an opening prayer, after which congregants confess their sins and are then assured of God's pardon for them. In response, the congregation sings a hymn of praise, more Scriptures are read, and the pastor delivers a sermon. This is followed by creeds, intercessions, offerings, the doxology, and sometimes the Lord's Supper, before the service is closed with a final hymn and benediction. These churches emphasize the importance of attending during Christian holidays.

The problem with contemporary liturgy is that it generally welcomes God into the worshipers' own presence on their own terms. It emphasizes the attributes of God that modern people find acceptable to the exclusion of other attributes. In this arrangement, the church loses its own distinctive qualities in order to compete with other institutions that offer human fulfillment and self-help. This quality is easily recognized by branding slogans such as: "You Belong Here" or "Creating Life Change."[1] Traditional liturgy, on the other hand, welcomes worshipers into God's presence on His terms. It highlights the full spectrum of God's revealed attributes as people conform themselves to a higher order of being.

Protestant liturgical calendars also provide a helpful alternative to the recent string of specially recognized days that celebrate sexual perversion and undermine American heritage. For a long time, Christians in the United States enjoyed a status where even secular institutions exclusively recognized virtuous holidays. Now that pagan forces have weaponized our own calendars against us, it is important to rethink the way we mark time.

As Halloween became more ghoulish in certain parts of the country, evangelicals in the 1980s started introducing or emphasizing alternatives such as harvest parties, Trunk-or-Treat, or Reformation Day. That way children had something to celebrate without compromising their Christianity. Today, the need for alternatives is much

---

1   "Home," McLean Bible Church, accessed June 10, 2024, https://mcleanbible.org/; "Calvary Church with Skip Heitzig," Calvary Church | Osuna, accessed June 10, 2024, https://calvarynm.church.

greater. We can diminish the influence of pagan celebrations by increasing the importance of Christian ones.

Most American Christians celebrate the Resurrection, Thanksgiving, and Christmas. Contrast this with the first Episcopal *Book of Common Prayer* from 1779 which featured over thirty periods of fasting or feasting besides Sundays. Most evangelicals do not recognize things like the Feast of Stephen, the Feast of Saints Peter and Paul, All Saints' Day, or Lent—but perhaps we should.

Its easy to dismiss these events, since mainline churches who still recognize them are generally compromised. But it is important to remember that their liturgical calendars did not cause their compromise any more than the grandeur of their architecture or music did. They gave up biblical authority, along with many in the upper classes they came from, but kept many of the traditions built on that authority. While traditions do not guarantee orthodoxy, for centuries they did reinforce it. To reject traditions simply because the meaning behind them can be forgotten is to reject the wisdom of the past. Instead, Christians of all people should seek to understand the purpose of valuable traditions before dismissing them. Nowhere in the church is this more needed than in the music ministry.

Traditional hymnody aligned worshipers with both God and each other. Hymns are written to express truths about God or to God in the context of corporate worship. Their melodies are generally memorable, their vocal range is achievable for all parts, their rhythm complements the singing, and their form is reverent. Hymns do not simply praise God, but also explain why we should praise Him. Consider the rich Trinitarian theology in hymns like "Come, Thou Almighty King," "Now Thank We All Our God," and "Angels from the Realms of Glory."

In contrast, Paul S. Jones, the long-time music director at Tenth Presbyterian Church in Philadelphia, explained in his 2006 book *Singing and Making Melody* that much of the modern praise music is very different. "Melodies tend to be monotonous or to move in extreme ranges. Harmony often is simplistic and consists of repeated standard chords that have little direction or contrapuntal logic. . .

[and] the soloistic nature and rhythmic complexity of most CCM pieces will elude the congregation, rendering successful unison singing difficult." He summarized that "hymns clash with the spontaneity, simplicity, and style that have come to rule in the post-modern evangelical church," an era Jones described as "me-focused."[2]

Christians who desire their worship to reflect the intentions of their Creator in a symphony of corporate praise would do well to rediscover hymns. Paul commands Christians in Ephesians 5:18b-19 to "be filled with the Spirit, speaking to one another in psalms and hymns and spiritual songs, singing and making melody with your heart to the Lord." This does not mean modern songs should not be incorporated, but they should be carefully selected to complement the purpose of corporate music.

This means singing should not be a private or a spectator experience. Churches that transform their buildings into dark conference halls intentionally draw focus from the congregation to a stage performance, even though Scripture instructs singing "to one another." It means rejecting music the congregation finds too difficult to follow and lyrics that are erroneous, confusing, or nebulous. It may mean changing from styles that overwhelm, distract, or discourage singing in favor of instrumentation. Fortunately, there are many resources to help churches make a transition from a more self-focused and numbing personal experience to a God-focused and vibrant corporate setting. Much of the problem with today's worship music is that it is driven by a Christian celebrity industry, yet this industry is not limited to its music.

People will naturally organize themselves into hierarchical arrangements. However, modern "pop culture" and the accompanying veneration for celebrities corrupts this behavior by selecting leaders based upon optics instead of virtue. Possessing a weak moral character is generally advantageous in ascending the ranks of managerial institutions, because it allows one to suppress ethical concerns and natural duties in order to attain institutional loyalty and success.

---

2 Paul S. Jones, *Singing and Making Music: Issues in Church Music Today* (P & R Pub., 2006), Kindle Location: 44683, 3226.

Sadly, there is little exception to this dynamic in major Christian institutions, as whistle-blowers from Cru and the Southern Baptist Convention can attest.[3]

This state of affairs currently works to select ladder-climbing careerists over qualified leaders. Using the powerful resources these institutions provide—such as validation from other respected names, publishing networks, conference circuits, media opportunities, and an array of content-producing mechanisms—corrupt or weak men can easily portray themselves as faithful and strong to an unsuspecting audience.

For example, it should seem odd that Russell Moore wrote a book entitled *The Courage to Stand*, even though his pattern is to stand with major media forces against traditional Christians. Similarly, Al Mohler wrote a book called *The Conviction to Lead*, yet his leadership seems to frequently lack conviction.[4] Situations like this are not unusual at all in the Christian industry. Unfortunately, it is this industry that often dominates church hierarchies.

Even in the case of independent Bible churches, there is typically an unacknowledged administrative class beyond the local church that influences both the leadership and the congregation. It could be associated with a certain seminary or conference, and it is likely evident in obvious places such as lobbies, libraries, and lessons. For example, a pastor who quotes a particular teacher in almost every sermon, or frequent advertisements for events associated with a parachurch ministry, or books displayed from an exclusively narrow range of authors—these can all signal the existence of an informal chain-of-command. Some church members were surprised to feel the pressure emanating from these hidden hierarchies during the

3 Russell Fuller, "What Happened at Southern Seminary?" (Be Not Conformed Conference, Deforest, WI, June 18, 2023), https://www.youtube.com/watch?v=MmtMiTqXInM; John Knox, "CRU, Formerly Campus Crusade for Christ, Fired Two of Its Employees after They Voiced Concerns about the Group's Stance on LGBT Issues," *Not the Bee*, March 16, 2020, https://notthebee.com/article/cru-formerly-campus-crusdade-for-christ-fired-two-of-its-employees-after-they-voiced-concerns-about-the-groups-stance-on-lgbt-issues.

4 Jon Harris, "Russell Moore Playlist," accessed June 10, 2024, https://www.youtube.com/playlist?list=PLqA7HoggRbpxoGrCyAskdf_ZYQyIVXJgr&jct=VF0Fllq9JeEHU7W256ZrajY6xpahqw; Jon Harris, "Al Mohler Playlist," accessed June 10, 2024, https://www.youtube.com/playlist?list=PLqA7HoggRbpyjpnwkggMp0prqTgfsaxXk&jct=-rpYonFTlUb0ybxtA-MNWO80egynbw.

lockdowns of 2020, as local pastors chose to follow the opinions of Christian celebrities over the concerns of their own congregations.

It is certainly not wrong to be influenced by wise people. The problem we face is that Christian organizations are not generally interested in providing wisdom as much as they are in their marketability. Christians should certainly use helpful products from ministries. But they should not be under the allusion that famous expositors, Christian music artists, and other Christian celebrities are the pinnacle of spirituality. Nor should they think that Christian celebrities deserve a loyalty above local leaders whom congregations have vetted according to biblical standards.

Sadly, many churches choose their own leaders based upon showmanship, business savvy, and personal connection rather than virtue. Whether someone attended the right institution, happens to be a dynamic speaker, or can parse a Hebrew verb should come second to the standards laid out in 1 Timothy 3 and Titus 1. Christians need to think about practical ways they can honor the depth of character God prioritizes over the more superficial qualities prized by corporate boards and market forces.

One way to do this is to host more local conferences and retreats while attending fewer national events. Another recommendation is to identify gifted people in a church who can write music and create discipleship materials tailored for the local congregation instead of exclusively using mass-produced content. Pastors can also help by referencing a broad array of Christian voices, especially those from the past, when delivering sermons. Regardless of how Christians approach major organizations and church celebrities, we must achieve a healthier, more accountable, and more traditionally-rooted leadership class.

GOVERNMENT

This book has already emphasized the importance of resisting Babel and the dangers of uniting principles that disregard natural relationships. My key focus is the promotion and preservation of high-trust communities with local accountability. It is not difficult to see how globalist forces have contributed to undermining social stability. What is more challenging, however, is proposing solutions, and this is mainly for one simple reason: those in power often view alternatives to the systems that benefit them as threats. This may include those who want to apply fascistic, monarchical, and theocratic schemes that threaten the liberal order. Yet, as someone writing about America who prizes American traditions, I wish to offer proposals from America's tradition of decentralization.

Of course, the United States as we know it would not exist today if it were not for a class of men who prioritized local arrangements over a distant king and were willing to risk everything to defend that choice. It is crucial to consider the historical context in which the Founding Fathers drafted the U.S. Constitution. They sought to move away from the centralized control of a constitutional monarchy with its unwritten constitution, opting instead for a decentralized republic with a written one. Their vision was not of an all-powerful government dictating every decision, but rather an alliance of States united for mutual benefits like defense, trade regulation, and immigration control. This structure was designed to reduce corruption with mechanisms to remove corrupt officials, while also respecting the diverse interests of various regions.

Of course, Americans have moved away from this arrangement in a myriad of ways that space does not permit me to elaborate on in this volume. Consider this as one example: Originally, each congressman was meant to represent just 30,000 people—a number smaller than some modern megachurches. Now, the ratio has ballooned to one congressman per over 760,000 constituents. It is no wonder even elected officials are often able to operate with little accountability. Yet, while I recognize the importance of discussing topics like the scale of representation, term limits, and conventions of states, I have decided to narrow my focus to three underutilized tools that I think Christian conservatives should be more aware of in resisting centralized tyranny. It is in this spirit that I aim to promote greater local

control while maintaining the necessary strength to combat globalist threats.

One effective way States can resist unconstitutional encroachments
from the general government is through the Anti-Commandeering
Doctrine. James Madison articulated this idea in Federalist Number
46. He said States could obstruct "unwarrantable measures" emanating from "the federal government" through "refusal to co-operate
with the officers of the union." In recent years States have successfully used this rationale to defend themselves from assuming liability
for radioactive waste, adjudicating firearm background checks, and
expanding Medicaid. Recently, State and local officials in Missouri
used this doctrine to fight what they believe are threats to the "rights
of law-abiding citizens to keep and bear arms," especially during the
Biden administration.

On June 14, 2021, Missouri Governor Mike Parson signed the
Second Amendment Preservation Act into law. The act declared "as
invalid all federal laws that infringe on the right to bear arms" protected by the State and Federal Constitutions. This included certain
taxes, tracking and use laws, as well as confiscation orders. State
and local officials who enforced invalid federal laws were subject
to a $50,000 civil penalty.[5] Multiple Missouri counties and munici-
palities accompanied the legislation with decrees of their own. The
Camden County Commission passed an ordinance declaring their
county to be a Second Amendment Sanctuary, thereby nullifying certain firearms regulations and penalizing those who applied
them.[6] Actions from the Bureau of Alcohol, Tobacco, Firearms
and Explosives (ATF) justified these actions in the minds of many
Missourians later that year.

On November 9, 2021, twenty armed and tactically equipped
ATF agents raided a gun shop in Camden County, Missouri, for

---

[5] Mary Grace Bruntrager, "HB85–Creates Additional Protections to the Right to Bear Arms," Missouri
Senate, August 28, 2021, https://www.senate.mo.gov/21info/bts_web/bill.aspx?SessionType=R&Bill
ID=57629955.

[6] Noah Davis, "Camden County Becomes Missouri's First Second Amendment Sanctuary County," Sanctuary
Counties (blog), January 23, 2021, https://sanctuarycounties.com/2021/01/22/camden-county-becomes-
missouris-first-second-amendment-sanctuary-county/.

selling firearms without allegedly administering background checks.[7] According to investigators, the owner Jim Skelton made a comment about selling guns out of his truck during a compliance inspection. This triggered a series of investigations in which ATF agents claim Skelton illegally sold firearms.[8] Skelton accused the agency of using entrapment techniques to justify their raid.

He said two undercover agents posing as a couple falsified documents when purchasing firearms at Skelton's Tactical. In compliance with the law, Skelton would not sell firearms to anyone but the buyer. In this case, however, a female agent deceptively signed Federal paperwork stating she was making the purchase, while the male agent physically handed over the money. As a result, the ATF confiscated Skelton's records along with around $180,000 worth of firearms.[9]

The following year Jim Skelton's brother, Ike Skelton, campaigned in part on the issue of gun rights and became the Camden County Presiding Commissioner. He made national headlines in 2023 for defying the ATF when they requested information on the Federal Firearms License holder's zoning and business licensing. Skelton believed the ATF was trying to find minor unrelated infractions to shut down small businesses selling firearms. "It's easier for them to enforce their unconstitutional edicts if they only have to enforce them on the big box stores. . . that comply with Federal rules," he stated.

Skelton, along with other county officials including the sheriff, signed a joint letter to investigator Amy Borkowski, informing her the ATF was "unconstitutional" and they would not assist her in violating citizens' God-given rights. Skelton followed the letter with a press conference claiming they did not recognize the ATF and warning citizens not to assist the agency. Sheriff Tony Helms pledged to defend the 2nd Amendment rights of Camden County

7 Bureau of Alcohol, Tobacco, Firearms, and Explosives
8 Sam Zeff, "Missouri County Official Who Declared ATF 'Unconstitutional' Has Family History with the Feds," *Kansas City News* and *NPR*, April 17, 2023, https://www.kcur.org/news/2023-04-17/missouri-county-official-who-declared-atf-unconstitutional-has-family-history-with-the-feds.
9 Jim Skelton, "What's Burnin with KB Ike Skelton Segment," interview by Kevin Burns, November 11, 2021, https://www.youtube.com/watch?v=Iu_gJMGymbQ.

residents. 1ˢᵗ District Commissioner James Gohagan added: "The only thing the ATF is good at really is murdering innocent dogs."[10] Camden County's actions are a good example of the Anti-Commandeering Doctrine in practice. In the words of Ike Skelton, "[The ATF] can go try to enforce what they want to enforce, we're not going to help them." Lesser magistrates are not obligated to support government-sponsored tyranny. Because multiple levels of government in Missouri sponsored laws to protect firearm rights, even if the state's Second Amendment Preservation Act is struck down, there are still multiple counties standing in the ATF's way. Tying up Federal agencies in court for years can easily stall tyranny until the election of a new administration more favorable to Constitutional rights.

Another underutilized tool states can use to frustrate the centralizers is interposition (or nullification) whereby a state nullifies a general edict it deems to be unconstitutional. Unlike anti-commandeering, where state officials refuse to enforce unconstitutional mandates, interposition invalidates unconstitutional mandates within a state's jurisdiction. In recent years, liberals have used this tool to promote marijuana legalization and sanctuary cities despite Federal laws. Yet Conservatives are reluctant to use it, often opting to sue the general government—which increases its perceived legitimacy—when they believe it has overstepped its bounds.

Interposition rests on the nature of the Constitution as a compact created by the several states under which they delegated a definite and limited array of powers to a central authority. The Tenth Amendment of the Constitution says: "The powers not delegated to the United States by the Constitution, nor prohibited by it to the States, are reserved to the States respectively, or to the people." In Federalist 45, James Madison observed that these "delegated" powers were "few and defined," while the powers remaining with the

---

10 Dissident [@DieOnFeet], "Camden County, #Missouri Ban #ATF (Anti-Gun Federal Agency), Prohibiting County from Cooperating with ATF, Preserving 2nd Amendment. The 2nd Amendment Grant Americans the Right to Bear Arms: Not for Fun, but to Keep Gov't at Bay. Https://T.Co/X05jqBqmQ1," Tweet, *X*, April 12, 2023, https://twitter.com/DieOnFeet/status/1646286941560659969.

States were "numerous and indefinite."[11] Unfortunately, the record of history shows the centralized government repeatedly overreaching into powers not delegated to it. When this takes place, States are justified in nullifying these efforts.

Before the Civil War, there were more significant attempts to nullify federal laws, the most important of which were the 1798 Kentucky and Virginia Resolutions. Authored by Thomas Jefferson and James Madison, respectively, these resolutions challenged the Alien and Sedition Acts. Madison argued in the Virginia Resolution that the Acts exercised "a power not delegated by the Constitution" and infringed upon "free communication among the people."[12] This tendency to threaten nullification often swayed public opinion and inspired negotiated solutions.

In 1807, New England invoked these "Principles of '98" in opposition to the Jefferson administration's trade embargo. The issue resurfaced in 1814 during debates over whether the federal government had the authority to conscript state militia members into the federal military. Massachusetts Senator Daniel Webster argued that, should the military conscription bill pass, it would become the "solemn duty" of state governments to defend their authority over their own militias and "to interpose between their citizens and arbitrary power."[13] In the early 1830s, South Carolina's opposition to the Tariff of Abominations and the Force Bill—which aimed to enforce a tariff they deemed unconstitutional—culminated in the Nullification Crisis. South Carolina argued that the tariff, which primarily benefitted Northern industries, was inconsistent with the Constitution's provision for promoting the general welfare. In the 1850s, Wisconsin's Supreme Court and Legislature both applied the same reasoning to effectively nullify the 1850 Fugitive Slave Act.[14]

---

11 James Madison, "Federalist No 45," accessed December 24, 2024, https://avalon.law.yale.edu/18th_century/fed45.asp.

12 James Madison, "The Virginia Resolution," December 24, 1798, Bill of Rights Institute.

13 Daniel Webster, "Daniel Webster's Speech on the Conscription Bill," in *The Letters of Daniel Webster* (Haskell House, 1969), 67.

14 Tom Woods and Clyde Wilson both have good treatments of state interposition. See: Thomas Woods, *Nullification: How to Resist Federal Tyranny in the 21st Century* (Simon and Schuster, 2010); Clyde Wilson, *Nullification: Reclaiming Consent of the Governed* (Amazon Digital Services LLC–Kdp, 2016).

Opponents of interposition argue that the Supremacy Clause of the Constitution—declaring the Constitution as the "supreme law of the land" and binding states to it—renders interposition unconstitutional. However, this argument assumes the very point it seeks to prove. The question at hand is whether the laws in question are themselves constitutional. Another objection is that the General Welfare Clause forbids interposition, since it grants Congress the authority to do whatever it deems necessary for the general welfare. Yet this is a misreading of the clause. James Madison himself criticized such an interpretation, calling it an attempt to subvert the foundational principles of the general government by turning the clause into a blank check, rather than a guiding principle.[15] Some advocates of broad federal power look to the Elastic Clause (also known as the Necessary and Proper Clause) as their justification. However, this clause does not grant new powers. It simply asserts that existing powers should be executed through appropriate laws.[16] Finally, some contend that states might abuse their power to nullify laws they wrongly deem unconstitutional. While this is a valid concern, it is often overlooked that the same potential for abuse exists within the central government, where the risk of tyranny is arguably greater.

I have thought for years that interposition is a tool deep Red States could use to nullify unconstitutional Supreme Court decisions that directly attack the created order, especially on issues like abortion and sexual perversion. While the power disparity between the states and the centralized authorities in Washington, D.C. has grown since Appomattox, the underlying principles remain the same. The potential for using this tool to provoke public debate or to force compromise, as it was in the early years of the Republic, still exists. Some of these ideas are making somewhat of a comeback even in elite circles.

I remember watching Catholic libertarian Tom Woods debate in

---

[15] "Bounty Payments for Cod Fisheries, [6 February] 1792," *Founders Online*, National Archives, https:// founders.archives.gov/documents/Madison/01-14-02-0192. [Original source: *The Papers of James Madison, vol. 14, 6 April 1791 – 16 March 1793*, ed. Robert A. Rutland and Thomas A. Mason. Charlottesville: University Press of Virginia, 1983, pp. 220–224.]

[16] Jonathan Elliot, ed., "Archibald Maclaine on the Elastic Clause," in *The Debates in the Several State Conventions on the Adoption of the Federal Constitution* (Lippincott, 1888), 141.

favor of state secession at the Yale Political Union in 2017. Before the debate, Woods warned that Leftist forces might try to shut it down. But to everyone's surprise, not only did the protesters fail to materialize, but Woods won the debate by a landslide, securing twice as many votes as the opposition. And this happened at Yale, of all places.

Although secession and interposition are distinct concepts, both represent decentralized forms of resistance. In today's political climate, these ideas have become unconventional and are often excluded from polite discourse. Simply reviving the debate over such tools could be a victory in itself, helping to build public support for further resistance against centralized power. I am under no illusion that the Yale Political Union is motivated by a commitment to God's order, organic communities, or Christian virtue. But perhaps they are open to more decentralized approaches that allow California to be California and Alabama to be Alabama. In a time when Christians are one election away from losing significant religious freedoms, it is important to revive and nurture the decentralization traditions that have been a part of America's past character.

Secession may be the most controversial tool worthy of discussion, given that there was already a war to prevent one region of the country from attempting it. While it is clearly a final resort, not a first step, in addressing disagreements with the general government, it deserves serious consideration for many of the same reasons that nullification does. However, secession is more than just a political tool. In a certain sense it may be inevitable, given current circumstances. This makes it all the more important to understand.

The inevitability I refer to relates to the "Big Sort" currently underway in the United States, where people are self-sorting according to cultural similarity and political views. This represents a secession of the heart, as people choose to cut the attachments that have bound them to one place and establish themselves in another. Many Red States are getting redder and Blue States are getting bluer. This is happening organically, to the dismay of some and the enthusiasm of others. I myself have concerns about the change this brings to some local regions, but I also understand it as a reaction to globalism and one that is not likely to stop anytime soon. What this means for the possibility of secession is that the conditions which first led thirteen colonies to secede from Great Britain in 1776, New Englanders to consider secession at the Hartford Convention in 1814, and Southerners to actually secede in 1860-1861, are starting to reemerge as strong regional political identities make their return.

The idea of the "proposition nation" was never strong enough to hold the country together, partly because groups of people have fundamentally different views on what social hierarchies should look like. While opposition to the Soviet Union and later the War on Terror did provide temporary national solidarity, this was always destined to fade once the external threats diminished or when half the population perceived the Deep State to be a greater threat. The reality is that, broadly speaking, there are at least two radically different visions for the future of the United States—visions that cannot coexist indefinitely without one eventually dominating the other. This is where political secession could become a viable tool, offering a way to avoid conflict and promote peace, should the situation require it and circumstances make it possible.

Secession, like interposition, is grounded in the idea that the Constitution is a compact created by the states for their mutual benefit, and therefore, it is accountable to them, rather than the other way around. The 1783 Treaty of Paris, which ended the Revolutionary War, specifically named each state as an individual party to the agreement. This was a common practice at the time, reflecting the view that the states were distinct, sovereign entities. Prior to the Civil War, many Americans even referred to the United States in the plural form, saying "The United States are" rather than "The United States is," emphasizing the independent nature of the states within the Union. When states like Virginia, New York, and Rhode Island ratified the Constitution, they explicitly reserved the right to withdraw from the Union if necessary, indicating that they saw secession as a legitimate option. Given these historical and legal precedents, there are strong arguments that secession could be considered constitutionally permissible.[17]

However, while something may be technically correct, that does not mean it is prudent. If Red States lack the strength to nullify unconstitutional edicts, there is little hope they can stand up to the general government and form their own country, not at this point at least. On a smaller scale, movements like the Greater Idaho movement and the proposed Pacific State of Jefferson help keep the idea of redrawing maps to match cultural realities in the public eye. Depending on the geopolitical winds, America could experience the equivalent of Brexit or the collapse of the Eastern Bloc in the near future. Both of those events surprised many of the so-called experts when they happened. There is no reason Christians should not know more about this topic and start seeing it as a possible option, should circumstances favor it.

In online discussions within the New Christian Right, it is common to see calls for banning practices like abortion, pornography, and blasphemy, and for using national power to enforce these moral standards. Figures like the "Christian Prince" or a hypothetical "Protestant Franco" are sometimes mentioned as potential solutions to present challenges. Like these younger Christians enthusiastic for a return to Christian political principles, I also believe in policies that restore God as the moral center of the nation and reinforce the divine order He established. To add to the list of issues: I also have conservationist concerns about ways we might be physically damaging the world God gave us through disruptive environmental practices like the overuse of plastics. While it would be great to see Christian priorities carried out on a national level, it is important to note that Christians can pursue many of their admirable goals on the local level with fewer resources and more chances for success.

While I deeply appreciate the willingness to take bold actions to protect what is good, true, and beautiful, I do not want to stray too

---

[17] For further reading on this I recommend *Is Davis A Traitor* by Albert Taylor Bledsoe. Jefferson Davis was never tried for treason, but if he had been, this book contains the legal defense regarding the permissibility of secession that Davis's lawyer would have made.

far from the principles that have shaped America. One of those principles is the genius of our federal system. The structure of government may be less important than the values it upholds, but I believe the local level should be a priority. The high-trust society that once thrived in small-town America is something I want to preserve. This may require more heavy-handed measures to address challenges that threaten order in high crime areas or protect the country's sovereignty against globalist forces. However, if there is a way to restore and protect the high-trust communities that still exist—by reducing government interference and allowing these communities to govern themselves—this would be ideal. Returning to a more federal arrangement seems like the most practical path to achieve this and one we can appeal to even when we are playing defense. At the very least, it is worth consideration.

Personal Conduct

Charting a path forward for individuals, families, and the social institutions they are part of on a small scale is challenging, given the abundance of valuable ideas on the subject. To focus my recommendations, I would like to highlight a few key areas related to spiritual, mental, and physical health. Each of these areas is interconnected, and modern Americans, including professing Christians, are by-and-large lacking in all of them. Simply put, people today tend to be less disciplined, more fragile, and less stable than they were in America's past. This is even more reinforced in my mind as I grew up hearing stories of strength and valor from the Greatest Generation. It is often said that today's generation could not have won WWII—and I tend to agree. Our capacity for sacrifice and solidarity has diminished, and I believe disorder on the home front has much to do with it. But by God's grace, this can be reversed.

I want to emphasize first and foremost that if you are reading this book and you do not know where you will spend eternity, you are already on unstable footing, even if you are physically capable. The Apostle Paul wrote to his younger protégé Timothy that "bodily discipline is only of little profit, but godliness is profitable for all things, since it holds promise for the present life and also for the life to come."[18] This does not mean that you cannot behave in orderly ways in other areas of life simply because you are disordered spiritually, but it certainly does not help.

Unbelieving fathers who "know how to give good gifts to [their] children," are concerned with the welfare of their families, and generally provide for their homes.[19] But they are still unbelieving. They may possess certain natural instincts that accomplish earthly good, but they are not capable of accomplishing heavenly good that pleases God. This means they do not "have the Spirit of Christ" or "belong to Him."[20] Scripture teaches that the consequences for sinful thoughts and actions is eternal separation from God in hell.[21] God is holy and just and can therefore not abide sin in His presence. If He were to simply overlook violations of His law, He would cease to be a righteous God. Therefore, in order for Him to remain just while still punishing the sin committed by man, He sent the second person of the Trinity, Jesus Christ, to become a man, to take the sins of His people onto Himself, and to pay the penalty God required of sinful humans. This is the message of the Christian gospel—that despite our sins, God made a way to be forgiven through the death of His Son.[22] Paul wrote that God "made Him who knew no sin to be sin on our behalf, so that we might become the righteousness of God in Him."[23]

Someone can be strong physically, right politically, or culturally enriching, which are all wonderful things, but still be on their way to everlasting judgement. I want to see a return to culturally Christian norms, but I do not believe this kind of recovery is possible, and would have little interest in it, if it did not result in more people knowing God through Christ. Part of my interest in preserving cultural Christianity is not just maintaining a safe and beautiful

---

[18] 1 Tim 4:8
[19] Matt 7:11, Luke 16:27, 1 Tim 5:8
[20] Is 64:6, Rom 8:8, 9.
[21] Rom 6:23, 2 Thess 1:8-9, 1 John 5:1
[22] Rom 2:5-8, John 3:16-17, Eph 5:7
[23] 2 Cor 5:21

society for my children, although that plays into it strongly. It is also to ensure there is a constant public reminder that God is just and Christ is merciful. The two go together. This is what I think of when I see "In God We Trust" signs in courtrooms, hear church bells or invocations at civic ceremonies, pass by Christmas trees and manger scenes in public, and so forth. These things are not just part of our birthright as Americans—they are signs that point to something greater.

As we seek to restore a worthwhile earthly citizenship, let us not as Christians forget to beckon all men to enjoy the heavenly citizenship God has for those who love Him. The more people who truly love God there are in a country, the better the morals of its citizens and the greater the capacity for establishing an ordered liberty. Even if many churches seem to imply that one's spiritual journey ends when one is reconciled to God through Christ, this is in fact the beginning of a sanctification process whereby the Holy Spirit assists believers in carrying out moral imperatives that truly do please God.[24] This is the fulfillment of a Christian's purpose on this earth, according to Paul, who declared, "For we are His workmanship, created in Christ Jesus for good works, which God prepared beforehand so that we would walk in them."[25] If we as patriotic Americans want sensible, righteous, and godly citizenry, we should support efforts to convert souls to faith in Jesus and to walk with Him. We should also wisely steward the bodies and minds He gave us.

Although bodily discipline is not directly profitable for the life to come, it is nonetheless profitable for temporal life. The Bible repeatedly references the importance of physical health and its connection to spirituality. Proverbs 3:7-8 says that humility and righteousness are "healing to your body." The Proverbs 31 woman is girded with strength, as evidenced by her strong arms.[26] The Bible also emphasizes the physical strength of some of David's mighty men, who could "handle a large shield and spear" and were "swift as the gazelles

---

[24] Gal 5:16-17
[25] Rom 8:29, Eph 2:10, 2 Cor 7:1
[26] Prov 31:17

on the mountains."[27] In addition, the Apostle John prayed that his friend Gaius would "be in good health" and Paul gave medical advice.[28] To think the authors of Scripture were unconcerned with physical health is to ignore what the Bible teaches.

It should go without saying that unwise lifestyle choices lead to sinful habits, and sinful habits lead to physical weakness. Proverbs 1:32 is correct in stating that "the waywardness of the naive will kill them, and the complacency of fools will destroy them." The reality is that people trust themselves too much. Scripture calls this pride. We often believe we are able to handle things like mind-numbing drugs, technology that triggers dopamine, and junk food. The evidence suggests that we cannot. All around us are strategies and programs for fighting gambling, screen, sex, alcohol, and drug addictions. One does not need to be a Christian or religious to notice how threatened our civilization is by the wasted time, compulsive immaturity, and irresponsibility that these lifestyle habits produce. While this book is not intended to be a guide to recovery, I do want to point people in the right direction.

First, Scripture links the new identity a Christian receives upon conversion with their aversion to sin. Christians are instructed to see themselves as "alive to God," "obedient children," and "new creature[s]" who are no longer characterized by sinful behavior.[29] This does not mean they never sin, nor does it mean they can attain perfection this side of heaven. But it does mean that sin is no longer part of who they see themselves as. Their desires have changed in such a way that they long to please God. This makes sinful actions undesirable. I often think that Christians who lack resistance to sinful habits have trouble upstream realizing who they are. They are like the man James described as looking in a mirror and forgetting just "what kind of person he was."[30] It is important to know who you are first as the motivation behind your actions.

This would also apply to natural identities like being a boss,

---

[27] 1 Chron 12:8
[28] 3 John 1:2, 1 Timothy 5:23
[29] Rom 6:11, 1 Pet 1:14-16, 2 Cor 5:17
[30] James 1:23-24

parent, sibling, or citizen. No matter who someone is, they have responsibilities to God and others which should limit choices that get in the way of those responsibilities. The drug addict who unexpectedly gets pregnant should change her lifestyle whether she is a Christian or not, simply because of her identity as a mother. A government official should not receive bribes, because part of who they are should be serving their constituents' best interests and not special interests. Remembering who Americans are as a people who sailed oceans, won wars, and survived depressions should translate into a national character of independence and bravery. Visualizing who you are, and aiming to be the best version of that person, goes a long way in adjusting your habits.

Second, this means that simply stopping habits that disconnect you from God and others is not enough. They must be replaced by something. Paul repeatedly emphasized the importance of replacing old ways of life with better new ones. In Ephesians 4:22-24 he put it this way: "Lay aside the old self, which is being corrupted . . . [and] be renewed in the spirit of your mind, and put on the new self, which in the likeness of God has been created in righteousness and holiness of the truth." Paul then gave a list of specific examples of what this should look like, which included things like former liars telling the truth, former thieves sharing with others, and filthy talk giving way to thanksgiving. The passage culminates with replacing drunkenness with being filled with the Holy Spirit.[31] Modern examples could include things like volunteering for a charity instead of doom scrolling, or investing in proximate relationships instead of achievements on video games.

Healthy habits can be difficult at first, but it is more difficult to live without them and suffer the consequences to body and soul. I would suggest taking inventory of your life, assessing your goals, and thinking through who you are and who you want to be. Let your goals then drive you to concrete actions. Things like getting sleep, connecting with God, exercising, and eating right should be

---

[31] Eph 4:25-5:18

non-negotiable. They may look slightly different for different people, but they are foundational for basic functioning, handling the trials of life, and standing ready to help others.

This leads me to a growing concern I have over personal habits related to entertainment and vocabulary. What some may consider to be inconsequential compared with the obvious problems we face as a people, I believe to be symptoms of an underlying problem that will jeopardize our gains should we let it fester. Those who fight for public order should exemplify personal order. Younger conservatives, as evident by the "trad wife" and "manosphere" movements, are waking up to the importance of home life, physical health, and mental acuity, but they do not seem to have a problem with perverse language and raunchy entertainment.

Despite having less intercourse on average, our society is over-sexualized to the point that nearly every interaction can be thought of in sexual terms. We live in a world similar to how Paul described Cretans in Titus 1:15: "To the pure, all things are pure; but to those who are defiled and unbelieving, nothing is pure, but both their mind and their conscience are defiled." The distinction between sacred and profane has been all but eliminated, one dirty joke, one irrelevant mock, and one racy image at a time. One 2024 *Daily Mail* headline read that "up to half of all porn consumed in US is 'family themed.'"[32] The taboos surrounding sexuality are disintegrating, as are the boundaries concerning violence.

I remember attending the premiere of the PG-13 movie *The Fellowship of the Ring* in 2001. Toward the end of the film there is a scene showing Aragorn, one of the heroes, decapitating an ugly creature called an Uruk-hai. It was violent, but not gruesome by modern standards. The surprised audience let out a corporate gasp at the sight. Twelve years later, I sat in a theater not far away from where I had seen *The Fellowship of the Ring*. This time it was to see *The Hobbit: The Desolation of Smaug*, part of the same franchise. A

[32] Luke Andrews Senior, "Experts Slam America's 'Grim Fascination with Incest,'" *Mail Online*, March 29, 2024, https://www.dailymail.co.uk/health/article-13227585/experts-slam-americas-incest-obsession-family-themed-porn.html.

similar scene where an elf decapitates an Orc, showing his squirming body on the ground, elicited a corporate laugh from the audience instead of a gasp. The difference thirteen years made surprised me and it would be foolish to think that even though I did not laugh, this change has not also had an effect on me.

In a world of cheap sex and meaningless life, we should be the people who prize both. For most, this includes getting married and raising children, staying away from environmental hazards that threaten fertility, and doing what is possible to criminalize abortion and euthanasia. But it also means we should be concerned about what we consume and what we say. Jesus said the "mouth speaks from that which fills his heart," and the Bible has much to say about guarding the tongue.[33]

My concern is not so much with what we say, but why we say it. Symbols, terms, and fashions do change, and there is a traditional cultural element that accompanies many of our mores. Why are some words appropriate to describe a body part when others are not? Often, we do not remember. But in many cases there was a reason, and it is still reflected in public sensitivities regarding private matters. Maintaining a hierarchy of intimacy is important. A husband is able to talk to his wife about certain matters in ways another man should not. Men should not always talk the way they do with each other in mixed audiences. There is an added reverence for the kind of conversations that are appropriate within certain institutions like court buildings and churches.

The spirit today that concerns me, even among younger and middle-age conservatives, is a cavalier transgressive penchant for breaking standards simply to break them. Using language that upsets the old folks simply because it upsets them is a form of rebellion. There are plenty of good things to rebel against, unhealthy choices being one, but this should not be mixed in with rebellion against the ways older generations upheld valuable separations that younger people seem to disregard. A pastor who wants to talk from the pulpit about

---

33 Luke 6:45

his favorite curse word or a Christian college that wants to appropriate the middle finger as a way to supposedly oppose evil is simply left looking like a sheltered child who smirks the first time he uses a "bad word."[34]

There is nothing impressive or bold about upsetting the few traditionalists who are likely to get riled up by such a display. It just looks immature because it is. It accomplishes nothing more than subverting the very thing Christians and conservatives should be interested in doing: upholding godly standards. It also reveals the extent to which someone's mind has been exposed to such behavior, to the point that it is normalized.

The solution is not to become prudish about every minute detail one sees or hears. But there is a general caution one should have over who they spend time with, the entertainment choices they consume, and the kind of speech they use. Rather than obsessing about negative standards, i.e. what kinds of things one should not say or see, it is wise in personal conduct to follow Scripture's advice to seek a higher road. Paul gives an affirming standard for speech in Ephesians 4:29, which states, "Let no unwholesome word proceed from your mouth, but only such a word as is good for edification according to the need of the moment, so that it will give grace to those who hear." Another affirming standard for what believers should allow themselves to consume is in Philippians 4:8-9, which includes things that are honorable, pure, and praiseworthy. If something is consumed or said that does not meet this affirming standard—which matches the identity we ought be cultivating as Christians, gentlemen, or ladies—it is better left unwatched, unheard, or unsaid.

In conclusion, I urge you to engage in voluntary organizations, community efforts, meaningful hobbies, and, especially, church activities. It has been said that "a land without memories is a people without liberty." The ordered liberty that Christian conservatives seek will not emerge from a vacuum. It must be nurtured through

---

[34] Tullian Tchividjian on Instagram: "Why the Word 'Goddammit' Is My Favorite Cuss Word #prayer," 2024, https://www.instagram.com/reel/DAj_shwJelB/; *Wanted* (New Saint Andrews College, 2024), https://www.youtube.com/watch?v=qivXrESLO_U.

shared experiences. As people come together and develop ways of living in community, they become better equipped to withstand the threats posed by globalists, centralizers, and transhumanists. United by common purpose and history, they form a resilient bond that strengthens their collective identity.

Without genuine interaction, there can be no localism, no special places, and no real community worth protecting. As automation advances, social interaction becomes more of a choice than a necessity. While some tasks can be outsourced, a sense of togetherness cannot be. Often those who isolate themselves through technology are surprised at how much better they feel when they break free from their screen addictions. It is as if they have carried a burden they did not know existed, only to find it lifted and realize that this, truly, is the way life is meant to be lived.

I want you to live life to the fullest and then live forever with Christ. This life prepares us for the one to come, and in order to live this life we must regain a sense of reality. We must appreciate nature and reconnect ourselves to friendship and community. We must take our responsibilities seriously and reject philosophies that erase our obligations and attack the basis for our shared loves. We must wield power to meet threats, cultivate virtuous leaders, and restore masculinity to its proper place. Ultimately, we must reflect the divine order which teaches us something about the heavenly order to come.

19

WILL AMERICA EXPERIENCE A NATIONAL REVIVAL?

The answer to militant godlessness is militant godliness.

Leonard Ravenhill

As both the government and broader society become increasingly hostile toward basic morality, and as rising paganism penetrates into even fly-over country, it is natural to question whether Christian America is like the Old South, gone with the wind. Perhaps it is. Once a distinctly Protestant nation, the country evolved to be simply Christian, then Judeo-Christian, and now it seems to be a pluralist mix, especially in urban areas.

Yet America has seen times of genuine renewal in the past, such as during the Great Awakening or the Civil War, when thousands of people repented of their sins and came to a saving knowledge of Christ. Could we be on the brink of another Christian revival? To explore this question, it is important to consider how some modern influential Christians have incorrectly approached it, the nature of America's corporate relationship to God, and the current spiritual climate. While Christian media sometimes uses overly optimistic language on this topic, there really are compelling reasons to remain cautiously hopeful that a revival can take place.

THE RELIGIOUS RIGHT'S REVIVAL THAT NEVER WAS

From the 1980s through the early 2000s, many Religious Right leaders predicted Americans would eventually return to Christianity. I remember in my mid-teens hearing popular speaker David Barton tell an audience in Albany, NY, that despite moral and legislative set-backs, America was on the cusp of a national revival. One of his reasons for thinking this was an apparent increase in pro-life sentiment among young people. Republican politicians like Paul Ryan and Ted Cruz echoed this sentiment, claiming a pro-life momentum in the upcoming generation.[1] Of course, today, any increased support that may have existed has largely disappeared. Pew Research recently reported that "among adults under age 30, 76% say abortion should be legal in all or most cases."[2] Yet Christian Conservatives still sometimes appeal to the "pro-life generation" narrative as a sign of hope for the future.[3]

As America continues to move away from Christianity, the old guard of the Religious Right has increasingly searched for indications of a return to what they perceive as a Christian America. In 2023, Religious Right leaders like Michelle Bachmann, David Barton, and even Mormon Glenn Beck participated in "a civil 're-covenanting ceremony' where essentially, America remarries God."[4] This and other similar events assume America shares the kind of national relationship that God had with Israel throughout the Old Testament.

---

[1] *We Are the Pro-Life Generation*, 2016, https://www.youtube.com/watch?v=PZEx3NQzc1s; *Ted Cruz: This Is Most Pro-Life Generation* (MSNBC, 2016), https://www.youtube.com/watch?v=lZhOzTXecGI.

[2] "Public Opinion on Abortion," *Pew Research Center*, May 13, 2024, https://www.pewresearch.org/religion/fact-sheet/public-opinion-on-abortion/.

[3] For example: *Emotional Connection Forms A Pro-Life Generation* (Standing for Freedom Center, 2023), https://www.youtube.com/shorts/JLG0teqSD8U.

[4] "Declaration – First Landing 1607," accessed September 9, 2024, https://firstlanding1607.com/declaration/; This event assumed Rev. Robert Hunt dedicated America to God in 1607 in a covenant which promised to "take the kingdom of God to all the earth." In my research I could not locate a primary source for this covenant, although the language appears in the 2023 "Declaration of Covenant" and other Christian websites.

America's decline is a result of turning away from God, but if the country follows His laws again, He will restore it to a place of blessing. Like ancient Israel in her captivity and punishments, America will also remember her first love after times of trial and testing.

PROPHETS OF DOOM

Christian political leaders who anticipate this kind of revival seem to believe it will come through a collective moral awareness as a result of their efforts. They see themselves and their organizations as modern-day prophets, akin to Nehemiah rebuilding Jerusalem, Elijah in the wilderness, or Daniel in Babylon. They function as representatives of their people before God and of God before their people. At the same time, evangelical church leaders have moved leftward to incorporate liberal and social justice ideas. They view themselves as prophetic, yet they criticize the Religious Right for its political focus, particularly its support for the Republican Party. Donald Trump's presidential campaigns have escalated tensions between these groups, yet both of them make similar mistakes regarding America's relationship to God.

Both groups seem to believe that America has a covenantal relationship with God accompanied by a divinely appointed purpose. They also hold that the country's blessings are contingent upon its obedience to Him. The Religious Right focuses on issues like abortion and family values, while the evangelical Left emphasizes support for migrants and expanding women's roles. Despite their different priorities, both also believe their efforts will help America avoid judgement and find spiritual restoration.

Richard Mouw, a founding father of progressive evangelicalism, encouraged readers of *Christianity Today* to pursue a theocratic national order marked by pluralism.[5] Adam Russell Taylor, the president of *Sojourner's* magazine, wrote a piece claiming "the U.S. isn't a 'chosen nation,'" yet ironically he still thinks people should work

---

[5] Richard Mouw, "Theocracy Is Not the Enemy of Pluralism," *Christianity Today*, July 3, 2024, https://www.christianitytoday.com/2024/07/mouw-theocracy-is-not-enemy-of-pluralism/.

to make the United States' ideals of equality a reality for everyone.[6] While evangelicals on the Left tend to reject the "Christian nation" idea in favor of pluralism, they still adopt a spiritual view of what they think America's divine mission is.

THE AMERICAN COVENANT?

But unlike Israel, America does not possess a divine mission to show-case God's justice and redemption as a "light to the nations."[7] Neither is God obligated to fulfill a covenantal agreement with America that guarantees blessings for obedience and curses for disobedience. In the Old Testament, God treated other nations differently from the Israelites. Although He judged their sins, He also allowed them periods of prosperity in order to fulfill special purposes such as with Babylon in Jeremiah 25. God also rarely sent prophets to pagan nations and sometimes completely wiped them out in judgement. In contrast, He gave Israel swift judgment for sin, sent prophets to them as a sign of mercy, and offered them the promise of a lasting existence.

Evangelical elites on both sides of the political divide often see America in the similar way. They view the country as a perpetual union enjoying an ongoing connection to God despite sinful behavior. They believe He sends prophetic figures like Abraham Lincoln or Martin Luther King Jr. to address wrongdoing and bring blessings. For them, America's wrongs aren't just violations of a moral order, but are actually betrayals of a unique spiritual identity. Just as God gave Israel specific civil and ceremonial laws to highlight their special status as His chosen people, America must be inclusive and reject its bigotries. Leaders on both the Religious Right and the evangelical Left treat attitudes of racism and materialism as breaches of a sacred pact belonging chiefly to their country.

However, while the United States was birthed under Christian

---

6   Adam Russell Taylor, "The U.S. Isn't a 'Chosen Nation.' But Christians Can Still Be Patriotic," *Sojourners*, September 5, 2024, https://sojo.net/articles/opinion/us-isnt-chosen-nation-christians-can-still-be-patriotic.
7   Is 49:6-7, 51:4.

assumptions and has enjoyed a great deal of prosperity, these things do not mean it is "chosen" in the same sense as Israel. Any country that follows the proverbial truths contained in Scripture can generally expect a good result. Proverbs 13:34 says, "Righteousness exalts a nation, but sin is a disgrace to any people." God also generally punished nations for their wickedness.[8] So Christians should uphold moral standards and advance themselves politically. God can and does use these efforts to punish evil and promote good. But this should be done with a proper understanding and expectation.

When Ben Carson told the RNC that the promise from Isaiah 54:17, that "no weapon that is formed against you will prosper," applied to President Trump's survival of an assassination attempt, he applied a specific promise to America that was originally given to Israel.[9] When Raphael Warnock told the DNC that Kamala Harris would "heal the land" from "anti-democratic forces" and "Donald Trump," who he claimed threatened the progressive values of the "American Covenant," he also applied language traditionally associated with Israel to the American context. This common prophetic sentiment goes beyond mere imagery. There are people who really do view, beyond the obvious displays of providence and self-preservation, a special chosenness and divine destiny that lies under spiritual threat from political opponents. However, even if this were the case, why should current Christian leaders think they are the ones to restore America spiritually?

REVIVAL FROM THE OUTSIDE

I grew up listening to Religious Right leaders lament Christians' lack of participation in government. This was, and still is, a valid concern. But often their critique focused on the compromised American church. Progressive evangelicals bemoaned the same problem, except they thought conservatives who were involved in politics

---

8 Jer 18:7-8, 25:12-25.
9 *"No Weapon Formed against You Shall Prosper."–Isaiah 54:17 Donald J. Trump Is Alive and Well, Standing Firm to Be Our next President of the United States of America!*, accessed September 12, 2024, https://www.facebook.com/reel/511437397907070.

had nefarious intentions. For the Religious Right, churches are by and large anemic and pietistic. For the evangelical Left, churches are mostly controlled by Pharisees. Both groups tend to signal the need for church revival before political success. But did it occur to them that well-funded parachurch organizations integrated into Christianity's leadership class are more often products of the church establishment than they are prophetic voices to it?

Throughout the New Testament and church history, times of spiritual conversion or revival were often led by outsiders. None of Jesus' twelve disciples possessed a position in Israel's or Rome's religious hierarchy. Neither St. Patrick nor St. Boniface occupied priestly roles in the countries they reached with the gospel. The Protestant Reformers similarly reformed the church from the outside. Today's class of institutional theologians, celebrity pastors, and political figures can hardly say the same.

They might find it useful to position themselves as outsiders, but this is mostly for branding purposes. If the American church were really as corrupt as insiders like Russell Moore say it is, such as in his 2023 book *Losing Our Religion: An Altar Call for Evangelical America*, then he should not expect revival to come from the influential evangelical organizations he helped shape, such as The Southern Baptist Theological Seminary, The Ethics and Religious Liberty Commission, and *Christianity Today*. Yet it has been in Christian institutions and with their blessing that he has acted in what he considers to be a "prophetic" capacity.[10]

BUILDING FROM SQUARE ONE

More importantly, fewer Americans are now even passively aware of Christianity, and unlike in Israel's past, there is no covenantal continuity or special national identity to tap into. Many influential parts of America have severed their connection to Christianity in ways

---

[10] In Russell Moore's 2015 book *Onward: Engaging the Culture Without Losing the Gospel*, he argues forcefully for Christians to "be prophetic" just like their "forebears in the abolitionist and civil rights and pro-life activist communities." See: Russell Moore, *Onward: Engaging the Culture Without Losing the Gospel* (B&H Publishing Group, 2015), 46.

that prevent a restoration. The popular church is also theologically weak to the point that only a tiny fraction of self-proclaimed believers hold to basic Christian beliefs.[11] In other words, most people will need to discover Christianity for the first time.

The fascinating thing is some people are discovering the Faith, and they're doing it apart from institutional Christianity. After 2020, a growing group of mostly disaffected secular liberals have moved toward the political Right as they rethink their guiding assumptions. This "red-pilled" experience has brought with it a renewed interest in religion. *The Wall Street Journal* published a headline in December, 2024 that "Sales of Bibles Are Booming, Fueled by First-Time Buyers and New Versions." Many recent high profile expressions of curiosity in or conversion to Christianity are also happening in ways that are completely outside the boundaries of elite evangelical influence.

In 2023, JP Sears, a successful internet comedian, announced his own journey from skeptic to embracing God and religion due to the obvious evil he sensed in the world around him. That same year, celebrity tattoo artist Kat Von D renounced witchcraft, converted to Christianity, and got baptized at a small Baptist church in Indiana where she sings in the choir. In 2024, British celebrity Russell Brand, who participated in Transcendental Meditation and was known for his hedonistic lifestyle, announced his own conversion to Christianity and subsequent baptism. This accompanied growing skepticism about Covid treatments and government control. Nala Ray, a pornographic actress, also converted to Christianity that year, got baptized, deleted her OnlyFans account, threw out her immodest clothing, and got rid of her signature red hair. More recently, Denzel Washington was baptized, Gwen Stefani publicly announced her intention to pray every day during the Christmas season, and Tim Allen announced he was reading through the Bible for the first time.

Unlike expressions of faith during the Jesus Movement of the 1970s, in the 2020s there is little to gain from saying positive things

[11] George Barna, "American Worldview Inventory 2021" (Cultural Research Center, August 31, 2021), https://www.arizonachristian.edu/wp-content/uploads/2021/08/CRC_AWVI2021_Release06_Digital_01_20210831.pdf.

about Christianity, let alone from converting. Yet more and more, socially influential figures like Joe Rogan and Elon Musk, as well as more conservative political commentators such as Tucker Carlson and Charlie Kirk, are focusing their attention on Christianity. In 2025, Rogan even gave a platform to Wesley Huff, a Christian apologist who rose to prominence by challenging the arguments of modern mystic Billy Carson against Christianity. Notably, no major Christian ministry can claim credit for Huff's emergence. But perhaps no one recent influential figure has championed a pro-religion and pro-Christian message more passionately than Jordan Peterson.

Peterson has profoundly influenced young men to view religion as a meaningful framework. His 2017 lectures on Genesis attracted millions of views. I myself know a former atheist who abandoned his atheism after listening to them. However, Peterson's approach to concepts like heaven, hell, and the resurrection differ from Christian interpretations. He views Bible stories, through Jungian psychology, as universal myths that help people understand the world and improve their lives. Although Peterson has not explicitly embraced the gospel or publicly joined a church, he has increasingly started to treat aspects of Christianity like the Resurrection as objectively true.

CONCLUSION

There are various interpretations concerning what may be happening right now. It could simply be that secularism has left people without the moorings necessary to navigate trials and vice. The needs of the moment necessitate a return to religion. Young men are especially yearning for challenge, purpose, and guidance in navigating a world that sees their masculinity as a threat. But as a Christian myself, I cannot help but consider another possibility that may also be true.

Some of this uptick in interest is legitimately resulting in what appear to be fruitful conversions, and every one of those is a special move of God's saving grace. This does not necessarily mean a true revival is around the corner, but it may be—and if it is, I would expect God to work in this way. No Christian organization, celebrity pastor, or Religious Right figure can take credit for what is happening right now. Only God can, and He is described in Scripture as opposing the proud and giving grace to the humble. It also says He "has chosen the weak things of the world to shame the things which are strong."[12] It would be in keeping with His character to choose tax collectors, fisherman, simple monks, and even formerly pagan kings to accomplish His spiritual purposes, rather than those who occupy the chief seats in a compromised religious establishment.

America is not Israel. But God has blessed her in unparalleled ways historically with the light of the gospel, the influence of the church, and a supply of godly men. Americans should agree with George Washington that "it is the duty of all Nations to acknowledge the providence of Almighty God, to obey his will, to be grateful for his benefits, and humbly to implore his protection and favor."[13] Perhaps He is not done with America yet.

---

[12] James 4:6, 1 Cor 1:27.
[13] George Washington, *George Washington Papers, Series 8, Miscellaneous Papers -99, Subseries 8A, Correspondence and Miscellaneous Notes: Correspondence and Miscellaneous Notes, 1773 to 1799. /1799, 1773*, Manuscript/Mixed Material, https://www.loc.gov/item/mgw8a.124/.

APPENDICES

THE RHETORIC OF JESUS

For Christians, conflict with a world-system that opposes Christ is inevitable. Jesus Himself taught, "Blessed are those who have been persecuted for the sake of righteousness," and that "the world has hated [His disciples] because they are not of the world."[1] It should come as no surprise when unbelievers, invested in their sins, see Christians as a threat and seek to suppress them. Because of this, Jesus likened His followers to "sheep in the midst of wolves."[2] Given this reality, it is crucial for believers to heed Jesus' instruction to be "shrewd as serpents and innocent as doves." In such adversarial circumstances, wisdom is essential. Paul further emphasized this by urging Christians to let their speech be "with grace, as though seasoned with salt, so that you will know how you should respond."[3]

Sadly, many professing believers interpret this as a call for Christians to accept a subordinate role assigned by secular elites, where only their charitable qualities are highlighted, while their more controversial beliefs are suppressed. Christians who accept these terms promote a one-dimensional version of Jesus—one who

---

[1] Matt 5:10, John 17:14
[2] Matt 10:16
[3] Col 4:5-6

invites children to come to Him and preaches "Blessed are the peacemakers," but avoids overturning tables and engaging in direct confrontation with His enemies. On the other hand, a smaller minority of self-identified Christians, often ripe for media attention, reject this posturing. They engage in what can only be described as aggressive denunciations, yet these are often devoid of any persuasive substance.

Understanding how Jesus treated those who vigorously opposed Him, particularly the Pharisees, is crucial for modern Christians seeking guidance on how to respond to threats from their social enemies. However, Jesus' approach to His opponents should not be seen as a one-size-fits-all strategy for every situation. He made clear distinctions between the leaders of the religious establishment who opposed Him and those who blindly followed it. Jesus resisted the proud while extending grace to the humble, even patiently teaching Nicodemus, a member of the Pharisees. In this, Jesus perfectly exemplified the pattern outlined in 1 Thessalonians 5:14: "Admonish the unruly, encourage the fainthearted, help the weak, [and] be patient with everyone."

As a result, Jesus knew His audience and treated them like people. He did not win arguments for the purpose of vain self-promotion, but did so because of an awareness of those listening who would benefit and whose condition He could lift to a higher understanding of truth. He listened to His opponents' arguments and crafted statements that suited them. He was able to identify root issues and admonish in measured ways that fit the circumstances. In short, if the purpose of rhetoric is to "perfect men by showing them better versions of themselves, links in that chain extending up toward the ideal," as Richard Weaver taught, then Jesus was the perfect rhetorician.[4]

It is long overdue for modern Christians to move beyond a cherry-picked version of Jesus who exists solely to passively serve humanity, and instead to fully embrace the complete picture of

---

4   Richard Weaver, *The Ethics of Rhetoric* (Echo Point Books & Media, 2015), 158.

Jesus—the one who confronts the ideas and enemies that oppress our neighbors. This is a vital part of loving those around us, and Jesus did not suspend His work of loving others when He engaged with the Pharisees. Christians who are active in modern social and political struggles should look to Jesus as their example if they hope to be successful. In this spirit, here are seven ways Jesus handled His major opponents, the Pharisees.

1. DO NOT TAKE QUESTIONS AT FACE VALUE

First, Jesus, did not take their questions at face value. Matthew 22 recounts the Pharisees' plot to trap Jesus "in what He said" and thus discredit Him. It is worth mentioning that the Herodians, a sect loyal to King Herod and opposed to the Pharisees' political interests, found common cause with this attempt to discredit Jesus. This means these were not simply religious disputes but also featured a political dimension. In order to accomplish their purpose, the Pharisees, along with the Herodians, asked Jesus if it was "lawful to give a poll-tax to Caesar."

This put Jesus on the horns of a dilemma. If He were to say it was lawful to pay the tax, then He would offend those opposed to Roman rule and undermine the claim that He was in fact the Messiah with the authority to overthrow Rome. If He were to say it was not lawful, then He would be in trouble with the Roman authorities. What Jesus said in response amazed His audience.

Instead of accepting the terms of the challenge, Jesus impugned the motives of those asking the question, challenged the premise of it, and took an offensive posture against their hypocrisy. He said, "'Why are you testing Me, you hypocrites? Show Me the coin used for the poll-tax.' And they brought Him a denarius. And He said to them, 'Whose likeness and inscription is this?' They said to Him, 'Caesar's.' Then He said to them, 'Then render to Caesar the things that are Caesar's and to God the things that are God's.'"

Many of today's Christians cite this passage as evidence that Christians should leave politics to unbelievers, but the reality is that Jesus was engaged in politics. He publicly pointed out that two politically motivated groups failed to live up to their own standards by not serving the God they claimed to worship. While operating within and benefitting from Caesar's economic system, they neglected to align themselves with God's moral order. Jesus anticipated their trap and turned the tables, putting them on trial instead of Himself, because He refused to accept their question at face value.

Modern Christians would do well to likewise anticipate traps from their own political enemies, such as when media members ask questions like, "Why do you hate women?" or "How can you believe in a religion that supports some form of evil?" Christians would do well to suppress the urge to prove themselves worthy of the media's standard and instead ask questions that challenge the liberal philosophy.

2. CHOOSE THE RIGHT SETTING

Another aspect of Jesus' shrewd dealings with the Pharisees was His discernment in choosing the right conditions for engagement. There is a mistaken perception among some segments of the dissident Right that conflict should never be avoided. While in an ultimate sense this can be valid—the truth is worth defending and only cowards shy away from it—there should also be wisdom in choosing the right setting for certain conflicts. There are numerous examples of this from Jesus' ministry.

In John 7:1, we learn that Jesus "was unwilling to walk in Judea because the Jews were seeking to kill Him." His brothers, who did not anticipate the threat, encouraged Him to go to Judea and attend the Feast of Booths. Rather than going with them, Jesus suggested they go ahead, creating the impression that He would not attend the feast. However, once the feast began, Jesus showed up unnoticed in the temple and began teaching. By doing so, He avoided the risk of being confronted with a small group entering the city, and instead revealed Himself within the safety of the crowd. This strategic move meant that if the Jews who sought to kill Him were to act, they would have to do so in full view of everyone—something they were unwilling to do. Jesus did not avoid conflict, but He did choose the ground on which He was willing to fight.

Jesus did something similar in Luke 4. After informing members of the synagogue in His hometown of Nazareth that He would not perform miracles there because of their lack of faith, it says they "were filled with rage" and attempted to "throw Him down [a] cliff." Yet as they tried to carry out their plan and chase Him out of the synagogue, the text says that "passing through their midst, He went His way." Jesus' evasive behavior did not reflect cowardice. What He said to offend them had already demonstrated His own bravery, yet this fortitude was mixed with another cardinal virtue—prudence.

It is worth noting that not only did Jesus avoid unwanted conflicts, but He also chose conflicts He wanted. He could have avoided conflicts with the scribes, Pharisees, and Herodians by not healing on the Sabbath. Yet He did so numerous times, even justifying His behavior to them.[5] In Luke 14, He responded to opposition by exposing the fact that the spiritual shepherds of Israel cared more about their own livestock than they did the people under their care. He challenged: "Which one of you will have a son or an ox fall into a well, and will not immediately pull him out on a Sabbath day?" Scripture records that "they could make no reply to this."

Modern Christians should carefully consider the controversial situations they enter, especially when they have a choice. Not every challenge is worth accepting, as some can place participants at a significant disadvantage. For example, think about how media outlets can edit interview footage to make someone appear to have said something they did not. Allowing bad-faith actors to control one's public image is unwise. There are times when a disagreement is necessary, but not in a context where social etiquette gives an unfair advantage to Christianity's enemies. Often, a certain level of decorum is expected within one's home or public forum that limits the ability to take a more aggressive stance. Personally, I have learned to be cautious about whom I invite on my podcast for this

---

5 Mark 3:1–6, Luke 6:6–10; 13:10–17; 14:1–6; John 5:1–18

reason. There are many people I would happily debate, but only in a neutral setting. Additionally, it's important to consider the terms of a debate. A challenger may appear to act in good faith but have ulterior motives, such as attempting to smear a Christian's reputation rather than engage in meaningful discussion. Choosing the right setting is crucial.

3. Use Coded Language at Times

It is no secret that the media frequently accuses conservative politicians of using "dog whistles" to communicate with what they perceive to be as the more nefarious elements of their base. For example, Donald Trump was often accused of signaling support for racists, misogynists, and homophobes, which, more often than not, seemed to imply that he was appealing to conservative Christians, a group the media was intent on unfairly vilifying. I have often thought that the media tends to read motives into people's words that are not there, simply because they and their liberal allies are accustomed to using "dog whistles" to appeal to their own base. They portray their enemies as irredeemably evil, while casting their own nefarious allies as either misunderstood or noble. While there is, of course, a dishonest way to use coded language, there is also an honest way—one that perhaps Christians can learn from.

Jesus often used parables to ensure that the prideful would not understand His message, while the humble would. However, in Matthew 21, Jesus told the Parable of the Wicked Tenants, which the Pharisees seemed to grasp. In the story, a landowner rents his vineyard to vine-growers to produce a profit. When the harvest came, the landowner sent several servants and eventually his son to collect the produce. Each time, the wicked vine-growers killed the messengers. Jesus then asked His audience what the appropriate punishment for the murderers should be, and they responded that the landowner should "bring those wretches to a wretched end" and replace them with righteous vine-growers.

Jesus then linked this story to the messianic Psalm 118, which says,

"The stone which the builders rejected has become the chief corner-stone." For those who were paying attention, the message became clearer. The vine-growers represented Israel's religious leaders who rejected both the prophets and the Messiah. The text notes, "When the chief priests and the Pharisees heard His parables, they understood that He was speaking about them."

Jesus initially exposed the Pharisees in a subtle, indirect manner, using parables and veiled critiques. However, in Matthew 23, just two chapters later, He is very direct and overt in His condemnation of them. This shift reflects the changing nature of Jesus' ministry. As the Pharisees' opportunity to accept Him closed, Jesus began to reveal His true identity more openly. This gradual revelation allowed Jesus to build a case against the Pharisees without unnecessarily provoking them.

Christians living in the modern West must exercise shrewdness in the same way. While they should never shy away from the truth, they are not required to reveal every offensive belief in every situation. Some more radical approaches to online dialogue within certain circles of the chronically online New Christian Right argue that stating the unvarnished truth is always the best response. This may make sense for those with anonymous accounts or individuals who can avoid the consequences of being canceled by the Left, such as those who are self-employed or have little public influence. However, for Christians who are making a significant impact in areas dominated by liberal influence, it is important to carefully consider how overt they should be in expressing all the truths that challenge the world system. In some cases, it may be wiser to express the truth in a more veiled manner. This does not mean failing to challenge incorrect assumptions, but it may mean doing so in a more prudent manner.

4. Shift Conversations

One of Jesus' most admired rhetorical traits was His ability to address the heart of a matter. When a rich young ruler asked Jesus what he must do to "inherit eternal life," instead of presenting the entire gospel message—as many evangelists might do today—Jesus responded with a question: "Why do you call Me good?" He then probed further, asking whether the young man had kept God's commandments. The brilliance of this approach lay in how it allowed Jesus to identify the man's idol—his wealth—and reveal what was truly preventing him from inheriting eternal life. The young man's issue wasn't that he did not understand God's requirements, but that he refused to place his faith in God, choosing instead to rely on his riches.

This ability to shift a conversation from what someone may want to discuss to what truly matters is also evident in Jesus' encounters with the Pharisees. In Mark 2, Jesus performs one of His early miracles by healing a paralytic. Instead of simply healing him, Jesus first forgives his sins and connects the two actions. This provoked the Pharisees, who accused Him of blasphemy, arguing that only God can forgive sins. Jesus, perceiving their challenge, chose not to directly defend His divinity or His role as the Messiah. Instead, He shifted their focus to the miracle that had just occurred before their eyes. He asked, "Which is easier, to say to the paralytic, 'Your sins are forgiven,' or to say, 'Get up, pick up your pallet and walk'?" This forced the Pharisees to confront the evidence that Jesus was using divine power. It is much easier to claim that someone's sins are forgiven because there is no physical proof to verify it. However, healing someone physically is a tangible act that can be verified— and in Jesus' case, it was.

If Christians today, in a world where Christianity is constantly challenged, could shift conversations toward the evidence that supports the truth of Christianity—or highlight the emptiness of non-Christian religions and philosophies—it could make a significant impact in apologetics. While Christians should always be willing to answer good-faith questions from unbelievers, it is often wise to remind people of what they already know. The rich young ruler knew he was failing to keep God's law, despite initially claiming otherwise. The scribes knew Jesus had healed a man, even though they doubted His ability to forgive sins. Similarly, we should remind unbelievers of what they know: that they live in a world designed by a Creator who has also given them a moral law that they fail to keep.

I recently argued that Christian apologists should be cautious about granting 21st-century egalitarians the moral authority to judge biblical standards. Attempting to prove that women were treated well in the Bible or that biblical slavery aligns with modern concepts of labor arrangements is a losing battle. This becomes even more apparent when trying to reconcile biblical teachings with modern views on sexuality. Instead of engaging in these difficult comparisons, it is more effective to highlight the moral disasters of the modern world, which are often the result of these egalitarian assumptions. From modern forms of slavery, such as civil slavery, debt bondage, generational welfare, pornography addiction, the prison system, and outsourced sweatshop labor, to issues like "transing kids," family breakdown, the opioid crisis, open borders, the murder of children in the womb, euthanasia, and impersonal warfare, there is more than enough moral evil to be concerned with. Christianity, far from being the cause of these problems, offers the solution. It provides a template for the kind of ordered liberty that could help society address these pressing issues.

5. Claim Moral High Ground

In shifting the conversation, Jesus often claimed the moral high ground. Again, early in Jesus' ministry in Mark 2, the scribes and Pharisees challenged Jesus for eating with sinners and tax collectors who were social outcasts. (Perhaps a modern equivalent of a social outcast, contrary to how most modern pastors interpret the world, would be sharing a meal with perceived racists and misogynists, not guys with tattoos and prostitutes). Jesus responded to their challenge by questioning their care for sinners. He said, "It is not those who are healthy who need a physician, but those who are sick; I did not come to call the righteous, but sinners." This exposed how the Pharisees failed to take care of the spiritually sick under their charge. When all they saw was the association Jesus had, they failed to recognize the reason for that association, which was to accomplish the moral duty of helping those who needed help.

Christians today can use this tactic to expose their political enemies. Often those who operate in the political sphere with Christian values are accused of failing to care for the poor or another aggrieved group. This is often linked to whether or not they support a certain government policy. For example, caring about the poor must include allowing unvetted migrants to cross the border illegally and consume resources not belonging to them. Yet the same people who often make this policy claim refuse to allow these poor individuals into their communities. When Governor Ron DeSantis symbolically sent a bus of illegal migrants to Martha's Vineyard in 2022, and they were summarily sent to other places, it exposed the fact that the same class of people clamoring for others to receive these people were unwilling to do it themselves. This, in essence, was a way for more conservative minded Americans to claim the moral high ground as they were trying to solve the policy problem.

Similar parallels can be seen in other moral issues such as abortion. While those who support abortion claim they are concerned about unwanted children, Christians are engaged in helping adopt these children and supporting policies that make raising children easier. This is morally preferable to killing a child before they have the opportunity to live. The bottom line is that those who hate Christianity and claim the moral high ground do not possess such a position, and Christians should not go into discussions assuming they do. Instead, Christians should assume that the principles in the Bible on things like natural obligations and punishing murder are true, and as a result they possess the moral high ground.

6. Challenge Unqualified Authority

Related to the last point about claiming the moral high ground is also the instinct Christians should have to challenge unjustified or unqualified authority. My father often says that just because someone has letters after their name does not mean they necessarily know what they are talking about. This instinct has served me remarkably well. I remember a professor from my grad school days taking offense when I affirmed this teaching. However, one conversation with him proved my instincts to be correct. Often, academic experts are only experts in a narrow field. It is rare to find the renaissance man who possesses the wisdom stemming from a wide breadth of knowledge. Sometimes experts in a particular field do not even know what they should know.

Jesus pointed this out in Matthew 12 after the Pharisees tried to use the behavior of His own disciples against Him. They said that it was unlawful for them to pick grain on the Sabbath. In response Jesus directly challenged their understanding of Scripture and the law of God. The disciples were not in violation of Mosaic Law. Rather, they had good precedent in following the example of David, who ate consecrated bread, and the priests themselves, who performed duties on the Sabbath that would qualify as breaking the law if it were to be interpreted according to the Pharisees' logic. The Sabbath did not exist for its own sake as a moral end in itself. Rather, it was intended to facilitate spiritual good for man.[6]

For our purposes, the key portion of this story is what Jesus said in verse 7, "But if you had known what this means, 'I desire compassion, and not sacrifice,' you would not have condemned the innocent." Essentially, Jesus demonstrated that the Pharisees did not understand the very law they claimed to be experts in. Jesus makes a similar case in John 4 when He tells them, "If you believed Moses, you would believe Me, for he wrote about Me."

When a supposed expert opposes Christians or Christianity or Christian principles, but does not know what they are talking about, it is permissible to expose them for this—whether or not they are socially revered. Christians should challenge the claims of scientists, professors, and other alleged experts by discrediting their knowledge in the field if they show themselves to be ignorant. This is not an ad hominem attack. Jesus actually does answer their objection. But He concludes from the nature of their objection that they should not be trusted as experts.

---

6 Mark 2:17.

7. Expose Logical Absurdity

In Mark 3, Jesus demolishes one of the scribes' arguments against Him by showing its fallacy directly. Jesus had recently begun His itinerant ministry, called the twelve disciples, and started healing people and casting out demons. In response, the scribes claimed that He was possessed by Beelzebul, which was a title for Satan meaning "Lord of the Flies," whose power did not come from God but from an evil source.

In response, Jesus asked them a question. "How can Satan cast out Satan?" He then proceeded to expose the absurdity of their claim by using the imagery of a kingdom fighting itself. Satan and his cohort of demons are united in purpose. If they were not, then they would channel their energy into fighting among themselves and would no longer be a threat. By simply taking their challenge to its logical conclusion, Jesus exposed its fallaciousness.

Modern Christians would benefit from learning basic logic, if they have not already. While the Bible is not a logic textbook, there are instances where the Prophets and Apostles employ logical reasoning. Recognizing inconsistencies and absurdities can help believers defend their faith. For instance, when someone argues that being confident in one's ethical beliefs is a sign of arrogance, it can be pointed out that this very argument would be itself arrogant, since the person making the claim is equally confident in their own ethical stance.

In conclusion, Jesus demonstrated an ability to avoid traps, shift the conversation, and discredit His opponents in ways modern Christians do not find natural to themselves. Jesus did not see any conflict between behaving in this manner and loving one's enemy and praying for those who persecute. In fact, it should come naturally for Christians to love others by challenging destructive behavior. This would include exposing those with ill intentions. It is worth noting that Jesus saved His most forceful denunciations for those who used their authority to lead others astray. It is time for modern Christians to do the same.

SAME-SEX ATTRACTION

While there are many examples I could draw on to show how Christians have embraced a false understanding of love that undermines the created order, the soft-peddling of homosexuality is perhaps one of the most subversive and egregious.[1] It has become especially common within evangelical circles to normalize it as a legitimate form of love referred to as same-sex attraction. Christians from earlier generations would have found it unfathomable that their spiritual descendants would use the idea of love to approve of actions that God disapproves of.

Surprisingly, even voices that are generally orthodox seem uncertain about whether experiencing same-sex attraction is sinful. There is often an underlying, uneasy stance that goes something like this: "While having a same-sex orientation or attraction is not sinful in itself, acting on those impulses is." Some thinkers articulate this general framework differently by reducing same-sex attraction to a non-sinful temptation, while conceding that sexual lust or desire for

---

[1] For more concrete examples see: Jared Moore, *The Lust of the Flesh: Thinking Biblically about Sexual Orientation, Attraction, and Temptation* (Free Grace Press, 2023).

those of the same sex is sinful. In either case, the idea of experiencing a non-sinful homosexual inclination—however small—is accepted. Thus, the impression is given that sexual desires in general are amoral.

Some defend this view by grounding the sin of homosexuality in man's choice. They imply that unwanted homosexual desires are not sinful until someone entertains them. However, the Apostle Paul in Romans 7, under the authority of the Holy Spirit, claimed that he did not want his own sinful practices, yet they were still sinful because they missed the mark of God's holy standard.[2] To understand the error baked into this generally accepted teaching on same-sex attraction, one must first understand what Scripture teaches on sinful passion, desire, and temptation and how they deviate from love.

According to the *Theological Wordbook of the New Testament*, the Greek term *Pathos* refers to things like "passion" and "impulse." In all three New Testament uses of the term—in Colossians 3:5, 1 Thessalonians 4:5, and Romans 1:26—it refers to sexual passion.[3] Greek scholar Alexander Stouter describes it as "state or condition" of lust. We get English words like empathy and pathology from this term. It is perhaps the closest approximate language we have approaching what modern people reference when they describe "orientation" (i.e, pathologically experiencing a pattern of attraction).

The Greek word *Epithumia* simply refers to a desire, lust, or craving. *Epithumia* is used in both positive ways and negative ways throughout the New Testament. Paul said his desire in Philippians 1 was to be with Christ, yet in Ephesians 2 the same word is used to refer to sinful desires that invite God's wrath. Both sinful *Pathos* and *Epithumia* are condemned in Romans 1 and Colossians 3:5.

Peirasmos is the word commonly used to refer to temptation in the New Testament. When the Devil tempted Christ in Matthew 4, or when the author of Hebrews stated Christians "do not have a high priest who cannot sympathize with our weaknesses, but One who has been tempted in all things as we are, yet without sin," this

---

2 Rom 7:15-16.
3 Gerhard Kittel, Gerhard Friedrich, and Geoffrey Bromiley, *Theological Dictionary of the New Testament: Abridged in One Volume* (Wm. B. Eerdmans Publishing, 1985), 801.

term constitutes the experience of a sinless person. Therefore, experiencing temptation in itself does not necessarily indicate the internal presence of sin.

However, James 1:13-15 says, "Let no one say when he is tempted, 'I am being tempted by God'; for God cannot be tempted by evil, and He Himself does not tempt anyone. But each one is tempted when he is carried away and enticed by his own lust. Then when lust has conceived, it gives birth to sin; and when sin is accomplished, it brings forth death." According to this passage, the source of temptation to evil is a lust which is present in fallen creatures but not in God. We can conclude that temptation is not the source of sin, but it does expose desires that could be.

At this point it is important to make a distinction theologians make between inner and outer temptation. When Satan tempted Jesus, the appeal was to achieve godly ends in ungodly ways. Jesus only had godly desire, so Satan could not appeal to evil desires resulting from an inner sin nature, or to unnatural desires downstream from previous sinful experience. We could say the same about Adam and Eve before the Fall.

Augustine makes this distinction in *The Confessions* when he tells the story of lusting to "thieve . . . compelled by no hunger, nor poverty, but through a closedness of well-doing, and a pamperedness of iniquity."[4] Proverbs teaches that "men do not despise a thief if he steals to satisfy himself when he is hungry."[5] In contrast, Augustine stole simply to enjoy "the theft and sin itself." Both scenarios illustrate sinful behavior, but of the underlying desires only one is sinful. To desire food is a natural good. According to Jesus, even evil fathers naturally give their son a fish instead of a snake when their son is hungry.[6] Accomplishing good ends through evil means is sin. But accomplishing evil ends through evil means is worse.

This is similar to the situation Romans 1 describes concerning same-sex attraction. Paul highlights this experience as a primary

---

4 Augustine, *The Confessions of St. Augustine*, (P. F. Collier & Son, 1909), 27.
5 Prov 6:30.
6 Matt 7:10-11.

example of both the progression of and judgement for idolatry, the end of which is an "unnatural function." In other words, same-sex attraction serves to illustrate the result of a descent into idolatry in ways that opposite-sex attraction does not.

Before addressing male homosexuality, Paul emphasizes lesbian experience as a way to shock his readers concerning the depths to which idolatrous creature-worship can take people. The chronology of the text teaches that preceding this sinful action are sinful "lusts" and "degrading passions." Preceding them is a previous sinful idolatrous experience. This is wholly different than heterosexual attraction, which humans are naturally designed to experience within the bounds of marriage. Heterosexual attraction is not by definition sinful or resulting from sin, whereas homosexual attraction is always sinful according to Scripture. What is the conclusion then?

According to Scripture, although any erotic attraction outside the covenant of marriage is sinful, same-sex attraction is not in the same category as opposite-sex attraction, because it results from idolatry and its purpose is to achieve unnatural ends. This means that temptation to commit such acts reveal underlying sin. There is no scenario taught in Scripture in which any kind of homosexual yearning is justified. The answer for those who struggle with same-sex attraction—as Paul struggled with the sin he was responsible for but did not want in his mind—is to repent, confess it, resist it, flee it, pursue righteousness, ask God for deliverance, and pursue marriage with a godly person of the opposite sex.[7]

If Christians are struggling to maintain clear boundaries in familial relationships and responsibilities, it is no wonder they also struggle to understand the importance of national duties. True love does not erase legitimate order and hierarchy. Rather, it upholds and reinforces them. God is love, and His will for us is to love others—but that love must align with the order He has established. Otherwise, we risk misdirecting or distorting our duties, loving the wrong things, or failing to love at all.

---

[7] 1 John 1:9, Hebrews 12:4, 2 Ti 2:22, Matt 6:13, 1 Cor 7:2.

THE FALL OF A LEADER: LESSONS FROM STEVE LAWSON'S REMOVAL

Published September 20, 2024 at Truthscript

Yesterday the elders at Trinity Bible Church in Dallas, Texas, announced that their lead preacher, Steve Lawson, was involved in an "inappropriate relationship" with a woman. This revelation was serious enough to lead to Lawson's departure from TBC and likely his broader ministry career. Ligonier Ministries, where he served as a teaching fellow, and The Master's Seminary, where he held the position of Dean of D.Min. Studies, have removed him from their respective websites.

This news has sent shockwaves through the Reformed evangelical community, particularly among those who have long appreciated the ministries of R.C. Sproul (Ligonier) and John MacArthur (Master's). I've received numerous messages from friends expressing their astonishment, with one asking me if it was true. Sadly, it is. The reaction earlier this year when Alistair Begg affirmed his support for attending a same-sex wedding was similar. It raises a troubling question: How can someone who taught the Scriptures so effectively find themselves compromised on such fundamental moral issues?

But for the Grace of God

One of the helpful things to remember first, and a warning I've noticed coming from wiser men, is to consider the deception of sin. As a child, I remember the familiar teaching: a lie becomes bigger the longer you tell it. All sin is like this. James 1:14-15 says, "But each one is tempted when he is carried away and enticed by his own lust. Then when lust has conceived, it gives birth to sin; and when sin is accomplished, it brings forth death."

Sin doesn't begin with the most egregious violations of God's moral order; it often starts with small, gradual steps away from His clear teachings. It is quite literally "to miss the mark." The arrow may only be an inch off the first time. Solomon presented sexual temptation in Proverbs 7 as cunning, persuasive, and flattering. It does not consider the potential consequences until it is too late.

For Steve Lawson, it is too late to avoid some serious consequences, but that doesn't mean it's too late for you if you're struggling with similar temptations. The potential for grievous sin is always close to a heart that thinks too highly of itself. We must remember the tools God has provided to help us gain victory over temptation—no matter what form it takes. Steve Lawson was surrounded by theology, adored by fans of expository preaching, and stood at the pinnacle of Reformed evangelicalism. Yet in the end, his battle was the same every common person faces: choosing between his own flesh and his God.

Courage as a Window to Character

While acknowledging the allure of temptation for a prideful heart is crucial, it doesn't completely address a pressing question: Why are scandals arising more frequently in circles that seem otherwise theologically sound? When King David fell into sin with Bathsheba, it was preceded by a lapse in another duty. In 2 Samuel 11:1, we see that David stayed home when he should have joined his army in battle. This decision ultimately placed him in a position to see Bathsheba bathing from his roof and allowed for an immoral relationship to develop. My lack of surprise regarding Lawson's situation partly stems from my observations of social justice movements within evangelicalism over the past few years. Reactions to these movements have served as a barometer for individual courage, revealing deeper insights into character. When social justice came knocking, did they stay home, or did they go to battle?

In the case of Steve Lawson, he would not sign the Dallas Statement on Social Justice. He did not weigh in on social justice, at least not publicly, to my knowledge, until 2022, when he received a question at a Bible study. He expressed his disapproval in a somewhat general way without naming names. I was encouraged at the time.[1] However, a few months later, Lawson endorsed Paul David Tripp's book, *Do You Believe?* This surprised me, especially since it was well-known that Tripp attended Epiphany Fellowship, led by the author of *Woke Church* and reparations advocate Eric Mason. Tripp had also controversially stated in 2018 that he had been complicit in advancing an "incomplete gospel," because he had preached "the gospel of God's grace" for his entire ministry, but left out "the gospel of [God's] justice."[2]

Phil Johnson, CEO of Grace to You, expressed concerns about Tripp's issue during the infamous Shepherd's Conference Q&A panel in 2018. In *Do You Believe?* Tripp even complained about how he's called a Marxist when he addresses racial injustice, seeing this response as the symptom of a disconnect between Christians' theology of grace and justice and their practical lives. Yet attacking this supposed disconnect is what Lawson endorsed. He said of Tripp's book, "In this important book, Paul Tripp puts his finger on a live nerve in the body of Christ. He addresses the dangerous disconnect that often exists between sound doctrine and sound living."[3]

---

1 https://www.youtube.com/watch?v=qXFz0bGUKGQ
2 https://www.paultripp.com/articles/posts/my-confession-toward-a-more-balanced-gospel
3 https://www.amazon.com/Do-You-Believe-Historic-Doctrines-ebook/dp/B097J1D27Y/ref=tmm_kin_ swatch_0?_encoding=UTF8&qid=&sr=

For the record, this doesn't mean that Lawson is "woke." It means he, unlike John MacArthur, failed to protect the sheep from "wokeness" when it mattered and continued to preach alongside people like Ligon Duncan and Tim Keller without squarely facing the issue.[4] At key moments, like when his influence could have helped the men I knew who confronted Al Mohler for allowing CRT ideas at Southern Seminary, he was absent from the battlefield.

THE ILLUSION OF IMAGE

This may offend some, but Steve Lawson fit my own personal impression of someone whose image was made for the upper levels of the Reformed evangelical conference circuit long before this incident. Some of this comes down to what some may consider petty things. But taken as a whole I don't think they are. Expositors on the conference circuit are generally revered for their accurate preaching and professional persona.

Lawson presented well with his wardrobe of overfolded pocket squares, cuff links, signature striped ties, and tailored suits. His preaching was technical, sophisticated sounding, and left little room for practical asides. He fit the image of a specialist in handling God's Word. I almost thought I could see a glow coming from his well-lotioned hands, soft from turning pages. He was not what you would call a wartime leader. His very clean-cut image signaled all was well. For these reasons, and others relating to my own impression of Lawson's softer mannerisms and what seemed like overly scripted messages, I never cared for his preaching.

My overall impression was that there was an overproduced quality to Lawson that seemed to conceal who he was, something I never wondered about in preachers like John MacArthur or R.C. Sproul. For example, I knew MacArthur's wife was Patricia, his grandkids distracted him from his work much to his delight, and personal

---

4 https://jakarta2020.stemi.id/speakers; https://puritanconference.org/speakers

stories from his own experience. His views on politics and other cultural matters flowed naturally from the pulpit.

Lawson was different. He was the kind of expositor who played well with others on panels, spoke from study more than experience, avoided politics, and focused on threats to the Reformed evangelical brand, like charismatic theology and Arminianism, more than on general threats facing all American Christians, like social justice.

While Lawson traveled extensively, often without his wife, he juggled an impressive array of responsibilities: writing books, leading One Passion Ministries with its Center for Expository Preaching and *Expositor Magazine*, and participating in conferences alongside his academic roles at Master's and Ligonier. Lawson's focus allowed him to master the formula, satisfy the expectations of his peers, and create the materials that positioned him at the top of his field.

Now that I've sufficiently offended all the Steve Lawson fans who genuinely gleaned from his ministry, let me also say that Lawson was a gifted speaker and most of what I heard him say was true. I do not for a second minimize the way God used him to communicate truth. Neither do I remotely blame anyone for not seeing Lawson from my perspective.

I bring my impressions up now to ask a larger question: Is it possible, even in the most conservative Christian circles, that there is a pressure to emphasize image, group acceptance, and the accolades of prominent ministries over virtue? This is a genuine problem in all managerial institutions today. But I think some Christians tend to believe their organizations aren't affected by these forces. We are accustomed to thinking the larger ministries are more heavily vetted, and therefore safer, than the smaller ones. I can tell you in no uncertain terms that all my research on social justice confirms the exact opposite of this.

I'm concerned that when someone makes it big in evangelicalism, we give approval to them mostly based on superficial qualities and technical skills. The limelight will always encourage pride. That's unavoidable. And pride will always open the door for temptation. But we are given qualities to look for in elders. Someone can be a good teacher yet fail to defend biblical truths effectively. They can be gentle but lack discernment. It is difficult to detect some of these important weaknesses in conference settings, where only certain qualities need to be manifested.

FORMULAS DON'T PROTECT

If there's a point to be made, aside from seeing Lawson's fall as a warning, I think it is this: Formulas will not protect us. Lawson fit a common mold in a certain quarter of evangelicalism that emphasizes expository preaching, a plurality of elders, cessationism, and Calvinistic soteriology. These qualities are what many in these circles think make someone "solid." Not only did Lawson check all the boxes, but he looked the part. The problem was that his character was lacking. Some of the deadliest threats are not addressed by believing the right things on these issues or carrying institutional credibility.

I pray for Steve Lawson with the assumption that he is a Christian caught in sin and in need of truly spiritual people to help restore him to repentance, as Galatians 6:1 instructs. But I fear for American Christianity. Our leadership class is thin at the highest levels and in desperate need of replacement by godly men. As many have said to me, "John MacArthur can't live forever, but who will replace him?" I'm increasingly coming to the opinion that God will work all of this out. After all, the gates of hell will not prevail against Christ's church. But are we prepared to embrace a different paradigm? One less formulaic and more virtue-focused? Perhaps a newer paradigm looks like one that rewards sacrifice for truth more than avoiding necessary conflicts. One that's less technical and more practical.

Perhaps the disappointment some of us feel right now is a good opportunity to thank God for that local pastor who never made the limelight but was faithful. Maybe it is time to elevate that person in our minds and with our resources over more distant celebrity-level pastors. At the end of the day, this is ultimately a good reminder to put our confidence in God and not men.

RUSSELL MOORE
LOSES HIS RELIGION

Published August 4, 2023 at *Truthscript*

R ussell Moore, the Editor in Chief of *Christianity Today*, recently authored a critique of the current state of evangelical-ism called *Losing Our Religion: An Altar Call for Evangelical America*. In decades past, rank and file evangelicals might take someone with Moore's credentials seriously. Moore served as the President of the Ethics and Religious Liberty Commission of the Southern Baptist Convention for eight years. Before that he taught theology at the largest Protestant seminary in the country. Yet in 2023, this pedigree can actually serve to decrease one's credibility in the minds of many conservative evangelicals.

Some of Moore's own former supporters now see his brand of evangelicalism as controversial. The obvious question is, "What happened?" How did someone who climbed their way to the top of conservative Christianity find themselves on the fringes? The question stretches beyond Russell Moore. Other evangelical elites like Beth Moore, David Platt, and Matt Chandler could ask the same question, as they have watched their audience divide and shrink for the past few years. Moore's answer can be summed up with the reverse of a common breakup line: "It's not me, it's you."

As the title of the book suggests, evangelicals are in the process of losing their religion to a false political gospel and need to come back to the faith. Unlike them, Russell Moore and those who agree with him "never changed."[1] He writes, after undergoing lengthy "heresy trials" during his time working for the Southern Baptists, "I hadn't changed my theology, or my behavior, at all. What I had done, as the president of my denomination's public policy agency, was refuse to endorse Donald Trump." In Moore's mind, he "paid the price" for the sharp political divide President Trump exposed.[2]

It is important to remember that three months before his departure, a Southern Baptist task force determined that Moore's organization was "a source of significant distraction from the Great Commission work of Southern Baptists." The report cited things like participating in the partially Soros-funded Evangelical Immigration Table, filing an amicus brief to support a mosque, failing to support the religious liberty of California churches during Covid-19, and a general tone of condescension and unresponsiveness. Moore's opposition to President Trump was only one factor in determining mission drift.[3] This lack of self-awareness on Moore's part can almost be considered the theme of his book.

If Moore were to apply many of his critiques against politically conservative evangelicals to himself, he would be found guilty. For example, Moore accuses Trump-supporting evangelicals of relativism when they justify their endorsement using the lesser-of-two-evils approach. He thinks these conservatives believe "immorality is necessary to combat even worse immorality."[4] That is certainly not the rationale most Christians who voted for Trump used. Yet Moore himself employed a similar approach to shame evangelicals for failing to sacrifice popularity in order to "preach the gospel" like Martin

[1] 94.
[2] 3.
[3] "Report to the SBC Executive Committee by the ERLC Study Task Force," January 16, 2021.
[4] 113.

Luther King Jr. In this case, Moore preferred a man with heretical theology and major character deficiencies over his own evangelical siblings who did not publicly support the Civil Rights Movement.[5]

Moore also critiques ends-justifies-the-means thinking, yet supported things like attending gay wedding receptions in order to be a witness.[6] He attacks what he calls "conflict entrepreneurs" who seek to gain an audience based on controversy. Yet this could be an apt description of what Moore did to rise to the level he is at now.[7] Moore believes people in the church are normalizing "crazed and irrational conspiracy theories," yet he also aggressively promoted the Covid vaccine and treats white supremacy as a pervasive threat.[8] One might ask Moore, "And if I by Beelzebul cast out demons, by whom do your sons cast them out?"[9]

Of course, Moore does not see himself as engaged in the very thing he objects to. Instead, he is one of the heroes of the story, courageously accepting the underdog position for the purpose of telling the truth. He draws a parallel between his situation and the situation outlaw country artists like Johnny Cash and Waylon Jennings found themselves in. They were exiled from Music Row and free to write more authentic songs "that seemed real to them." They breathed new life into a failing genre by breaking established rules and embracing something pure. In the same way, Moore says "American conservative Protestantism [is also] seeking revival."[10] In order to get there, evil and corruption must be opposed.

In accomplishing this, Moore awkwardly promotes "winsomeness" while simultaneously describing his political enemies in terms severe enough to make the most boisterous Fundamentalist blush. He compares "American conservative Christianity" to Mordor and describes politically conservative evangelicals as controversy-craving

---

5 Jon Harris, *Christianity and Social Justice: Religions in Conflict* (Reformation Zion Publishing, LLC, 2021), 40-41.
6 125; Tamara Audi, "Southern Baptists, Gay Community Break Bread at Conference," *The Wall Street Journal*, October 30, 2014, https://www.wsj.com/articles/southern-baptists-gay-community-break-bread-at-conference-1414691923.
7 80.
8 55-56.
9 Luke 11:19.
10 134-135.

power-hungry psychopaths.[11] They suffer from irrational fears such as "the supposed loss of the greeting 'Merry Christmas' in stores."[12] They allow conspiracy theories to "keep people from life-saving vaccines."[13] They are the people who failed to oppose slavery and segregation, cover up sexual abuse, and embrace a false political gospel by adopting "nationalistic movements" that swapped the "blood of Christ for blood-and-soil."[14] So much for the winsomeness, gentleness, and reasonableness Moore claims he supports.[15]

The root problem, according to Moore, is that conservative evangelicals are too invested in this world and as a result pursue political power at the expense of their theology. This is why they see the culture war as a spiritual war.[16] They got to this point most recently during the Covid-19 lockdowns when churches closed and members swapped their church communities for online communities, which in turn radicalized them on race and healthcare issues.[17] Moore does not seem to see the irony that he supported these lockdowns in the first place. Yet he believes he knows the solution for the recent divisions he helped create.

American Christians, Moore contends, must see themselves first as "part of the global Body of Christ" instead of "white middle-class Americans."[18] Once they embrace this "exilic identity," they will realize the United States is not the "Promised Land," and they will not concern themselves with their own social marginalization.[19] If a Christian figure existed who wished to advise totalitarian regimes in pacifying the believers under their authority, they would not be much different than Russell Moore. His assumption that temporal and eternal identities are somehow in competition with each other serves to neutralize Christian political resistance to evil. Interestingly,

---

[11] 6, 59, 117.
[12] 77-79.
[13] 3.
[14] 2, 151, 74-77.
[15] 124.
[16] 23, 97, 84.
[17] 43.
[18] 163-164.
[19] 97.

this all comes from a man who ran the Southern Baptist's political-engagement arm.

What Moore fails to consider is that perhaps the divisions in evangelical Christianity have more to do with people like him than they do the vast majority of evangelicals who supported Trump. Pew-sitters prevented from attending church watched their pastors hold racial reconciliation sessions over Zoom. Some of their own leaders marched with Black Lives Matter during the height of civil unrest. Nothing like this happened in recent memory on such a large scale. As a result, common people did lose faith in their spiritual leaders, which Moore sees as the crux of the problem. Yet it is worth noting they also lost faith in medical and political authorities at the same time and for similar reasons. One wonders how Moore does not see this clearly, but his ability to ignore his own role in problems afflicting the church may be unmatched.

This is easily seen in how Moore interacts with the people he criticizes. He does not even try to demonstrate why their arguments are wrong and his are right. Instead, he vilifies them by impugning their motives and claiming the moral high ground for himself. For example, he assumes the legitimacy of a contested *Houston Chronicle* story outlining abuse within the Southern Baptist Convention, and then proceeds to hammer those who disagree with it. Instead of addressing reasons for their disagreement, such as those expressed in Megan Basham's article critiquing the abuse narrative, he portrays his opponents as hypocritical "Alt-Right fundamentalist groups" who simply think the MeToo movement is a Marxist tool of the devil. In other words, they indirectly support abuse and he does not.[20]

At times he characterizes his opponents in embarrassing ways. He says at one point during the January 6th protest for election integrity, "American flags were thrown down and replaced with Trump and Confederate flags." To be sure, there were a variety of flags, including state, regional, and historic ones, but there were an overwhelming number of national banners as well—way more than are visible at

---

20 4.

leftist protests, where they are sometimes more likely to be burned than displayed.[21] Though it is an odd question to ask about someone who spent the majority of their adult life in evangelical institutions, one wonders whether Moore actually knows the working-class evangelicals he critiques.

One group Moore may know something about are the evangelical elites he maintained a club membership with for so many years. After working with guild-members to his right, he now seems to harbor disdain for them. Without naming names, Moore tells personal stories that reveal corruption behind closed doors. A "respected older Baptist leader" told him that in order to "play the game" right, he should "give [Southern Baptists] 90 percent of the red meat they expect" before focusing on things that mattered to him like supporting racial justice and refugees.[22] Moore claims that two respected Southern Baptist leaders (possibly Paige Patterson and Al Mohler) used intimidation tactics.[23] At one point he says that "some of the most ferocious of denouncers of sexual immorality 'in the culture' are sexual nihilists inside."[24]

It is hard to know whether such vague and general accusations are accurate, but they do reveal a pattern. In 2018, David Platt resigned from the Southern Baptists' International Mission Board. In his final address to trustees he stated:

"I hate the politics of the SBC. And I don't say that as an outsider. I say that as an insider these last four years. Some of the lowest points in my leadership have been when I found myself participating in them — jockeying for position, continual self-promotion, backroom deals followed by spin in the front room, strategizing like brothers are your enemy, feeling like others see you as their enemy ... getting to the point where you wonder if you can trust anyone even as you start to wonder how trustworthy you've become."[25]

---

[21] 41.
[22] 3-4.
[23] 111.
[24] 121.
[25] David Roach, "Platt's IMB Farewell: 'Rise above' SBC Challenges," Baptist Press, September 28, 2018, https://www.baptistpress.com/resource-library/news/platts-imb-farewell-rise-above-sbc-challenges/.

Platt's indictment of the Southern Baptist upper echelon is as unhelpful as Moore's, since he also left out specifics. Yet it does raise questions. Perhaps some of Moore's cynicism, displayed when he rebukes Christian organizations for platforming atheist James Lindsay and those who reject "aspects of Trinitarian dogma" (possibly Owen Strachan and Bruce Ware), is due to the fact that he himself is part of a group that ignores theological errors in order to move the needle politically.[26] Moore cannot separate himself from the threats he claims Christians face.

Perhaps this sad conclusion is the major take-away from his book. Despite Russell Moore's desperate attempt to absolve himself of responsibility for the divisions in Christianity, he simply cannot do it, and his efforts seem pathetic. There are more opportunities for the gospel with politically conservative and culturally Christian people than there have been in a while. Yet for them Moore expresses only disgust. He instead mimics many of the same talking-points exvangelicals use to justify their rejection of Christianity. Perhaps it's not Evangelical America that lost its religion, but left-wing evangelical elites like Russell Moore.

---

[26] 82, 151.

How Trump's Victory Affects the Civil War in Evangelicalism

Published December 2, 2024 at *The Federalist*

O ver the past decade, a clear political divide has emerged within American evangelical Christianity. Institutional leaders have increasingly aligned their organizations with the leftist ruling class, while many in the pews maintain more conservative views and resist these shifts. Trump's recent victory has intensified this balancing act for leaders and further deepened the divide within the movement.

Signaling approval for the left's cultural dominance while maintaining Religious Right credentials has never been easy. In the 2010s, the strategy was to expand the definition of pro-life to include issues such as racial justice and left-leaning immigration policies. To pick one example among many: McLean Bible Church Pastor David Platt wrote positively, in his 2020 book *Before You Vote*, about a Christian who cared about the life issue but would not vote for a Republican pro-life candidate. This is the same D.C. beltway pastor who shut down his church for Covid-19, and marched and spoke at a Black Lives Matter-style protest that same year. Platt, along with many evangelical leaders, gave the impression that Christians were expected to push the needle left on a range of issues while pushing right was, at the very least, optional.

Platt's signaling against Trump — when he essentially apologized to his congregation for the "hurt" he may have caused related to issues like "racial division and injustice" after praying for Trump — was only possible as long as theoretical lip service was paid to pro-life and pro-family issues. This allowed evangelical elites to project an image of transcending the political divide, when they were in fact choosing a side.

LUKE-WARM CHRISTIAN INTELLECTUALS

In 2024, white evangelicals once again voted for the president-elect in large numbers. Yet many individuals who see themselves as the evangelical intellectual vanguard are unable to see why evangelicals would vote for Trump and are reviving the narrative that he poses a threat to Christian values. Russell Moore, the editor-in-chief of *Christianity Today*, chalked Trump's victory up to an infatuation Americans have with entertainment. Evangelical *New York Times* columnist David French encouraged Christians to stand courageous in the face of MAGA's cruelty. Like he had in 2020, Pastor John Piper of Desiring God once again insinuated a moral equivalency existed between Trump and his Democrat opponent when he tweeted that the results showed God had "delivered us from one evil" but "now tests us with another."

In a recent Gospel Coalition article shared by former Vice President Mike Pence, McLean Bible Church Associate Pastor Joe Carter makes the case that Trump's nomination of Robert F. Kennedy Jr. to run the Department of Health and Human Services (HHS) signals "that the GOP has fully shifted from the pro-life party to one that's unapologetically pro-choice." Carter went on to chastise the pro-life establishment for its lack of principle and encourage them to "reject any temptation to trade moral clarity for political favor."

Yet when President Joe Biden issued an executive order to protect abortion through the HHS, Carter told Christians that the order would not "have much effect on the [abortion]" since the Dobbs decision had kicked the issue back to legislatures. Carter also said that on abortion, "aside from nominating Supreme Court justices, most of what [presidents] can do is purely symbolic." Apparently, the pro-life movement has more to fear from a Trump HHS than they did from a Biden HHS. And this despite the fact that RFK Jr. is open to appointing an "anti-abortion stalwart to a senior position in HHS" and restoring "anti-abortion policies from the first Trump administration." This "punch right, nuance left" approach is still the default setting for many evangelical elites.

Evangelical Publications Mislead their Flock

In the world of the evangelical elite, people such as Carter are able to pour cold water on Trump's core demographic from the inside. Organizations such as The Gospel Coalition, Christianity Today, and the Southern Baptists' public policy arm — the Ethics and Religious Liberty Commission (ERLC) — must retain some pro-life and pro-family positions, but they subversively bend public opinion toward the left in every other available avenue, whether on red flag laws or comprehensive immigration reform. According to the Gospel Coalition, an evangelical opinion-shaping outlet, the religious right joined the Republican Party because of their "self-centered framework," and the Biden administration's transgender normalization push in schools is "flawed," but Trump's policies will lead to the "same place."

Southern Baptist Leaders Moderating

Yet it is important to note there may be a few leaders adjusting their political approach as they realize Christian public opinion has not supported their positions. This is especially visible in the Southern Baptist Convention (SBC).

J.D. Greear, who served as the president of the SBC from 2018 to 2021, insinuated numerous times that Trump was somehow racist and his policies incompatible with Christianity. For him, central elements of the Black Lives Matter movement, including taking "a deep look at our police systems and structures," was a "gospel issue," and promoting "diversity, equity, and inclusion" in the church was "an essential part of discipleship and the responsibility of every follower of Jesus." Yet he was able to say there was "much to be hopeful for" in the wake of Trump's win.

Pastor Dean Inserra of City Church in Tallahassee, Florida, who some SBC insiders say will likely run for president of the denomination, opposed supporting Trump in 2016 on the basis that he had marriage issues and made "derogatory statements toward women and toward ethnic minority groups." Yet he surprisingly expressed that Christians in America should line up more with the Republican Party after the 2024 election.

One of the most telling post-election Southern Baptist statements came from Nathan Finn, a professor at North Greenville University and ERLC fellow. During Trump's first term, Finn had put his name on left-leaning statements related to Trump and the Charlottesville rally. Yet in the aftermath of Trump's 2024 victory, he maintained a positivity about Trump's more racially diverse coalition. Finn said that "demographics [were] not destiny," socioeconomic factors determined outcomes more, and churches needed to be welcoming to members of different economic and, by implication, political groups. The interesting part of this strategy is that the goal of making congregations politically diverse, and thus appealing to Democrats, is still present. What's missing is the diversity language that used to accompany such calls. It is possible that Southern Baptists may be backing off some of their more overt racialized language.

A LASTING SOLUTION

Evangelical leaders, denominations, and organizations will have to navigate the next four years with the understanding that their base of support is a central part of Trump's coalition. My advice to rank-and-file evangelicals is to consider who attempted to steer their futures toward disaster and respond accordingly. Some leaders will remain steadfast in their leftward direction, others will moderate just enough to placate their base, while some may genuinely return to their Religious Right roots.

Unfortunately, it takes time to discern whether good changes are sincere. Pew sitters should think twice before allowing leaders who compromised on government Covid-related overreach, Critical Race Theory, and other left-leaning movements to continue leading their organizations. Jesus Himself said, "He who is faithful in a very little thing is faithful also in much; and he who is unrighteous in a very little thing is unrighteous also in much."

Christians should also consider raising new leaders from uncompromised up-and-coming organizations such as the Center for Baptist Leadership, Truthscript, and American Reformer. Fresh faces who are loyal both to God and their congregations will close the growing political divide within evangelicalism faster than any attempt to reform the current leadership class. This will also strengthen communities in red areas dominated by Christian conservatives, since a healthy church has historically held the state accountable. More than just the future of evangelical Christianity hangs in the balance.

Made in United States
Troutdale, OR
02/22/2025

29219103R00176